THE
DEMOCRACY
GAP

Recent Titles in
Contributions to the Study of Mass Media and Communications

The News as Myth: Fact and Context in Journalism
Tom Koch

Cold War Rhetoric: Strategy, Metaphor, and Ideology
Martin J. Medhurst, Robert L. Ivie, Philip Wander, and Robert L. Scott

Foreign Policy and the Press:
An Analysis of *The New York Times'* Coverage of U.S. Foreign Policy
Nicholas O. Berry

Sob Sister Journalism
Phyllis Leslie Abramson

The Course of Tolerance:
Freedom of the Press in Nineteenth-Century America
Donna Lee Dickerson

The American Trojan Horse:
U.S. Television Confronts Canadian Economic and Cultural Nationalism
Barry Berlin

Science as Symbol: Media Images in a Technological Age
Lee Wilkins and Philip Patterson, editors

The Rhetoric of Terrorism and Counterterrorism
Richard W. Leeman

Media Messages in American Presidential Elections
Diana Owen

The Joint Press Conference:
The History, Impact, and Prospects of American Presidential Debates
David J. Lanoue and Peter R. Schrott

The Media in the 1984 and 1988 Presidential Campaigns
Guido H. Stempel III and John W. Windhauser, editors

THE DEMOCRACY GAP

THE POLITICS OF INFORMATION AND COMMUNICATION TECHNOLOGIES IN THE UNITED STATES AND EUROPE

Jill Hills
with
Stylianos Papathanassopoulos

CONTRIBUTIONS TO THE STUDY OF
MASS MEDIA AND COMMUNICATIONS,
NUMBER 30

GREENWOOD PRESS
NEW YORK • WESTPORT, CONNECTICUT • LONDON

Library of Congress Cataloging-in-Publication Data

Hills, Jill.
    The democracy gap : the politics of information and communication
technologies in the United States and Europe / Jill Hills with
Stylianos Papathanassopoulos.
      p. cm.—(Contributions to the study of mass media and
communications, ISSN 0732–4456 ; no. 30)
    Includes bibliographical references and index.
    ISBN 0–313–26170–9
    1. Telecommunication policy—United States. 2. Telecommunication
policy—Europe. I. Papathanassopoulos, S. II. Title.
III. Series.
HE7781.H547   1991
384′.068—dc20   90–22396

British Library Cataloguing in Publication Data is available.

Library of Congress Catalog Card Number: 90–22396
ISBN: 0–313–26170–9
ISSN: 0732–4456

First published in 1991

Greenwood Press, 88 Post Road West, Westport, CT 06881
An imprint of Greenwood Publishing Group, Inc.

Printed in the United States of America

The paper used in this book complies with the
Permanent Paper Standard issued by the National
Information Standards Organization (Z39.48-1984).

10 9 8 7 6 5 4 3 2 1

To family and friends

Contents

Preface

This book originated from my teaching of technology and communications at City University in London. The writing of it has been much delayed. Hopefully, the end product has benefited from that delay. Certainly, in the intervening period I have learned a great deal from students and from colleagues in the field. To all those who have directly or indirectly contributed go my thanks. In particular, I would like to thank Stylianos Papathanassopoulos. Currently undertaking military service in Greece, he bears no responsibility for the final version of this book, but did provide an indispensable starting point for it. Others who have contributed are Marion Banks, Larry Stone, Fritz Phillips, and Constantine Sfiktos, to name but a few. To them and to my past and present students my thanks for teaching me so much. I am also indebted to those who took part in the European Consortium of Political Research sessions in Götenborg, Amsterdam, and Mannheim. In particular, my thanks to Edgar Grande, Rob Van Tülder, and Mogens Kuhn Pedersen for their arguments and cogent thinking. My thanks also to Eun Ju Kim and Bergitte Magnussen, who helped with the boring bits. I am indebted to financial support from the British ESRC (Grant RE/00/23/2196) and from the Nuffield Foundation. Finally, my thanks to my family, who allow me the personal space to write, and to my granddaughter, Stephanie, who, at eighteen months, has been consistent in her determination to help.

THE
DEMOCRACY
GAP

Introduction

This book is about political choices—choices surrounding the new technologies of telecommunications and broadcasting. Who is determining how they are implemented and why? Who is benefiting by them? It is often assumed that technology determines social organization. But, if that were so, then each new technique would contain within itself the parameters of human action. No matter what its cultural or historical past, each society would be circumscribed by the very technique itself. Were that the case, then the outlook for human choice would be limited and the prospects for social advancement pessimistic.

This book does not subscribe to that view. Rather, it sees technology as a combination of both techniques and organization, in which the organizational and distributional aspects of the technology are fluid. Although as the world grows smaller the same techniques may be adopted in widely divergent cultures, the organizational part of the technology can vary from culture to culture, nation to nation, and institution to institution.[1] It is with the distributional possibilities of the new technologies, and with the political and economic interests that bargain and conflict over those possibilities, that this book is concerned.

The question of the neutrality of technology is one that occupies philosophers, but to some extent it is also a matter of everyday observation.[2] The introduction of word-processing equipment into an office can be followed at one end of the management spectrum by the congregation of all such operators into one "pool," with control exercised via computer over measured output and numbers of mistakes. Using different management criteria, the introduction of the equipment can be followed by a retention of the existing organization and the utilization of the technology to reduce typing loads and to increase time for more self-discretionary and self-disciplined activities on the part of the secretaries. Although the logic necessary to use the word-processing software may be inherent in the package, and therefore certain human/machine interactions may be prescribed by the equipment, neither form of social organization is set by the word-processing equipment itself. Rather, the organization of new technology and the distribution of resources and power that results from its introduction are the result of political and economic interests. These interests are aroused by the possibilities of redistribution that the technology brings with it. That redistribution may be on the level of the workplace or the home, or within the domestic political economy, or on a global scale.

This book is primarily concerned with that redistribution at the level of international and domestic political economy. It focuses on the ways in which governments have attempted to innovate, organize, and control information technology, telecommunications, and broadcasting within their domestic political economies, and the ways in which they have sought to use these resources to gain political and economic advantage against other countries. The book looks, therefore, at domestic economic and industrial policy decisions that favor the interests of one technology against another, and at the actions of governments in international economic institutions. Because of space limitations, its analysis is limited primarily to the United States and Western Europe, particularly the European Community. Its focus is on the information technology, telecommunications, and broadcasting sectors—three sectors that now have the technological potential to come together into one electronic distribution system.

The primary focus of the book is on the politics of innovation pursued through the mechanisms of technology push, market restructuring, and standardization. Restructuring takes the form of the introduction of competition. Technology push and market restructuring in the form of liberalization are strategies often seen as competing with, rather than complementing, one another. The former is seen as extending the control of governments over companies, the latter as loosening it.[3] This book argues differently. It contends that both technology push and market restructuring can lead to increased government control, and that market restructuring may well be done in the interests of those who have benefited from technology push. Both mechanisms are industrial policies.

Technologies are created by the economic interests and demands of scientists and manufacturers. They need both legitimacy and markets.

Legitimacy is gained through ideological and bureaucratic backing by governments—the incorporation of technology into national aspirations for competitive advantage in military, economic, and political power. Moreover, in a world where the economic power of technological leadership is increasingly linked to national security and national prestige, so industries and bureaucrats form alliances in the interests of promulgating the "national" version of any one technology. The technology itself becomes a social construction, its characterization incorporating the hopes and dreams of national revival.

Such has been the history of information technology. It has come to be seen as a savior of western industrialized nations.[4] In its conceptualization as a technology to renew economic strength, it has become the vehicle for chauvinistic policies designed to retain or restore national advantage. David Haglund and Marc Busch have coined the term "techno-nationalism" to describe this combination of objectives.[5]

This book argues that the technological innovation that governments in the industrialized world have backed through research and development funding in the new information technologies primarily centers on technology unrelated to market demand. It is primarily technology developed for other political, military, or chauvinistic reasons. Governments subscribe to the technology-push concept of innovation, and give it legitimacy.

However, technology also requires markets to become economically viable and widely distributed. Governments can provide these markets by intervention, either to buy the technology themselves through public procurement, or through the creation of the market conditions that allow the new technology to enter. Mature markets are those most suitable for such restructuring. They present the opportunity for new products to replace the old, and for new investment to generate increased economic activity. Often monopolies as a result of previous government policies are suitable candidates for the entry of competition. Whereas such markets may previously have been funded by government investment, their restructuring attracts new private entrepreneurs to invest in and utilize new technology. Telecommunications and broadcasting are two such markets.

Within this book it becomes obvious that in the past in Europe, there was a general consensus surrounding the parallel concepts of broadcasting and telecommunications. Both technologies were regarded as "public goods"—goods held in common, paid for in common, accessed by all, and benefiting everyone. The social organization of both technologies has been along the lines of national boundaries. Both have been regarded as natural monopolies. Telecommunications was shielded by the huge investment in infrastructure necessary for competition, and broadcasting by the perception of spectrum scarcity. Governments have directly or indirectly controlled both. Both telecommunications and broadcasting have been linked to concepts of national security and the military, but broadcasting has also contained aspects of a cultural defense, defining and promulgating a view of what holds one nation of people together as against another. So fierce has been the view of broadcasting as a forum for the expression of national solidarity and as the national information source for citizens, that for the last 70 years, in democratized but fragmented Western Europe, governments have retained public service broadcasting organizations to fulfill these roles.

Almost inevitably, the representational function of public service broadcasting organizations—acting as a mirror of the breadth of opinion within society—has brought them into conflict with government perspectives on what constitutes unbiased information. Moreover, just as the telecommunication monopolies were engineering-led, demonstrating rather little interest in the customer, so the broadcasting monopolies were often unresponsive to the changing tastes of their viewers. Up to the point of a conjuncture of advertiser pressure, a mature market, a European recession, and financial crisis, public service broadcasting had survived a variety of challenges. However, new technology and the potential entry of multinational capital have increased the attack.

Governments differ in how far an economic bias in broadcasting policy has replaced the previous cultural bias, but in general policy has been concerned with the attraction of private interests into the market through the use of new technologies of distribution. These private interests then become stakeholders in the policy process, reaffirming the trends toward liberalization and commercialization.

Although the concept of the public interest is notoriously hard to define, it has to do with governments protecting those who have no voice in the proceedings, and with an overall collective interest, going beyond sectional interests, and with responsibility to the young, weak, and poor. Traditionally, such concerns have involved the regulation by governments of the content of broadcasting. As this book illustrates, such a definition of the public interest has been abnegated in the United States by the Federal Communications Commission (FCC), which argued that the public interest is simply the collation of private choices. As Mark Fowler and Daniel Brenner said in 1982,

> The perception of broadcasters as community trustees should be replaced by a view of broadcasters as marketplace participants. . . .

Instead of defining public demand and specifying categories of programming to serve this demand, the Commission should rely on the broadcasters' ability to determine the wants of their audiences through the normal mechanisms of the marketplace. The public's interest, then, defines the public's interest.[6]

In situations where the marketplace defines the public interest, it is a short step to argue that the public interest is defined by what people will pay. Payment determines value, which determines public interest. Hence, the license fee on broadcast receivers, which is prevalent as a means of financing public service television, and which as a universal, affordable, flat-rate fee benefited those who watched the most television—the poor— could legitimately be jettisoned in favor of the more lucrative pay-per-view.[7]

Telecommunications as a public good also involved governments in emphasizing the importance of the penetration of the technology in assuring access to all citizens. In turn, cross-subsidies lowered the costs of such access to the residential subscriber while increasing the costs of those using long-distance and international service. New technologies, mature markets, pressure from multinational users and manufacturers and the United States, and the need for a huge investment to modernize the networks have led to the ending of this consensus. Moreover, as in the case of broadcasting, no alternative image of the future has been put in its place.

One can see in the programs designed by governments to attract private capital to these markets an underlying reconstruction of what is meant by the term, *public control*. While that control in Europe previously relied on organizational forms of public ownership that linked broadcasting and telecommunications to the state and substituted indirect for direct intervention, the new control mechanisms are more direct and legalistic.[8] Public monopolies are being replaced by competition between these entities and private enterprise. In turn, the method of control has also changed from that inherent in the organizational form of public ownership to a system of rules encompassing both the structural regulation of the market and the behavioral regulation of individual companies. Political control is spread wider across sectors and deeper into the corporate strategies and accounts of dominant companies.

In telecommunications, the previous monopoly also held the power of determining rules and standards for the networks, services, and equipment it controlled. Those powers are being split off from the previous monopoly, with regulatory bodies being formed and rules instituted to govern competition. However, as evident from the history of the Federal Communications Commission in the United States, such regulatory bodies are institutionally weak. They lack the power base of electoral accountability to offset the lobbying of large business.[9]

The public-good concept of broadcasting produced a market in Europe where the importance of a free market for opinions took precedence over that of a free market for advertisers. It produced a constrained market for television advertising in Europe compared to that of the United States. In the United States, the economics of broadcasting (in which numbers of entities compete for the same advertising finance), coupled with the entry of new technology, has led gradually to the rolling back of regulation of both market structure and behavior. In turn, concentration among different media—newspapers, magazines, radio, films, video and television—threatens the very plurality on which the free marketplace of ideas was built. As these multimedia conglomerates spread their activities internationally, so in Europe a similar threat arises from a failure of regulation.

In broadcasting, the entry of competition may take several forms. The vertical integration of program making and transmission may be broken, or parts of the previous monopoly sold off, or new competitors licensed. In seeking to attract entrepreneurs who will enter these markets and utilize new technology, governments must seemingly loosen their previous control over the markets. The companies that can afford the cost of being first in the market with the new technologies are those with huge financial resources, with which they can bargain with governments. However, while governments lose the indirect control that they previously exercised over their domestic market, market restructuring produces its own form of extended control. Licensing of new competitors involves the state in determining which company shall have market access and gives the state agency the right to choose between companies and managements. Choices between competing and substitutable technologies, such as optic fiber versus radio or satellite versus cable, allows the state to favor one company over another. In the competition for market entry, governments pick the winners. Hence, regulation of market structure brings with it the potential for clientelism with specific companies or individuals, and for a form of micro-corporatism to develop.[10]

This book draws its intellectual framework from a number of different strands of academic discourse. In the field of international relations, reacting against the realist school (which defined power in primarily military terms), interdependency theorists have contended that nongovernment organizations, such as multinational corporations, were as important as governments; that the issues were not hierarchical; and that military power was not dominant. Instead, interdependency theorists gave precedence in their analysis to diverse economic issues, which are separated by differing networks of participants. These networks were sometimes linked by the overlapping participation of actors or linked as issues in order for one to gain legitimacy from another.[11] On the other hand, some neorealists have looked to changes within domestic political and economic systems for an explanation of international behavior.[12] It is within this latter tradition that this book was written, while taking from the interdependency theorists the notion of different networks of personnel involved in different issues at different times.

The concept of networks is useful as a descriptive mechanism but does little to explain alterations in policy.[13] Networks change and interlink, but why? For that explanation it is necessary to conceptualize the state as being more than a unitary being, and instead as made up of numbers of agencies and competing fragments.[14] These fragments are more easily identifiable in federal political systems, but also exist in even the most unitary of states.[15]

Each fragment may have its own interests in legitimacy, survival, and expansion, and may create alliances.[16] Each alliance may also be driven by its own perception of the public interest. In addition, the influence of specific individuals and the noncoherence of their personal opinions must also be taken into account.[17]

For policy change to occur, the views of these competing bureaucratic coalitions must gain legitimacy. Two mechanisms are evident. First, coalitions form between interests in the state and private economic interests, with each set of interests able to communicate and reinforce the opinions of the other. Clearly, these coalitions gain saliency according to the relative economic power or perceived potential of the economic interests. In turn, such perceptions of potential emanate from trends within technology and within the international and domestic economy. They are opposed by stakeholders in the "old" technology, who can either utilize or prevent the utilization of the new technology. Hence, there are a wide variety of potential coalitions between parts of the state bureaucracies and economic interests involved in the introduction of any new technology into a previous monopoly market. Political trade-offs must be made between technologies, protagonists, and differing policy goals.

The second mechanism is the use of ideology to legitimate political interests. While political parties fulfill this function, it is possible also for coalitions to mobilize around the traditional ideas of the state's relations with industry as expressed through history. What is acceptable in France, for instance, with its history of *dirigisme* (guidance), will not necessarily be acceptable in West Germany or the Netherlands. Similarly, in the

United States and Britain, with their predominantly liberal market ideologies, the legitimacy of state actions can always be challenged by those who will suffer from them. In general, the political ideologies of specific governments cannot be taken as a reliable predictor of action; rather, the historical core ideology of a state seems to have greater salience in the potential legitimacy of policy change and implementation.[18]

However, the framework outlined above relates primarily to the nation state and domestic economies. Currently, there are factors that are weakening the control of governments over their domestic markets. While world trade has expanded in the postwar world, that expansion has been on the basis of intra-sectoral demand and differentiated products within sectors. Cross-national alliances and mergers buy entry into markets, while cross-national cooperation in research and development reduces risks and aids inventories. However, the more international the industry becomes, the more its interest may diverge from the narrow national interest, and the more difficult it will be to control. This vulnerability on the part of governments leads to a desire to place favorably within the new competitive market structures their own companies, as with the West Germans with satellite programmers or the Americans with their additional controls over so-called foreign network communications operators. Techno-nationalism is prevalent. One can see in it a response to the increased penetration of the domestic economy by international economic forces.

Faced with this erosion of their power, governments have begun to regroup. Both technology push and regulation have begun to move to the level at which economies of scale are sufficient to ensure the viability of companies. In Europe, this is the level of the European Community. However, the locus of control is also moving to international, multilateral forums, such as the International Telecommunications Union (ITU) and the General Agreement on Trade and Tariffs (GATT)

The shift is due in some cases to the characteristics of the technology. As equipment has become delinked from the networks to which it attaches, and as economies of scale require global marketing, so it becomes necessary for manufacturers to deal with the same interfaces worldwide. National standards determined by governments for telecommunications or broadcasting networks fragment the market and conflict with the global proprietary standards of computing and consumer electronics equipment that were determined by the manufacturers themselves. International standards agreed on between governments can replace both national and proprietary standards, and can be used to replace the market advantage of existing dominant global manufacturers. They are a mechanism for the redistribution of economic power between manufacturers and governments within the international economy.

However, while international standards determined by governments may replace the power that they lost over national standards, the international spread of networks has another feature that reduces the control of nation states over their domestic economies. International or regional standards determined externally become applicable internally, and whereas such standardization was previously limited to hardware in the network, the advent of competition means that the terms of access to nationally controlled networks must be internationally defined.

Similarly, where the paths of satellites can overlap nations, they pose a threat to sovereignty. Whereas international communication in telecommunications was previously conceptualized as communication that linked national systems ending at the border of a sovereign state, broadcasting has always recognized the possibility of one state's communications impinging on the sovereign control of another. In particular, the industrialized West has considered it a right to broadcast into the states of those it considers ideologically weak or hostile. However, while in the past it has been governments that have produced propaganda and distributed it mainly to developing countries and the Communist bloc via shortwave radio, the technology of its transmission has constrained television within national borders. Today, broadcasting and data transmission by satellite have placed invasive power in the hands of private companies, and the countries whose sovereignty is threatened are both industrialized and industrializing.

A similar trend is evident in the telecommunications sector. Whereas the sovereign rights of countries to decide on the form of organization of the technology within their state boundaries is accepted in the international treaties of the ITU, the reality is of increasing pressure for a reconceptualization of international telecommunications. Private companies demand the right to establish private international networks that would breach the territorial rights of states. Thus, international telecommunications becomes not state to state, but company to company, communications. This reconceptualization of the boundaries of the nation state has been taken the farthest by the United States. The American administration has been pushing both within the ITU and within GATT for the right of its international large users and service suppliers both to provide international communications to third parties and to establish operations within other countries. Increasingly, private economic power is pitted against national sovereignty.

This book does not review either GATT or the ITU in any detail, but the issue has been raised here because it applies to the European Community (EC) as well. Within the EC, these competing conceptualizations of integration versus national sovereignty reflect in the telecommunications and broadcasting fields the wider concerns over political unity. The view of the European Commission (the administrative agency of the EC) concerning integrated networks and their standardization competes with national governments' desire for a minimum of harmonization. Although de facto governments lose power to international institutions in which some consensus on trade-offs between interests is necessary, they attempt to use those same institutions both to legitimize actions within the domestic economy and to pursue national goals. Thus, at the EC level, while the prospect of regional mercantilism or techno-nationalism at a regional level may unify member states, the derogation of sovereignty and alliances with national manufacturers and suppliers divides them.[19] Therefore, member states still seek to retain national control over the social organization of the technology, while the liberalization of markets and weak cross-national regulation promulgated by the commission undermine that very domestic control.

Given the larger boundaries of the operation of private capital, national organization may be ineffective precisely in the domestic control it seeks. In what may appear paradoxical, governments who face losing power to international institutions may institute even fiercer control of the areas over which they *can* wield power. A weakening of the state by private multinational economic power goes hand in hand with a strengthening of the state over national economic interests.[20] Regulation replaces the control of public ownership, and market access replaces the previous state subsidies to industry.

Europe is at an intermediate stage of regulation in both broadcasting and telecommunications. While in telecommunications, the specification of standards in particular has moved to the European level, the policy consensus that must precede the regulation of European-wide networks is lacking. Moreover, despite efforts by the European Commission to create a wider regulation, regulation of broadcasting still clings to national boundaries. Hence, despite evident cross-national multimedia concentration and the dangers it poses to the free representation of opinions within Europe, its regulation remains a national matter. It therefore continues to be unregulated.

What this book is attempting to document and explain, then, are policies within the domestic economies of the United States and of member countries of the European Community, together with actions of the EC itself. The book relates these policies to the wider international issues of the standardization and market introduction of technology and to their impact on the social organization of the technology. There is no single factor that can explain why a particular technology is used in a particular way in a particular country to the benefit of particular interests at a particular time. Rather, a range of international and domestic factors, including the political system itself (whether federal or unitary), the importance of industrial and trade policy, the strength of trade unions and civil service personnel, the overlap with employment and broadcasting policy, and national cultural consensus on what is equitable have all contributed to differences in the timing and organization of technology push and the restructuring of markets. In addition, in an internationalized market, the desire of governments to retain control, to limit foreign investment, and to gain competitive advantage remains a potent force.

Yet what is documented in this book may well be an irrelevance in that process of gaining competitive advantage. While there is always a gap between government policy and its impact, in promoting innovation, governments place themselves in the hands of companies. As chapter 2 points out, the understanding of what leads to innovation and entrepreneurial activity has diverged from the technology-push strategies of governments. Market restructuring that leads to concentration may well contradict such attempts at innovation.

The technologies with which this book is concerned are those that emerge from the enabling technology of microchips and microprocessors. Their introduction has spawned the potential convergence of telecommunications, computing, and image processing into an electronic information industry that allows the possibility of both worldwide information-delivery networks and individual control procedures. In fact, despite having been debated for 15 years, such a convergence has not yet happened, and existing stakeholders have been able to defend their technological territories. Although telecommunications switches have become equivalent to central processors, data processing and telecommunications markets are still remarkably separate. Nevertheless, the potential of such a convergence creates political conflict, particularly where entry to markets is government-controlled.

Potential technological convergence in the communications sector occurred first between traditional voice and data communications brought about by the digitalization of switching technology. Switches are the equivalent of signals on railway lines, directing the access of traffic. Once voice transmission is digitalized, it cannot be distinguished from data transmission. Although the latter comprises only 10 to 15 percent of the total market, nonetheless it is the area of growth.

Second, the transmission of voice, data, and images via satellite or optic fiber is now possible. It then becomes possible to store images on computers with the aid of compact video discs. The Japanese in particular aim to combine digital satellite transmission of television with computing and telecommunications in one consumer product. Hence, while telecommunications has traditionally been seen as the transmission of signals from point to point on an interactive basis, and broadcasting as one-way transmission from point to multipoint, the two are less and less distinguishable.

Optic fiber cable consists of micro-thin glass fibers, barely thicker than a human hair and able to transmit light signals with little distortion. The signal to be transmitted is connected at one end of the cable by tiny solid-state lasers or light-emitting diodes. Optic fibers have the advantage over the copper coaxial cable they replace of allowing many more times the amount of information to be passed down them. They reproduce signals almost perfectly and, because they suffer from little sound attenuation, they can be laid with fewer repeaters, to boost sound over long distances, than cable. Economically they are more viable than satellite transmission for long distances and heavy traffic, although satellites still retain their advantage for mobile communications and long-distance low-capacity routes.[21] Both are transmission elements only, and their efficacy is limited by switching capabilities and economics.

At each end of a fiber optic cable, the signals must be converted back into electronic form. The disadvantage is that while the cost of fiber itself has decreased, the optoelectronics associated with it are too expensive as of 1990 for a local telecommunications network that does not involve television transmission. Hence, the question of whether posts, telegraphs, and telecommunications administrations (PTTs) should be allowed to distribute television signals arises from the technology and economics of fiber optics.

Cable TV developed from community antenna television into a closed communications system, in which homes are collectively wired by coaxial cable via feeder and trunk lines to a central originating "head end."[22] Programs are distributed from the head-end to households via trunk lines and feeders.

The majority of cable systems use pairs of copper wires and a tree-and-branch architecture. Under the tree-and-branch system, signals are transmitted along a trunk cable that has branches and subbranches splitting off it at intervals. Each branch and subbranch has the same capacity as the original trunk. A decoder is provided to restrict access to certain channels. The architecture is widely used in Europe and the United States in comparison to that of the switched-star system, under which trunk lines distribute signals from the head-end to a number of local switching points. From these, drops to individual homes radiate out to subscribers in a star shape, with each switching point, hub, or node, serving anything from 12 to several hundred homes. The switched-star system allows fiber optics to be used throughout and, unlike tree-and-branch architecture, it allows interactivity.[23]

Satellite TV was conceived in 1946 by Arthur C. Clarke, who pointed out that an orbiting satellite would revolve around the earth above a fixed point at the same speed as the earth rotates on its axis, and could be used as a transmitting station. The first satellites were used for international point-to-point transmission; television transmission took up too much capacity. In the United States, the technology was expected to replace the fixed network of the American Telephone & Telegraph (AT&T) telecommunications monopoly. It was only because the satellites launched for this purpose were underutilized that they became available for broadcasting to cable head-ends.

Over the past three decades of satellite communications, the available technology has limited its use to the end user. There is a trade-off between the cost and power of the space segment and the cost and size of receiving equipment. Low-powered satellites are less expensive and have larger numbers of transponders than high-powered vehicles, allowing more channels to be carried, but the receiving equipment is very large and expensive.[24]

Originally, the term *direct-broadcasting satellite* (DBS) referred to direct-to-home broadcasts from high-powered satellites requiring 200 to 300 watts of transponder power. However, because of the limited capacity and high costs of these satellites, alternative technology was developed. By the mid-1980s, the broadcasts of low- and medium-powered satellites using 60 and 100 watt transponder power could be picked up with small, receive-only dishes. In fact, the United States has always had a form of DBS in that even the signals from low-powered satellites were intercepted by large receive-only TV dishes in backyards.

Inside the home, the reception equipment for DBS comprises a descrambler to decode the signal and a converter that both puts the DBS transmission into a form suitable for reception by the existing television set and allows channel selection and tuning. Satellites broadcasting on different frequencies from different orbital locations need separate decoders and reception dishes. Hence, competition between satellite broadcasters tends to stimulate the cable TV industry, which can transmit the competing schedules. Broadcast satellites can also compete with telecommunications through data transmission.

In general, in a bid to outpace the bypass of their networks by private user networks utilizing satellite transmission or cable TV, the PTTs have begun modernization of their telecommunications networks through optic fiber. The concept of the Integrated Services Digital Network is that of a digital pipeline for sending data, voice, and images through one terrestrial network. Currently, such networks are *narrow-band*; that is, they transmit primarily voice and data. However, broadband networks, which are able to transmit interactive video, are seen by the European Commission as the future technological infrastructure for Europe. Broadband can be supplied by either optic fiber or satellite.

High-Definition Television (HDTV) is a new standard developed by the Japanese for the upgrading of program production and transmission that would give greater picture clarity than current systems. Although developed for utilization with DBS, because of the width of radio spectrum it requires it may be more suitable for transmission via optic fiber.

However, the vision of a unified telecommunications/broadcasting network utilizing optic fiber is being challenged by the newer radio-based technologies. Mobile radio was based originally on the concept of broadcasting via one transmitter serving a wide area. It was limited in its capacity because users competed with each other. Cellular mobile radio is based on a large number of low-powered transmitters, each serving a cell. This technology allows the reuse of the same frequency within a small territorial distance. A central processor switches calls from cell to cell, allowing mobility. The number of users can be expanded by the splitting of cells once capacity is reached. Such splitting places burdens on the switching capacity of the central processor, but micro-cell technology is now being introduced.

The high up-front costs of cellular networks make them expensive to the user and critically dependent on attracting a large number of subscribers.[25] A digital system will allow increased capacity, and in the 1990s the current nationally incompatible systems in Europe are to be replaced with one compatible pan-European digital system. In Britain, micro-cellular technology, called CT2 (a telepoint system providing radio-based voice transmission from public base stations), is being developed as a form of bypass of the local fixed networks, while in the upgrading of Eastern Europe's telecommunications it is satellite and cellular radio that can provide the needed infrastructure most quickly. In addition, the combination of satellites and cellular technology have the potential for providing international land mobile systems.[26]

The introduction of these technologies takes place within national economies that are becoming increasingly linked into the international economy. The saliency of many of the political issues discussed in this book comes from the redistribution of power within the international economy. Underlying many of the issues is the rise of Japan as a manufacturer of the basic components to electronic equipment—the microchip—and the decline of the United States in that manufacture. The Japanese now hold 90 percent of the world market in DRAM (Dynamic Random Access Memory) microchips and American companies struggle to invest sufficiently in research and development (R&D) to retain their market share. Following a slump in the computer market in the 1980s, the American industry has seen a reduction in its R&D, the threatened takeover of some of its companies by the Japanese, and the reentry of the military to supplement R&D programs.

Europe is particularly weak in component manufacture, despite massive amounts of government funding.[27] It has lacked the government-controlled markets with which to create national advantage—a controlled market that HDTV equipment may well provide. In order to increase volume production and offset R&D costs, increased cross-national alliances between European companies (for instance, betweeen Philips of the Netherlands and Siemens of Germany; and between Philips, Siemens, and SGS/Thomson of France) have been features of the 1980s. Both the European Community (EC) and the United States are protectionist. While the EC protects its industry with tariff barriers, the United States has instituted an international bilateral agreement with Japan on prices of chips in third markets, and in 1990 is contemplating retaliation under the 1988 Trade Act against Japan for that country's failure to open its domestic market.

Turning to the manufacture of equipment, the products themselves are maturing, and with them the structure of both the broadcasting and telecommunications equipment industries. Oversupply in both industries is a problem. In Britain and the United States, indigenous television production has been virtually lost to foreign competitors, as has the manufacture of such customer premises equipment as facsimile, cellular mobile telephones, and key telephone systems.[28] These telecommunications-based products are increasingly equivalent to consumer electronics items, such as calculators or audio equipment, sold on price and design features, not technology. Hence, the market has been opened to the newly industrializing Asian countries, and to the entry of major consumer electronics companies such as Sony of Japan.

In telecommunications switching equipment, world oversupply has also forced rationalization and global concentration. In the United States, following the divestiture of AT&T, increased competition forced International Telephone and Telegraph (ITT) and General Telephone and Electric (GTE) out of the market. AT&T has also been losing market share, both domestically to Northern Telecom and internationally. Similarly, in Europe, concentration has resulted from mature national markets. Because of fragmented standards, the European switching industry is estimated to work at only 70 percent of capacity. Moreover, because of the investment necessary in the next generation of equipment, the world market is thought capable of supporting only nine manufacturers.[29]

During the 1960s and 1970s, America led in both the technology and market share of satellites and launches. However, the 1986 American space shuttle *Challenger* and the European satellite launcher *Ariane* disasters and the subsequent shortage of launch facilities has had a dramatic impact on the industry. Launches have been delayed for several years. Rising insurance costs have further impacted on the industry. Because the manufacture of the space segment is often tied to launches, the Europeans have gained on the Americans. American companies still lead in world market share for space segments, but France now ranks second, its industry bolstered by DBS and by the European Space Agency.

The maturation of computer products has also led to changes in the manufacturing industry, with concentration of a cross-national basis and the globalization of production. In the personal computer market, products compete on price as much as technology. Increasingly, products and their software operating systems are being standardized through international negotiation. One of the major battles of the 1980s has been that between the proprietary standards of International Business Machines (IBM) and those of the internationally approved Open Systems Interconnection, which allows computers of different manufacturers to communicate with each other. Another battle has been between IBM and AT&T over the latter's UNIX operating system. Standardization in the interests of compatibility goes hand in hand with strategies of product differentiation by major firms and increased intra-industry trade. Competition on price gives the advantage to mass manufacture by the Japanese and newly industrializing Asian countries. In the late 1980s, all the major American computer companies suffered a decline in profits.

It is evident from this short survey that the major rise in manufacturing capacity of the new information technologies in the postwar years has come in Japan. Both the United States and Europe suffer from a balance-of-trade deficit in these markets, primarily because in telecommunications their strengths lie in capital equipment rather than customer premises equipment (CPE); in other words, in those products developed with the aid of government subvention or purchasing. Yet it is in CPE that the market has expanded dramatically. In computers and telecommunications (particularly mobile radio technology), as well as in audiovisual and computer software products, the United States retains its balance of trade with Europe. In general, however, the proportion of the world market held by its high-technology goods has dropped, leading to the perception that U.S. technological leadership is failing.

In turn these reversals in exports have had an effect on international trade negotiations. American pressure on Europe has been centered on the opening of European telecommunications networks to competition. As the American manufacturing industry has declined in productivity and the trade deficit has grown, so services (particularly telecommunications-based services) and agriculture have increased in importance to the national economy. It is this emphasis on services that has indirectly led to the question of their liberalization in GATT's Uruguay round.

On the other hand, it is the very weakness of the European industries and the fragmentation of production behind national barriers that has led to the emphasis of the European Community on the creation of an open market by 1992. The overwhelming intention is to gain economies of scale sufficient to allow the community's industry to be competitive. The European Community's policy is predominantly guided by manufacturers, multimedia conglomerates, and national elites, for whose benefit the markets have been restructured.

This book is about the way in which the search for competitive market advantage is driving policy in information technology, broadcasting, and telecommunications; how technology is determining social organization through policy-making that favors the interests of large-scale private companies. The book links policies of research and development to those of market restructuring in telecommunications and broadcasting, and to the international standardization of Integrated Services Digital Network (ISDN) and HDTV. Each is concerned with government control of markets, with alliances between fragments of the state and economic interests, and with policy divorced from any public debate about its potential social impact.

In the United States, HDTV is linked to the potential threat of Japanese domination of the computer industry and to defense interests. In Europe, the issue of HDTV standardization is linked to European research policies, to West German and French development of satellites, to the opening of markets for the introduction of DBS, and to the future of consumer electronics companies.

ISDN is a further technology, promising much in its early days for the individual user but as yet hardly relevant to even small business. Developed to benefit PTTs, once again the economics are likely to limit access. Technical decisions taken by nonaccountable personnel restrict potential political debate. The perceived technological gap between countries has promoted a democratic gap within them.

The book casts doubt on the efficacy of government-led technology-push innovation coupled with market restructuring, which is evident throughout the major industrialized countries. Its beneficiary through the various stages from research and development to market entry is large-scale multinational capital. Underlying the strategy is an inherent political and economic weakness. Unless the new information technologies reach down to the individual company so that the individual worker is able to utilize them, they do little to alter the underlying factors that create competitive advantage and creativity—the diffusion, acceptance, and utilization of technology leading to further innovation.

While governments hold to a linear design of innovation, concentrating on the twin mechanisms of technology push and market restructuring, they lose sight of the horizontal aspects of innovation, the geographical, managerial, and educational infrastructure that underpins that process, and the social organization and distribution of benefits that enable its acceptability and utilization. In all these developments, the individual citizen's needs for information, entertainment, and communication have been lost to the concept of the consumer of products and services. While governments concern themselves with technology push, the infrastructure to utilize the new information technologies remains stagnant. Lack of money to access the new technologies, and lack of education and organization to enable them to be managed, used, or enhanced, precludes the diffusion of innovation on which more lasting competitive advantage, human advance, and creativity could be based.

In derogating power to large capital, and in conceptualizing its population as paying consumers, not citizens, governments increase access costs to the individual and lose sight of the informational underpinnings of the democratic process itself. Democracy becomes subordinated to private economic interests. Ironically, at the very time when freedom of speech and the democratizing effects of both broadcasting and telecommunications have become evident in Eastern Europe, those very freedoms are under threat in both the United States and Western Europe.

NOTES

1. See, for example, Frances Stewart, *Technology and Underdevelopment*, 2d ed. (London: Macmillan, 1978).

2. Hugh Ward, "The Neutrality of Science and Technology" (Paper presented to the Political Studies Association Annual Conference, Nottingham, April 1986); Mike Cooley, *Architect or Bee? The Human/Technology Relationship* (Slough, U.K.: Langley Technical Services, 1980).

3. Douglas Webber, Martin Rhodes, J. J. Richardson, and Jeremy Moon, "Information Technology and Economic Recovery in Western Europe," *Policy Sciences* 19 (October 1986): 319–46.

4. Cees Brandt, "The Social Construction of Information Technology" (Paper presented to the European Consortium of Political Science Joint Workshops, Amsterdam, 1987).

5. David G. Haglund, with Marc L. Busch, "Techno-Nationalism and the Contemporary Debate over the American Defence Industrial Base," in *The Defence Industrial Base and the West*, edited by David Haglund (London: Routledge, 1989), 234–77.

6. Mark S. Fowler and Daniel L. Brenner, "A Marketplace Approach to Broadcast Regulation," *Texas Law Review* 207 (1982): 60, quoted in Wilhemina Reuben Cooke, "Broadcast and Cable Deregulation in the United States," in CNRS, *La Déréglémentation des télécommunications et de l'audiovisuel* (Paris: CNRS, International Colloquium, May 1986).

7. See Vincent Mosco, "Introduction: Information in the Pay-per-Society," in *The Political Economy of Information*, edited by Vincent Mosco and Janet Wasko (Madison: University of Wisconsin Press, 1988), 3–26.

8. Joachim Scherer, "Historical Analysis of Deregulation. The European Case," in CNRS, *La Déréglémentation des télécommunications*.

9. U.S. Congress, Office of Technology Assessment, *Critical Connections: Communication for the Future* (Washington, D.C.: Government Printing Office, 1990), 85–87.

10. Alan Cawson, ed., *Organised Interests and the State* (London: Sage, 1985). On U.S. policy and corporate interests, see Jill Hills, "The Dynamics of U.S. International Telecommunications Policy," *Transnational Data Report* 12 (February 1989), 14–19.

11. Robert O. Keohane and Joseph S. Nye, Jr., "Power and Interdependence Revisited," *International Organisation* 41 (Autumn 1987): 725–53.

12. Stephen Krasner, "United States Commercial and Monetary Policy: Unravelling the Paradox of External Strength and Internal Weakness," in *Between Power and Plenty. Foreign Economic Policies of Advanced*

Industrial States, edited by Peter J. Katzenstein (Madison: University of Wisconsin Press, 1978), 51–88; Stephen Krasner, *Structural Conflict. The Third World against Global Liberalism* (Berkeley: University of California Press, 1985).

13. See Maurice Wright, "Policy Community, Policy Network and Comparative Industrial Policies," *Political Studies* 36 (December 1988): 593–612.

14. Eric A. Nordlinger, *On the Autonomy of the Democratic State* (Cambridge, Mass.: Harvard University Press, 1981), 11.

15. Chalmers Johnson, "MITI, MPT and the Telecom Wars," Working paper no. 21 (Berkeley, Calif.: Berkeley Board on the International Economy, 1987); Jill Hills, "Government Relations with Industry: Japan and Britain. A Review of Two Political Arguments," *Polity* 14 (Winter 1981): 222–48; Martin Rhodes, "Industry and Modernisation: An Overview," in *France and Modernisation*, edited by John Gaffney (Aldershot, U.K.: Avebury, 1988), 66–95; Godefroy Dang Nguyen, "France, Telecommunications—Intervention at the Crossroads," in *Handbook of Information Technology and Office Systems*, edited by A. E. Cawkell (Amsterdam: Elsevier, 1986), 518–38.

16. Graham Allinson, *The Essence of Decision* (Boston: Little, Brown, 1971); Robert J. Art, "Bureaucratic Politics and American Foreign Policy: A Critique," *Policy Sciences* 4 (December 1973): 467–90.

17. Glenn Snyder and Paul Diesing, "External Bargaining and Internal Bargaining," in *International Conflict and Conflict Management*, edited by Robert O. Matthews, Arthur G. Rubinoff, and Janice Gross Stein (Scarborough, Ontario: Prentice-Hall, 1989), 238–46.

18. Jill Hills, "Neo-Conservative Regimes and Convergence in Telecommunications Policy," *European Journal of Political Research* 17 (1989): 95–113.

19. R. Hrbrek, "Technology Policy as an Engine of Integration in the EC" (Paper presented to the 14th International Political Science Association, Washington, D.C., August/Sept. 1988).

20. Paul Taylor, "Consociationalism and Federalism as Approaches to International Integration," in *Frameworks for International Co-Operation*, edited by A. J. R. Groom and P. Taylor (London: Pinter, 1990), 172–84.

21. See Joseph Pelton, "Satellites and Fiber Optics in an ISDN World," *Space, Communications and Broadcasting* 6 (1989): 361–66.

22. In older European cable systems, a loop system where a cable was slung from one household to the next in series was used. Since it is difficult

to add new subscribers to such a system, however, it was gradually abandoned.

23. B. L. Sherman, *Telecommunications Management: The Broadcast and Cable Industries* (New York: McGraw-Hill, 1987), 8; John R. Bittner, *Broadcasting and Telecommunication. An Introduction* (Englewood Cliffs, N.J.: Prentice-Hall, 1985).

24. For an overview, see Jill Hills, *Deregulating Telecoms: Competition and Control in the United States, Japan and Britain* (London: Frances Pinter, 1986), 9–17; "International Satellite Broadcasting," *Financial Times*, 29 May 1990.

25. George Calhoun, *Digital Cellular Radio* (Norwood, Mass.: Artech House, 1988), 39–44.

26. Brendan Gallagher, ed., *Never Beyond Reach* (London: Inmarsat, 1989).

27. Ian Mackintosh, *Sunrise Europe. The Dynamics of Information Technology* (Oxford: Basil Blackwell, 1986).

28. See John Zysman and Laura Tyson, eds., *American Industry in International Competition, Government Policies and Corporate Strategies* (Ithaca: Cornell University Press, 1983).

29. Centre for Business Strategy, *1992: Myths and Realities* (London: London Business School, 1989).

2

Innovation, Technology, and Trade

INNOVATION AND TRADE

In today's world, innovation, trade, and politics have become interwoven. International trade has become very important, not only to the national economies of all the industrialized countries, but also to those developing countries looking to increase their national income. Since the 1970s, Japan has become the prime example of a country that has built national wealth on the basis of exports that offset its own lack of natural resources. Other industrializing countries, such as South Korea, are now seeking to follow the Japanese example.[1]

That they can do so is related to changes in manufacturing production and to the postwar activities of both multinationals and governments. The internationalization of American multinationals has aided the diffusion of technology away from the country that had possessed the immediate postwar lead in its development. Although the theory of the product life cycle as it has been applied to international trade suggests that the innovating firm could gather monopoly prices from the introduction of an innovatory product, export it, and, as the product matured, manufacture abroad to reduce costs,the reality has been somewhat different.[2] In fact, subsidiaries of multinationals have often had to create their own products to fit the needs of local markets. Technology has had either to be transferred away from the home country, or developed locally. The activities of multinationals have therefore aided technological diffusion away from the technological leaders.

Today, the pace of technological diffusion is such that the period in which any firm has the monopoly of an innovatory product or technology is limited. In order for the industrialized countries to keep ahead, their companies must innovate constantly. Not only new products but new processes and new methods of social organization must be found in order to maintain market leads. However, as the pace of diffusion has increased, the payback period of monopoly profits on any innovation has decreased. Two trends are evident. On the one hand, company strategies have been based on economies of scale to reduce the unit costs of research and development, and on the other hand, the increasing demand for differentiated products has led to flexible manufacturing and short production runs.[3]

The postwar openness of the world trading system has resulted in shifts of relative power between states as measured by their economic growth and exports. In particular, the U.S. share of world exports has declined, while that of Japan has increased. Moreover, within this overall decline in relative position, the American decline in high-technology industries and its deficit in trade since 1986 have caused the most concern. Because exports of such products as computers, office machinery, communications equipment, and electronic components form a larger proportion of sales (about 20 percent) than exports in other product categories, the United States is particularly dependent on exports in these markets.[4]

During the 1980s, the linkage between economic success, national pride, and national security has been marked. Attention has been directed to potential government strategies to develop industrial success. Japan has been taken as a model for a government-led industrial strategy.[5] Despite the problems involved in one country attempting to duplicate the socio-economic and institutional arrangements of another, in both the United States and Europe, the search has gone on for government mechanisms that will either retain technological leadership or redress the balance of the perceived "technology gap."[6]

Some analysts make a distinction between innovation policy and industrial policy on the basis of micro and macro economics. Industrial policy is seen as utilizing a wider set of mechanisms, such as those related to trade, which are not specifically targeted at innovation. However, in looking at the new communications and information technologies, it is difficult to make any such distinction.[7]

Nancy Dorfmann has argued that U.S. government support of innovation in such technologies as transistors and microelectronics was not through micro-economic support to the sector, but in its action taken under antitrust laws against IBM and AT&T, and in government procurement of the products.[8] In a similar vein, in reviewing R&D policy in Canada during the 1970s and early 1980s, Robin Mansell has argued that the policy failed due to lack of concern with market structure.[9] We argue in this book that the technology push of R&D funding by government in the new technologies has often been linked to market restructuring. Hence, we make no distinction between innovation and industrial policy.

In this chapter we review concepts of innovation, arguing that R&D policy practiced by governments has tended to assume a direct link between funding and innovation that does not exist. R&D funding has tended to go to the largest companies for high-technology projects often linked to defense spending and based on national prestige. Such technology push may never find its way to the market. Where it does, as with satellites in Europe, governments are obliged to restructure markets to make way for the new technology. In turn, when this is done in the interests of large business, it ignores the infrastructural requirements and social organization needed for the widespread diffusion and adoption of that technology.

WHAT IS INNOVATION?

The intervention of governments in markets to foster innovation is itself primarily predicated on a particular assumption—that a financial contribution to R&D expenditure will produce innovatory activity on the part of the firm and will then lead to new products, which in turn will lead to exports. However, a number of analysts suggest that the concept of innovation underlying this model is simplistic. Innovation is not the smooth process from research and development to product that is implied in the linear pattern that underlies many policies.[10]

An emphasis on high-technology products in communications and information such as microchips, computers, satellites, and fiber optics tends to obscure the benefits to be had in all industrial sectors from the use of microelectronics and communications.[11] Not only is R&D policy often at odds with a policy of diffusion, but economists and individuals in business have come to challenge the view that such expenditure automatically achieves increased innovation. Innovation may come from customers or suppliers, or from the technical or production departments, and involves a number of different stages.[12] The causal flow is unlikely to be unidirectional, in that the overall performance of the firm will affect the level of resources available for R&D.[13]

Internal organization and politics within the firm are important to the process of innovation.[14] The internal "culture" of the organization and its level of technological accumulation will both impact on innovatory performance,[15] as will its functional organization and internal political environment.[16]

Linkages within a company between research and marketing and between the company and its customers have been shown to be important factors in the innovatory process. If customers and users are necessary factors in demand-led innovation, then isolation from the market becomes a factor in preventing the development of new technology. Government research establishments and universities have been accused of such isolation, and of being staffed by static personnel.[17] In the context of this book, both post and telecommunications administrations and public service broadcasters have been accused of being divorced from the markets they serve. Similarly, defense-related research is accused of failing to provide spin-offs to the civilian market.

Spin-offs from defense R&D are likely to come from basic research, but expenditure on basic research within military budgets is very small, estimated at 1 percent. Even within companies, defense-related research tends to be isolated from internal linkages as well as from the civilian market, and is unlikely to foster innovation for the latter.[18]

Neither will an innovation necessarily be put into practice first by the firm that produces it. Because diffusion seems to rely heavily on contact between producers or users, the geographic proximity of firms with a mutuality of interest is a means of diffusing technology between companies. The proliferation of science parks in Western Europe and the "technopolis" strategy in Japan are government attempts to increase diffusion through geographical proximity.[19]

It is evident that theories of innovation have become more complex during the 1980s, both in terms of intra-firm innovation and in terms of diffusion of technology. In the concerns of economists, who are now anxious to promote the diffusion of new technology in industrialized countries, one can see many of the arguments of the development theorists of the 1950s relating to the spread of technology within the Third World. A similar emphasis is given to the role of opinion-formers, the way know-how is acquired by contact, the importance of networks, and the localized nature of innovation.[20] Moreover, just as it is currently acknowledged that developing countries without the necessary infrastructure of education and training will be unable to handle the transfer of modern technology or make indigenous that technology, so the infrastructure of education, training, management, and finance, which underpins technological innovation, is gaining a place in the discussion of comparative advantage among industrialized countries.

However, some authors go beyond even these formal requirements to point up how informal procedures of social organization within companies and within localities (features of the general political culture of a country), may impact on the flexibility and adaptation needed to implement and integrate new technology into working practices. Macro-sociological phenomena such as education, training, and industrial relations impact on micro-sociological characteristics of formal and informal structures, processes, and interrelationships at the levels of enterprises, organizations, and individuals. These in turn affect the implementation of new technology, and the technology itself becomes part of social relations. Carla Perez has argued that new waves of technology require new institutional patterns of organization.[21] Annemieke Roobeek has pointed out how differences in workplace organization, trade union structure, departmentalism, and training all impact on the pace at which technology will be accrued into working practices. In addition, the motivation of individuals is affected by the general socioeconomic and institutional environment in which they live.[22]

A similar approach, which emphasizes the importance of local technical culture and informal social organization to innovatory and entrepreneurial activity, has been taken by Gerald Sweeney in a study of less favored regions in Europe.[23] In addition, in a fresh discussion of Japanese economic success, David Friedman has challenged existing explanations of that success based on bureaucratic or market efficiency. He argued that both explanations are based on a thesis of convergence in industrial organization, and contended instead that

> If we view politics as the fundamental orientation people possess about justice, appropriate behaviour, and rights throughout society ... even seemingly minor workplace struggles ... have crucial importance in shaping industrial order.... As the definition of economic rights varies, so too will incentives to adopt some variant of mass or of flexible production. In this view, then, an economic order is the result of countless political choices made more or less consciously throughout the industrial system; it is an artefact of the definition of justice and fairness people adopt as they encounter the workplace and the market.[24]

Friedman went on to suggest that "the politics of resource allocation or rule creation ... is much less important than the politics affecting the definition of rights in the workplace and throughout industry." He argued that Japan's greater economic success stems from the greater diffusion of flexible manufacturing strategies in that country, and that this faster adoption is related to the "definition of rights and substantive justice accepted throughout Japanese society."[25]

Each of these authors contends that neither technology nor government innovation policies determine the extent of innovation, and that the social organization of technology will vary from country to country and even within countries depending on the socio-institutional and ideological environment. Governments play a central role in the creation of favorable conditions through their structuring of the capitalist framework within a country and their definition of rights and obligations.[26] The role of governments in innovation and diffusion of technology goes beyond technology push and market restructuring to infrastructure, and to those socio-institutional and ideological values that shape the social organization of technology. Decentralization, cooperation between people with diverse, high-quality expertise, and the sharing of information seem to be prerequisites for innovatory entrepreneurial activity. Nevertheless, despite the acknowledgment among academics that innovation is not a linear process, governments still tend to see policy in those terms.

INNOVATION AND MARKET STRUCTURE

Government financing of research and development in virtually all the industrialized countries tends to go to the largest firms. The question then arises whether these companies make the best use of the money and are the most innovative. Is their success in the competition for R&D funds simply the result of their size? Increasingly, economists are coming to accept the relevance of the political environment for the efficacy of government innovation policy and the possible misallocation of resources that may go with it. However, indirect mechanisms of financing R&D through tax incentives, which theoretically benefit small business, have been shown to be ineffective in that the money is not used for the purposes intended.[27] On the question of whether large or small firms are the more innovative, the evidence is somewhat unclear, partly because the indicators of innovation are themselves not clearly defined.[28]

What has been acknowledged is that market structure produces barriers to the entry of firms.[29] In particular, start-up companies will look for niches that require less capital than is at the disposal of existing companies. The infrastructure of capital available to companies is also a matter of concern to innovation policy. In particular, the venture capital market is better developed in the United States than in France, Britain, or Japan. In both the United States and Britain, a failure by companies to invest in long-term research has been linked to the structure of finance in which shareholders demand instant returns. Similarly, in France the dominant role of government financing of R&D is attributed to failures in the capital market.[30]

New companies will avoid activities in which patent rights limit access, and they will also look to sectors of the market where there are no economies of scope or scale that provide existing firms with a price advantage.[31] Economies of scale and scope are of particular importance in government decisions concerning whether a market sector is a natural monopoly.

A natural monopoly occurs in cases where the existence of more than one firm would produce a more expensive product to the consumer than if there were only one producer. Where governments judge there to be a natural monopoly, they substitute regulation for market competition to reduce prices toward marginal costs. However, regulation itself provides a barrier to entry, and therefore may hinder technological innovation.[32]

Consequently, for instance, the antitrust ruling that divested AT&T in 1982 was backed by research for the U.S. Congress which concluded that all markets except the local telephone network were potentially competitive. Competition in these markets could be substituted for regulation of AT&T as a monopoly.[33] Similar views have also underpinned changes in telecommunications in Britain and Japan.[34]

Proponents of liberalization therefore argue that by introducing competition, innovation will be increased: For instance, without liberalization, investment by AT&T and by British Telecom in fiber optics would not have been so intense. They also argue that competition is a better means of reducing costs in a maturing market than is regulation. Hence, a policy of market liberalization can be argued as being a policy of innovation.

The problem here is that in some markets, the dominant innovator has been the major purchaser, pulling its suppliers into new products in order to service new customers, or to service old customers in new ways. As has been demonstrated in relation to the U.S. Department of Defense's provision of a market for the first microchips, the demand pull of stable, protected, domestic procurement is important in the first stage of the innovation cycle when products are expensive. Where, as with liberalization, this relationship between supplier, purchaser, and customer is undermined by competition, the result may be an overall diminution in innovatory activity. Basic research may be ignored in the interests of short-term profits. Similarly, if only large companies train their personnel, the introduction of competition and fragmentation of the market may actually impact on the future infrastructure of innovation.

These matters are of particular concern in cases where home markets are small, and where, if they are fragmented further by the entry of competition, it may become uneconomic for companies to invest in R&D. However, even in large markets the incentives for the dominant company to invest in basic research may be reduced by competition. The impact of liberalization on the telecommunications industry is discussed in chapter 3, but in general, in the United States, Britain, and Japan, there are concerns that liberalization of the telecommunications market may well have a long-term damaging effect on the basic research done by AT&T, British Telecom, and Nippon Telephone and Telegraph.[35] Moreover, the entry of new companies may raise the problem of who will pay to train future technical personnel in a competitive environment.[36]

However, restructuring of previous monopoly markets does not necessarily lead to a competitive market either domestically or internationally. Oligopolies develop, which in turn require the very regulation that was previously rejected. Hence, liberalization is not a once-and-for-all answer to the problems of fostering innovation.

TECHNOLOGY STRATEGIES

In general, government strategies can be characterized into supply-side and demand-side policies. Supply-side policies include:

1. Technology push—involving R&D support either directly or indirectly for industry and subsidies to certain companies.
2. Market restructuring—involving increased competition or concentration.
3. Standardization—to enhance or protect suppliers.

Demand-side policies include:

1. Demand pull—involving the purchasing of products by government agencies.
2. Technology diffusion—involving the diffusion of knowledge and transfer of technology between firms or between universities and firms. This might involve products, processes, or people.

3. Infrastructure—involving the underpinning of technology diffusion by raising standards in the education process through the provision of training and finance.

DOMESTIC POLICIES

In the 1960s European governments became particularly concerned about the technological gap between their own industries and those of the United States, and about their technological dependence on that country. The gap was seen as stemming from the R&D subsidies given to manufacturers through the U.S. Department of Defense. Almost inevitably, the analysis led to a solution involving the British and French governments in the backing of their own national computer firms and the imposition of a technology- rather than market-oriented policy.

Since then, most governments have tended to favor supply-side strategies, with public funding of R&D taking pride of place, but with some public procurement. One major difference exists between the constraints faced by European governments and the American and Japanese—the size of their markets. With small home markets, funding of competitive R&D by European governments was seen as wasteful. Therefore, small home markets have inevitably led to "national champion" companies financed both by R&D and preferential purchasing. Because of the very fact that this leaves only one company representing the national interest in a high-technology market, once public money has been publicly invested it is difficult for governments to withdraw. In contrast, the American, Japanese, and subsequently, the European Commission's funding of companies' research has taken place within a form of constructive competition between companies or, where they are involved in precompetitive collaboration, between consortia.

An element of national chauvinism has been involved in R&D support, and is particularly evident in past French and British policies. However, since world economic leadership by the United States has gone into decline, that national chauvinism has become prominent there also. In 1985, reviewing the goals of federal R&D policy in the information-technology sector, the U.S. Congress Office of Technology Assessment commented, "Preserving U.S. technological competitiveness and leadership is still an important policy goal with implications that extend beyond purely economic advantage."[37] Technology, national pride, national security, and international power are crucially linked.

National policies of R&D support can be differentiated in a number of ways. One primary division separating policies in the United States, France, and Britain from Japan and West Germany is the former countries' emphasis on military research and funding. In 1979, Britain's funding of defense-related research took more than 50 percent of its R&D budget, America's took just under 50 percent, and France's took 35 percent. These figures compared to 11 percent on the part of West Germany. By 1984, the proportion of American federal support for R&D devoted to the military had risen to 65 percent. The comparable proportions in West Germany and Japan were 10 percent and 1 percent.[38]

Comparative statistics from the American National Science Foundation show that whereas the United States spends a similar proportion of its gross national product (GNP) on R&D (2.76 percent in 1986) as West Germany or Japan, when defense research is taken out of the calculation, U.S. R&D expenditure as a proportion of GNP falls well below that of the two latter countries, and below that of France as well. Only Britain invests a lower proportion of GNP on civilian R&D. In both West Germany and Japan, the rate of investment in civilian R&D has not only been ahead of that of the United States for 15 years, it has been growing at increasing speed in the 1980s.

A second differentiating factor between national policies is the amount of total investment in R&D that comes from government sources. Overall, more than 50 percent of the R&D expenditure of the United States, France, and Britain comes from government, while in West Germany the proportion is 40 percent. The U.S. National Science Board commented: "As the share of national R&D effort a country devotes to defense-related activities increases, the share of resources it devotes to business-related activities decreases."[39]

The linkage of defense funding to industrial finance in the United States stems from World War II and the concurrent development of a social complex of corporate capital, government, the military, and scientific research that underpinned the development and expansion of the federal government's support of the microelectronics and computer industries.[40] The launch of the Soviet *Sputnik I*, the Cuban missile crisis, and the Vietnam War all served to legitimate and strengthen defense funding of science and technology. In the late 1950s, during the Cold War, only 15 percent of federal R&D funding went to industrial R&D. However, there have been periods, particularly following the end of the Vietnam War, when defense funding of the microelectronics and computer industries decreased in real terms to below that provided by the industry itself. The percentage of federal R&D funds devoted to civilian purposes reached a high of 40 percent in 1980.

It was during this period that the microelectronics industry freed itself from defense procurement and funding of research.[41] Between 1975 and 1980, industry-financed R&D in the United States remained stronger than in Europe as a whole. However, the decline of the U.S. economy after the oil shocks of 1973 and 1979 provided a domestic momentum induced by the threat of international competition and a perception of failing American hegemony, which allowed the reassertion of the dominance of the military.[42]

Even before the Soviet invasion of Afghanistan in 1979, U.S. President Jimmy Carter, who had been elected on a platform of military cuts, ended his stay in office with defense spending beginning to increase once more. With the election of Ronald Reagan, the share of defense R&D within the total federal R&D expenditure increased by 23 percent between 1980 and 1985.[43] In 1985, the U.S. Department of Defense spent some $85 billion on military equipment and a further $27 billion on R&D. Of this amount, the electronics sector received $26 billion in procurement and $1.48 billion for R&D.[44]

The Strategic Defense Initiative program (SDI or "Star Wars") began in March 1983 with the announcement by President Reagan of his vision of a strategic defense that would establish in space a shield that could prevent nuclear weapons from reaching their targets. As it evolved, the SDI initiative relied on the development of three linchpin technologies: computer software, technology to discriminate between missiles and other objects, and cheap space launchers. Between 1984 and 1987, the R&D budget attached to SDI amounted to $9.4 billion.[45]

The "Star Wars" program has involved the funding of both company and university research. Defense funding of university research grew by 115 percent between 1980 and 1986, to $1,065 million.[46] This funding of university and company research has gone outside the United States to both Europe and Japan, thereby helping to skew research in those countries away from civilian technology.

Within the United States itself, military backing of R&D and procurement in the new technologies has gained in importance. In its 1988 report, the U.S. Department of Commerce noted the domestic slowdown in the market for optic fibers and optoelectronic components following the completion of the installation of fiber networks by the telecommunications long-lines companies. The department commented: "Perhaps the most promising market for fiber optics will be the government. . . . Military spending on fiber optics could reach a cumulative $2 billion by the end of 1990."[47] Concerning radio communication equipment, it stated, "The level of military procurement budgets will continue to be the single most important factor affecting growth." And in regard to computer systems, it pointed out: "The Defense Advanced Research Project Agency's Strategic Computing Initiative has spent about \$400m since 1983 on A1 oriented programs . . . and expert systems for development of 'smart' weapons."[48]

In a country with a liberal market ideology, where the only legitimate mechanism for the subsidy of industry is in the interest of "national security," numbers of civilian technologies have beaten their way to the military's door. Sematech, a consortium to research microelectronics, and companies seeking to develop microchips for HDTV have been supported by the military. And as detailed in chapter 8, the American Electronics Association made a bid for funding on the grounds that an economic catastrophe would overtake America if the computing industry were lost to the Japanese.

In Europe as well large electronics companies such as Thomson of France, the General Electric Company and Racal of Britain, and Siemens of West Germany are linked to the defense industry. France and Britain both spend large proportions (13 percent) of their military budgets on R&D, compared to 3 percent in West Germany.[49] In France and Britain there is also more isolation from the market than in West Germany or America because a greater proportion of the research is done in publicly owned institutions rather than companies.[50]

A considerable proportion of European national expenditure also goes for satellite research, with between 4 and 5 percent of national research budgets in France and West Germany, and 10 percent in Italy devoted to space. These sums reflect a desire by these countries to manufacture their own satellites, as well as contributions to the European Space Agency. While approximately 10 percent of national budgets were devoted to European collaborative projects in the 1970s, the great majority of this cooperation (outside the EC) was in space and defense.[51]

France has taken the lead in space research since the 1960s, linking it with its independent nuclear deterrent. The American SDI program was originally seen as a threat to European space efforts, and elicited from President François Mitterand of France a proposal for a European collaborative program in civil technology, called "Eureka." West German support seems to have come from similar fears of technological dependence on the United States and the impact American export controls could have on its trade with East Germany and the USSR. Separate from European Commission programs, and to some extent in competition with them, Eureka is predominantly funded by industry.[52] Despite its initial proposal that the collaboration should be civilian-based, defense technologies do not seem to have been excluded. In addition, the French government later withdrew their opposition to the participation of French companies in SDI.

This further trend toward defense-based research has led commentators to point out that America has been able to set the technological agenda for Europe. Mario Pianta has argued that the United States has sought a high-tech fix for the decline in American economic hegemony.[53] Although uncoordinated, it seems that the process of regaining American technological hegemony has led to attempts to incorporate and utilize both Japanese and European technology for American interests through that technology's linkage with military security. In these and other projects within Europe, the threat of Soviet aggression on the one hand, and Japanese economic aggression on the other, have been utilized to legitimate the reorientation of technological research toward these American interests. The promise of money to groups starved for research funds in a recession-plagued Europe provided the means of bypassing reluctant governments.

With realignment within Europe and the ending of the Cold War, it seems unlikely that an export market for military goods will be so easily available in the 1990s. It therefore seems probable that unless military R&D expenditure on new technology produces civilian spin-offs, it will necessarily decline in the United States, France, Britain, and West Germany.

DIFFUSION AND TECHNOLOGY CONTROL

Differentiating between national R&D policies, Henry Ergas has divided European governments and the United States into "mission-oriented" and "diffusion-oriented" countries, placing the United States, Britain, and France in the former category, and Sweden, Switzerland, and West Germany in the latter. He defined mission orientation as technology policy that is intimately linked to national sovereignty, focusing on goals of national importance. In contrast, a diffusion orientation has the principal purpose of diffusing technological capabilities throughout the industrial structure, thereby facilitating adaptation to change.[54]

However, in West Germany, as in the United States, France, and Britain, it is predominantly large companies that benefit from research funding, through sectoral-specific policies.[55] The French have been the most aggressive in instigating demand pull through public procurement; nonetheless, in all the major West European countries such demand-pull policies in support of national industries have operated either directly or indirectly. One could also argue that the European Commission has tried to use public purchasing by community institutions to engender such a pull. In the

1990s, an ISDN network that has been proposed between EC research collaborators has a similar intention.[56]

Public procurement is simply one way of ensuring the diffusion of a product, thereby benefiting the supplier.[57] However, for governments to attempt to diffuse technology through the market is a more complicated process, and one that has achieved little prominence in terms of expenditure. For instance, the EC spends only 6 percent of its R&D budget on this process. Nevertheless, to some extent all governments are now concerned with that domestic diffusion. Programs range from the transfer of technical personnel to small companies in West Germany, to publicity-style campaigns on value-added telecommunications services financed by the British government, and to decentralization in France, to changes in antitrust law in the United States and the EC's STAR program for the improvement of access to telecommunications in less favored regions (see chapter 6).

Industry-university and -research institute links have been pushed closer both in the United States and in Europe. However, problems arise because of the short-term nature of industry time spans compared to longer term perspectives in universities, because of the often very specific needs of industry compared with the generic view within universities, and because of problems of control over the project—who gains patent rights and who is allowed access to the technology.

In 1984, American antitrust law was amended to allow cooperation between American companies in precompetitive research. As a result of this amendment, and tax incentives for R&D, companies have been investing both in intra-industry consortia and in academic-industry groupings. According to the U.S. Department of Commerce, between 1984 and 1985, 45 new or proposed consortia were created.[58] Earliest among these, and taking advantage of the unofficial relaxation of the Carter years, was Semiconductor Research Corporation, founded by IBM. This consortium of 20 companies is funded entirely by industry. However, a similar alliance between semiconductor makers to ensure a supply of Dynamic Random Access Memory (DRAM) microchips failed in 1989 for lack of support from computer companies.

Another cooperative research institute, Sematech, was launched in 1988 with U.S. Pentagon backing, and has constructed a manufacturing facility for advanced semiconductor devices. Both the industry and the Pentagon argued that such a cooperative was the only way to prevent Japanese domination of the semiconductor market, and through it the computer and telecommunications industries. For the U.S. Defense Department, the major aim of the project was to stave off dependency on foreign suppliers for weapons components, while for the industry, the major aim was to find financing for R&D after two years of losses.[59] Fourteen companies had become members of the consortium by 1990. Although Sematech refused entry to U.S. subsidiaries of European companies, the problem of attempting to retain technology within one country is illustrated by its decision in 1990 to cooperate with its European counterpart, Jessi, a consortium backed by the European Commission.[60] Moreover, the problems in getting congressional funding for Sematech illustrate the difficulties of such federally financed efforts in technology transfer.

In both the United States and Europe, much of the activity to promote technology transfer and innovation has taken place at the local level. In the United States, cooperative projects have been set up with state funding. Just as regions and localities in Europe have attempted to finance their own industrial regeneration, so the American states have taken up the slack in federal funding of R&D. They are looking, as the Europeans look, for industrial regeneration through high-technology products and processes, and for a gain in competitiveness of traditional industry through the diffusion of technology. To some extent, the interest in endogenous industrial renewal replaces the attraction of branch plant manufacture, which is seen as a potential strategy for only a few areas. Only in Britain does the attraction of foreign investment, particularly by the Japanese, still form a central feature of government policy.[61]

However, these local consortia often lack the infrastructure of training and culture on which to build. Sometimes they arise simply as a result of political rivalry between cities. Commenting on 15 of these American consortia in 1985, Dan Diamanescu and James Botkin stated that the weakness lies not in the development of the technology—the technology push—but in the level of management within the firms themselves, where technology transfer has little priority.[62] Similarly, in Europe such initiatives have not necessarily led to either localized information networks or the creation of new firms. In the U.K. in particular, management training in innovation or even in the use of new technology is lacking.[63]

One problem is that the diffusion of technology is not necessarily in the interests of firms. In the United States, the specific aim of academic/industry consortia has been to withhold technology transfer to any but those institutions partaking in the consortia. Access costs then exclude small companies.

Unless one can stop the transfer of personnel between companies and countries, one cannot stop the diffusion of research findings and technology. However, it is possible to attempt to slow down the international diffusion of technology in order to retain monopoly profits for as long as possible. One mechanism used by companies is to not apply for patents for innovations, in order to maintain a cloak of secrecy.[64] Other mechanisms are possible at the international level by control of the free flow of information through privacy legislation or through "security" conditions attached to exports. In particular, during the 1980s the American government demonstrated concern with the international diffusion of American technology.

Whereas in Europe the presence of American companies has allowed them to benefit from inclusion in technology initiatives such as the EC's ESPRIT (European Strategic Programme for Research in Information Technology) program, the process of gaining access to Japanese technology has involved bilateral deals and pressure on Japan as a military ally. In 1982 the Japanese were pressured to hand over to the American government technology developed for the civilian market, which the United States claimed was "critical" military technology. The Japanese eventually agreed to this transfer of civilian technology.[65] Similar arguments were used again in 1987 when the Japan-U.S. Technology Agreement came up for renewal. In 1987, the American government cited as a problem the imbalance of U.S. technology exports to Japan compared to its imports, and complained that Japanese companies were filing an increased number of patent applications in the United States. The American government also objected to the numbers of Japanese postgraduate students at American universities who gained free access to research and technology and to Japan's seeming inability to fund such basic research.[66]

The 1987 agreement demanded not "equal access" but "symmetrical access" to Japanese public and private R&D, that the Japanese open up to American companies the technology that resulted from American original research, that Japanese government-sponsored R&D projects be opened to American researchers, and that the number of American researchers in Japan be increased. Since the Japanese have almost no university-based research, these researchers would have to be based in either government or industry research laboratories. The Japanese agreed to the last three demands, and also agreed to joint research in nine areas, including information technology, superconductors, and the development of data bases.

In Europe, such controls over technology transfer and diffusion have been implemented through the U.S. Export Administration Act, which underwent a number of revisions during the 1980s. Under its provisions, both American and non-American technology to be exported by American companies or individuals must be licensed. The American list of "military critical technology" to be covered was wider than that agreed to by the Co-ordinating Committe for Multilateral Export Controls (CoCom)

(North Atlantic Treaty Organization countries except Iceland and Spain), as was the list of countries that may not be exported to. The impact of the controls have been threefold: First, to limit European access to American technological research; second, to control the movement of technology and products within Europe; and third, to prevent the entry of foreign firms into certain sectors of the American market, such as semiconductors. However, American companies have been damaged by these controls, because wherever possible, European companies have gone to other suppliers.[67]

Hence, the research strategy currently adopted by a number of disparate elements in American government ignores alleged weaknesses in American R&D—its overemphasis on defense, its underfunding of civilian R&D and basic research, its poor production of scientific graduates and declining research facilities—and concentrates on protection against Japan's rising technological capability.[68] With perhaps less emphasis on technology control, but with a suspicion of both American and Japanese intentions, European innovation policies have followed a broadly similar track.

INFRASTRUCTURE

The level at which Japan and West Germany most diverge from the rest of the industrialized countries is in terms of the emphasis that each has placed on infrastructure. Both have high standards of education and training, systems of rewards for educational and training qualifications, and systems of social organization which, although different from each other, are predominantly consensual. Both also have a well-developed small- and medium-sized manufacturing business community.

In contrast, the United States, France, and Britain all suffer from a shortage of trained personnel. In the United States this shortfall has been compensated for since 1985 primarily by the recruitment of foreign personnel, both to research and development work and to university teaching. In academia, a major reason for this shortage is the decline in numbers of doctoral degrees, especially in engineering, awarded to U.S. citizens. In line with France and West Germany, the science and engineering workforce in the United States is aging compared to that in the U.K or Japan, suggesting that further shortages may occur in the future.[69]

Whereas the United States has been able to attract foreign personnel to fill its labor needs, Britain and France in particular suffer from a lack of investment in the educational infrastructure. All estimates by industry and government show a shortfall of trained personnel at all levels of the information-technology industry and a failure of companies to train their staff. Both the French and British governments have responded to what they perceived as shortcomings in higher education by a restructuring of the sector while a national curriculum has been introduced to schools in Britain in an attempt to raise standards.[70]

A problem for the European Commission is that while innovation may rely not only on technological push and market restructuring but also on the capacity to diffuse and integrate technology into everyday life, only initiatives regarded as "economic" are considered legitimate by national governments. Initiatives by the European Community in education have not been kindly regarded by national governments—particularly Britain, with its concern for sovereignty. Moreover, the British government still refuses to accept the European Social Charter, which would define the rights of workers within the new market structure. Spurred on by what is seen as a technology gap between Europe and the other industrialized countries, an industrial policy based on an internationalized market structure with an emphasis on technology push and economies of scale is being put into place by the European Community. However, that structure lacks the democratic control and the very underpinnings of social organization necessary for innovation.

CONCLUSION

In general, there is no evidence that the United States is losing its lead in technology in the information and communications industries; rather, other countries are catching up. The problem for the United States in 1990 is that, given political development toward democracy in Eastern Europe, the rationale for defense spending has been undercut. Such moves threaten the "industrial policy" component of the defense program—such as the development of HDTV and Sematech.

Additionally, the balance of advantage between Europe and the United States has changed. Not only will the 1992 opening of the EC market create a large population base, but as a result, Europe will now have a cheap, easily accessible source of labor and markets for its technology goods. European companies have already done more business in manufactured goods with the Eastern bloc than the United States, and it is evident that they are moving eastward to create an even greater concentration of capital. The prospect is one of greater competition between regional trading blocs, particularly in technologically intensive industries. As this book demonstrates, these "technological regions" are already being put in place, with technological standards being used instead of protective tariffs.

National and regional R&D policies have all had the same intent—to promote "domestic" companies and "domestic" manufacture. Employment remains a priority. Nonetheless, the restructuring of the global industry has implications for these policies, as the EC has found in its efforts to develop European industry. A foreign company with large numbers of employees can lay claim to be a domestic company, as IBM has done in France. It is difficult to determine what constitutes "domestic" manufacture when a product is designed in one country, parts are made in several others, and the product is assembled in yet another locale. "Local content" rules have been adopted by the EC to attempt to control the loss in sovereignty produced by the globalization of production and distribution. These local content rules relate to the manufacture of products such as television programs as well as to manufactured goods. Whereas in the past the American government has tended to rely on import tariffs and quotas, in the 1990s, increasing inward foreign investment already poses the problem of what is an "American" company in a globalized economy.

In the 1990s, the policies of national sovereignty through technological leadership may well give way to policies designed to retain the sovereignty of regional trading blocs. However, as the rest of this book attests, the globalization of the new communications and information technologies is inherent in their economics. Cross-national alliances and investment promotes domestic restructuring and involves governments in the reregulation of markets as they seek to retain national or regional political control of these internationalized growth technologies. At the time of this writing, the U.S. Justice Department has taken the unprecedented step of evaluating the global market share of companies before allowing a domestic takeover by a foreign company.

Much of national government policies in Europe are devoted to similar concepts of technology push and demand pull as in the United States, as are policies of the EC. While such policies may be efficacious at the start of the product cycle, the extended linkage between the provision of government funds and the actual production of goods for the market allows the entry of many political, cultural, and economic factors opposed to innovation. In general, there is a question mark over the extent of technological innovation that has been funded by government and the efficacy with which it has been converted into products or processes and diffused. In particular, an undue emphasis on large companies and on defense and space electronics, and a failure to spend on basic research or infrastructure may have helped weaken the long-term prospects of the British, French, and U.S. communications and information sector. Moreover, while Japan and West Germany have benefited from protectionism, they have also reaped the advantages of a political and cultural emphasis on education and training, as well as characteristics in their general societal system that aid technological diffusion. These consensual characteristics may already be changing under external pressures from economic and political developments. Hence, in all countries, new mechanisms of government policy aimed at innovation and a restructuring of thought are needed to combat the potential concentration, centralization, and exclusive organization of the technologies of information distribution documented in this book.

NOTES

1. See John Zysman and Laura Tyson, eds., *American Industry in International Competition* (Ithaca, N.Y.: Cornell University Press, 1983); Francis Rushing and Carole Ganz Brown, eds., *National Policies for Developing High Technology Industries* (Boulder, Colo.: Westview Press, 1986).

2. Raymond Vernon, "International Investment and International Trade in the Product Cycle," *Quarterly Journal of Economics* 80 (May 1966): 190–204.

3. P.A. Consulting Group, *Manufacturing into the Late 1990s* (London: HMSO, 1989).

4. National Science Board, *Science and Engineering Indicators 1987* (Washington, D.C.: Government Printing Office, 1988), 124.

5. See George C. Eads and Richard R. Nelson, "Japanese High Technology Policy: What Lessons for the U.S.?" in *Japanese High Technology Industries. Lessons and Limitations of Industrial Policy*, edited by Hugh Patrick with Larry Meissner (Seattle: University of Washington Press, 1986), 243–70.

6. Erik Arnold and Ken Guy, *Parallel Convergence. National Strategies in Information Technology* (London: Frances Pinter, 1986), 34.

7. Mary Ellen Mogee, "Knowledge and Politics in Innovation Policy Design," in *Government Innovation Policy: Design, Implementation, Evaluation*, edited by J. David Roessner (Basingstoke, U.K.: Macmillan, 1988), 37–48.

8. Nancy Dorfmann, *Innovation and Market Structure. Lessons from the Computer and Semiconductor Industries* (Cambridge, Mass.: Ballinger, 1987), 180, 214–17.

9. Robin Mansell, *Contradictions and Illusions: The Canadian Communication Policy Experience* (Vancouver: William H. Melody and Associates, August 1985, mimeographed).

10. See Roy Rothwell and Walter Zegveld, *Reindustrialization and Technology* (Harlow: Longman, 1985), 47–81.

11. Aaron Gellman, "U.S. National Policies for High Tech Industries. Some Lessons Learned," in Rushing and Brown, *National Policies*, 227–35.

12. Thierry Gaudin, "Definition of Innovation Policies," in *Innovation Policies. An International Perspective*, edited by Gerald Sweeney (London: Frances Pinter, 1985), 12.

13. Christopher T. Hill and John A. Hansen, "The Measurement of Technology and Innovation," in *Government Innovation Policy. Design, Implementation, Evaluation*, edited by J. David Roessner (London: Macmillan, 1988), 152.

14. Gaudin, "Definition," 12.

15. Keith Pavitt, "Patterns of Technological Change—Evidence, Theory and Policy Implications," Papers in Science, Technology and Public Policy (Brighton, U.K.: University of Sussex, Science Policy Research Unit, 1983); quoted in Rothwell and Zegveld, *Reindustrialization*, 72.

16. Roy Rothwell and Walter Zegveld give an overview of the literature; see Rothwell and Zegveld, *Reindustrialization*, 83–107.

17. See Rikard Stankiewicz, "A New Role for Universities in Technological Innovation," in Sweeney, *Innovation Policies*, 114–51.

18. Euan Maddock, *Civil Exploitation of Defence Technology* (London: HMSO, 1983).

19. Sheridan Tatsuno, *The Technopolis Strategy. Japan, High Technology, and the Control of the Twenty-First Century* (New York: Prentice-Hall, 1986).

20. See, for instance, Everett Rogers and James Dearing, "The Japanese Experience: Tskuba City" (Paper presented to the 40th International Communications Association Annual Conference, Dublin, June 1990).

21. Carla Perez, "New Technologies and Development," in *Small Countries Facing the Technological Revolution*, edited by Christopher Freeman and B. A. Lindall (London: Pinter, 1988), 85–97.

22. Annemieke J. M. Roobeek, "The Forgotten Dimension in the Technology Race" (Paper presented to the International Conference on the Theory of Regulation, Barcelona, June 1988).

23. Gerald Sweeney, "The Information Networks Designed to Support Technological Innovation in Less Favoured Regions of the Community" (Paper presented to the 40th International Communications Association Annual Conference, Dublin, June 1990).

24. David Friedman, *The Misunderstood Miracle. Industrial Develop-*

ment and Political Change in Japan (Ithaca: Cornell University Press, 1988), 17.

25. Ibid., 18.

26. Roobeek, "Forgotten Dimension," 24.

27. Helmar Krupp, "Public Promotion of Innovation—Disappointments and Hopes," in Sweeney, *Innovation Policies*, 48–79.

28. Albert H. Rubenstein and Eliezer Geisler, "The Use of Indicators and Measures of the R&D Process in Evaluating Science and Technology Programmes," in Roessner, *Government Innovation Policy*, 185–203; Dorfmann, *Innovation and Market Structure*, 244.

29. John Barber and Geoff White, "Current Policy Practice and Problems from a U.K. Perspective," in *Economic Policy and Technological Performance*, edited by Partha Dasgupta and Paul Stoneman (Cambridge: Cambridge University Press, 1987), 24–50.

30. See John Plender, "Malaise in Need of a Long-Term Remedy," *Financial Times*, 20 July 1990; Louise Kehoe, "Capital Plan for U.S. Electronics," *Financial Times*, 9 November 1989; George Hatsopoulos and Stephen Brooks, *The Gap in the Cost of Capital: Causes, Effects and Remedies* (Cambridge, Mass.: Ballinger, 1986); Martin Rhodes, "Industry and Modernisation: An Overview," in *France and Modernisation*, edited by John Gaffney (Aldershot, U.K.: Avebury, 1988), 70.

31. On barriers to entry, see Dorfmann, *Innovation and Market Structure*, passim.

32. Kenneth Flamm, "Technological Advance and Costs: Computers versus Communications," in *Changing the Rules: Technological Change, International Competition and Regulation in Communications*, edited by Robert Crandall and Kenneth Flamm (Washington, D.C.: Brookings Institution, 1989), 13–61.

33. U. S. Congress, House Majority Staff of the Subcommittee on Telecommunications, Consumer Protection and Finance of the Committee on Energy and Commerce, *Telecommunications in Transition: The Status of Competition in the Telecommunications Industry*, 97th Cong., 1st Sess. (Washington, D.C.: Government Printing Office, 1981.)

34. Jill Hills, *Deregulating Telecoms. Competition and Control in the U.S., Japan and Britain* (London: Frances Pinter, 1986).

35. See Flamm, "Technological Advance," 59–60; Jill Hills, "Techno-Industrial Innovation and State Policies on Telecommunications in the United States and Japan," in *State Policies and Techno-Industrial Innovation*, edited by Ulrich Hilpert (London: Routledge, 1990); Michael Noll, "The Effects of Divestiture on Telecommunications Research," *Journal of Communication* 2 (Winter 1987): 73–80.

36. In 1990 in Britain the commercial broadcasting and cable TV companies proposed an independent training institute.

37. U.S. Congress, Office of Technology Assessment, *Information Technology R&D. Critical Trends and Issues* (Washington, D.C.: Government Printing Office, 1985), 4.

38. Stockholm International Peace Research Institute, *Yearbook 1984* (London: Taylor and Francis, 1984), Tables 6.2–6.4.

39. National Science Board, *Science and Engineering Indicators 1987* (Washington, D.C.: Government Printing Office, 1988), 4; Eurostat, *Government Financing of Research and Development, 1970–79* (Brussels: CEC, 1980), 53–70.

40. Alfonso Hernan Molina, *The Social Basis of the Microelectronics Revolution* (Edinburgh: Edinburgh University Press, 1989), 36–61.

41. Dorfmann, *Innovation and Market Structure*, 215–16.

42. D. Dickson, *The New Politics of Science* (New York: Pantheon Books, 1952), quoted in Molina, *Microelectronics Revolution*, 26–27.

43. Mario Pianta, *New Technologies Across the Atlantic. U.S. Leadership or European Autonomy* (Hemel Hempstead, U.K.: Harvester-Wheatsheaf, 1988), 3.

44. Douglas Webber, Martin Rhodes, J. J. Richardson, and Jeremy Moon, "Information Technology and Economic Recovery in Western Europe," *Policy Sciences* 19 (October 1986), 322.

45. Council of Economic Priorities, *Star Wars. The Economic Fallout* (Cambridge, Mass.: Ballinger, 1988), 34–35.

46. Ibid., 78.

47. U.S. Department of Commerce, International Trade Administration, *1988 U.S. Industrial Outlook* (Washington, D.C.: Government Printing Office, 1988), Section 31, 7.

48. Ibid., Section 30, 4.

49. Council for Science and Society, *U.K. Military R&D* (Oxford: Oxford University Press, 1986), 7–15.

50. Bernd Huebner, "The Importance of Arms Exports and Armament Cooperation for the West German Defence Industrial Base," in *The Defence Industrial Base and the West*, edited by David Haglund (London: Routledge, 1989), 119–62.

51. Eurostat, *Government Financing*, 66; Chatham House, *Europe's Future in Space* (London: Royal Institute of International Affairs, Routledge and Kegan Paul, 1988).

52. John Peterson, "Eureka and the Symbolic Politics of High Technology," *Politics* 9 (April 1989): 8–13; Douglas Webber, Martin Rhodes, J. J. Richardson, and Jeremy Moon, "Information Technology and Economic

Recovery in Western Europe," *Policy Sciences* 19 (October 1986): 333–36.

53. Pianta, *New Technologies*, 78.

54. Henry Ergas, "The Importance of Technology Policy," in Dasgupta and Stoneman, *Economic Policy*, 51–96.

55. Webber, Rhodes, Richardson, and Moon, "Information Technology," 326.

56. *Telecommunications* 24 (June 1990): 20.

57. Paul Stoneman, "Some Analytical Observations on Diffusion Policies," in Dasgupta and Stoneman, *Economic Policy*, 154–68.

58. Dan Diamenscu and James Botkin, *The New Alliance. America's R&D Consortia* (Cambridge, Mass.: Ballinger, 1986), 5.

59. Loise Kehoe, "Pentagon Takes Initiative in War against Chip Imports," *Financial Times*, 27 January 1987; Loise Kehoe, "Chip Makers Ask Congress for Help," *Financial Times*, 2 March 1987.

60. Michael Skapinger and Loise Kehoe, "A Marriage of Convenience," *Financial Times*, 11 April 1990.

61. U.S. Congress, Office of Technology Assessment, *Technology, Innovation and Regional Economic Development* (Washington, D.C.: Government Printing Office, 1983), 9–10.

62. Diamenescu and Botkin, *New Alliance*, 27–44, 134–35.

63. *Financial Times*, 11 July 1990.

64. Giles V. Berlin and Sally Wyatt, *Multinationals and Industrial Property. The Control of the World's Technology* (Hemel Hempstead, U.K.: Harvester-Wheatsheaf, 1988), 3–23.

65. Jill Hills, "Foreign Policy and Technology: The Japan-U.S., Japan-Britain and Japan-E.E.C. Technology Agreements," *Political Studies* 31 (June 1983): 205–23.

66. *Japan Economic Journal*, 16 January 1988.

67. Stuart MacDonald, "Stunting the Growth. Information, Technology and U.S. Export Controls" (Paper presented to the Information Technology and New Economic Growth Opportunities Workshop, Tokyo, September 1988).

68. Eric Bloch, "Managing for Challenging Times: A National Research Strategy," *Issues in Science and Technology* 11 (Winter 1986): 20–29.

69. National Science Board, *Science and Engineering Indicators*, 66, 72.

70. Sig Prais, "Oiling the School System Machinery," *Financial Times*, 25 April 1990.

3

The Restructuring of
the Telecommunications Market

The introduction to this book argued that technologies are mediated by political, economic, and cultural factors. In particular, the social coalitions comprising economic and political stakeholders surrounding any one technology are important in determining the national distribution of welfare.[1]

In this chapter we look at the restructuring process in telecommunications in the United States and Western Europe. Policies do not strictly follow the ideological lines of governments, but all are concerned with competitive advantage.[2]

In the past, telecommunications networks were run by nationally based, mainly publicly owned, domestic telecommunications authorities (PTTs). The organizations saw their task as the extension of telephone penetration throughout their countries, starting first with urban connections and moving gradually into the countryside. Administrations have differed in the amount of importance they have attached to urban as opposed to rural, business as opposed to residential, and long-distance as opposed to local service, but, in general, in the industrialized countries a system of charging grew up in which the costs of access and of local and rural calls were kept down in order to increase penetration.

On an international basis, telecommunications has been organized along the lines of separate domestic systems, linked at the borders. Governments have been assumed to have sovereign control over those systems. Through the International Telecommunications Union (ITU), PTTs have extended this domestic control into international transmission through collaboration with each other both in investment in facilities linking countries and in the way they were regulated. Under the recommendations of the ITU's Consultative Committee on International Telegraph and Telecommunications (CCITT), it was forbidden for any other group than PTTs or Recognized Private Operating Agencies, such as AT&T, to provide international service to third parties. Bilateral agreements between countries determined how revenue from international traffic should be shared, but the general principle was established that the country with outgoing calls should pay 50 percent of the agreed amount to the country to which the calls were made.[3]

This accounting rate between countries did not have to reflect the actual cost of the call to the PTT or its charge to customers. In the majority of countries international tariffs have been held at a high level in order to reduce domestic tariffs or sustain equipment prices or because of the balance-of-payments implications of any surge in international calls (and therefore outgoing revenue) that follows a reduction in tariffs. The beneficiaries of this division of revenues have been European countries in particular, which have received more calls (and, therefore, revenue) from the United States than they have placed. International tariffs have traditionally subsidized national penetration goals and national manufacture. Thus, the international has been subordinate to the national.

In pursuing the goal of maximum penetration, PTTs have had the backing of trade unions, the general public, rural areas, and telecommunications manufacturers. Loss-making postal administrations have often been supported by the growth in telecommunications. The stakeholders in this traditional network organization—the postal industrial complex, as Eli Noam has termed them—have held considerable power in European countries.[4]

In this traditional framework the national PTT was also responsible for setting standards for equipment, and through national standards was able to erect nontariff barriers in favor of local industry.[5] Because national equipment markets were protected, the supply of equipment rested with a small number of manufacturers, all linked with the PTT, with which they conducted joint research and development. Hence, where companies expanded abroad, they tended to do so through takeovers of domestic companies or the establishment of local subsidiaries.[6]

For many years, large users, a few of whom supply most PTTs with at least 60 percent of their income, did not complain about this distribution of welfare. The cost of long distance on the public switched network was compensated for by the lower cost of leased lines, which were tariffed via a flat-rate fee. Governments also found control of the telephone service convenient, using it to meet social welfare objectives such as reducing rural isolation, and for macroeconomic objectives. Telecommunications has often been used as a milk cow by national treasuries which have called on it to make subventions to the national budget (as in France in the early 1980s). In addition, telecommunications policy has always been closely linked with the concept of national defense and sovereignty, and for this reason was left out of agreements on such matters as public procurement made under the General Agreement on Trade and Tariffs (GATT).

In general, each national PTT held a monopoly over the whole network—transmission, switching, and equipment. The United States was the only country with a privately owned network operator (AT&T) which was controlled through an independent agency, the Federal Communications Commission (FCC), and the only country with several international operators. In other countries, such as Finland and Denmark, private telephone companies have existed but long-distance service and overall control has been exercised by the state. In both Spain and Portugal, a privately owned telephone company has had a monopoly, but under state control.

Public ownership was considered a guarantee of the public accountability of the PTT. The actual political control of the PTT, and political interference in its day-to-day running, varied under this ownership, from a situation where the PTT was more or less autonomous in its finances (as in West Germany) to one where it was funded on a year-to-year basis following parliamentary discussion (as in the Netherlands and Britain). Other aspects of network operation, such as tariffs, were controlled in respect to macroeconomic policy but were not regulated in terms of "costs." In general, equipment was expected to last for a minimum of 20 years, and was depreciated over a long period, thereby keeping tariffs low and investment in new technology at a minimum. Because the PTT was itself in charge of the introduction of new services, acting as both supplier and regulator, it was able to allow entry only at the margins of its monopoly, if at all.

The first attempts at restructuring the telecommunications market came in the manufacturing industry. State-led concentration began in the 1960s in Britain, and was followed in the 1970s in France and Italy, and again in the 1980s in France. It became evident that a home market, fragmented between a number of manufacturers, could not give the returns needed to recoup R&D costs on digital technology. Export markets became increasingly important. At the same time, international travel began to undermine equipment monopolies. Following the liberalization of the American equipment market in the 1970s, illegal telephones appeared in Europe in increasing numbers, forcing PTTs to upgrade their handset offerings, and leading to the piecemeal liberalization of national equipment markets.

The first evidence of commercialization in network operation began with the establishment of legal space between the PTT and the government in Britain during the latter 1960s and the formulation of rules of conduct in terms of profit and loss. A second stage in Britain involved the separation of telecommunications from posts within the same organization. The third stage was to liberalize the equipment and network markets, followed by the privatization of British Telecom in 1984, when operation and regulation were separated.

It took some time for most other European countries to begin this process of commercialization of the PTT. In the 1970s, the French PTT began to set up its own subsidiaries, and the Socialist government of 1981 emphasized profit making for public enterprises. In the latter 1980s, the first three of these stages were being followed in West Germany, and also formed the basis for the European Commission's directive on liberalization. Steps toward restructuring are expected in the early 1990s in Belgium, Italy, and Portugal. Only in the Netherlands has this commercialization involved the formal reconstruction of the PTT into a state-owned company, but whether formally public or private, commercialization—in the sense of a search for revenue and profit—has taken place within the PTTs.

At the international level, one can begin to see a reconceptualization of the network. The first intimations of this reconceptualization came in the early 1980s when the International Telecommunications Union (ITU), the United Nations agency which is dominated by government-owned telecommunications administrations, was forced to recognize the private international networks set up by the banks and airline industries. These networks evidenced a move away from the idea of separate "billiard ball" systems, linked only at the borders, to a concept whereby international transmission was visualized as going from company A within country A to a subsidiary in country B, and perhaps crossing several national borders in between. This conceptualization challenges the impermeability of the sovereign control of domestic telecommunications, and has been the basis of American and multinational company demands for liberalization of regulations in the ITU and GATT. It represents a fundamental challenge to sovereignty without putting into place any international regulatory system to replace domestic control.

REGULATORY FRAMEWORKS

Liberalization and privatization are two separate processes; the first introduces competition into the market, while the second simply changes ownership without changing the structure of the market. Because of the difference in terminology and meaning of the same word in different languages, a confusion has arisen between the two concepts and between the relationship of political control to privatization. A company that has been "privatized" is not necessarily less controlled than it was under public ownership. In other words, liberalization (the entry of competition), privatization (the selling of shares in a previous public entity), and political control are separate variables that will differ in each country. Privatization also has a different connotation in Eastern European countries and those under previous authoritarian rule (such as South Korea), where it is seen as a means to the establishment of accountability and democracy.

Regulation, the imposition of rules by governments on industry, is usually divided into structural regulation—that is, regulation that controls the behavior of companies through the introduction of competition—and behavioral regulation, which provides controls when there is no competition. In general, the entry of competition into a market is seen as an alternative to the imposition of rules by governments. The assumption in Britain was that the market would impose discipline on the previous monopoly operator through competition. This so-called "structural regulation through competition" would avoid the need for regulation of the operator's behavior.[7] Therefore, when British Telecom (BT) was first privatized, the City of London's institutional investors were assured that behavioral regulation of BT would be conducted with a light rein. Similarly, in the United States, the original intention of the Justice Department during the AT&T divestiture was to effect a structural separation of AT&T through Judge Harold Green's court, which would preclude the need for further behavioral regulation.[8]

However, in neither country has structural regulation reduced behavioral regulation. In Britain, following a 1987 strike by BT engineers, the regulator came under fire for regulating in BT's interests. Subsequently, its regulation of BT's behavior has increased. Moreover, as the balance of power between large users and the dominant operator has swung toward BT, so, at their behest, the regulator has even intervened in assessing BT's behavior in what had previously been termed competitive markets.[9] Hence, BT's privatization has had no impact on the reduction of regulation, while liberalization itself has been shown to be ineffective in controlling company behavior. In other words, neither liberalization nor privatization, of themselves, alter political control.

Regulators may be based within a ministry, or formally separate from the ministry but still within the civil service, as in Britain, West Germany, and the Netherlands. Such a model is the system preferred by the European Commission. The model says nothing, however, about accountability.

Although the European regulators may be formally accountable to their parliaments, none are financially dependent on approval by those parliaments in the same way as the American FCC depends on Congress. Moreover, none are publicly elected as are American state utility commissioners.

The question of where to draw lines of demarcation between markets is one that concerns both governments and regulators. It is possible to conceive of telecommunications networks as comprising customer premises equipment, local networks, domestic long-distance networks, and international networks. It is possible to see them as comprising voice and data services or voice and enhanced services (or value-added services including some voice). Alternatively, the demarcation may be drawn between those supplying facilities and those who do not. In the United States, the FCC's Computer I decision separated voice from data, and the 1980 Computer II decision drew the line between basic and enhanced services. Neither ruling was effective because digital technology allows no distinction between the carriage of voice and data. The 1982 Modified Final Judgment, which divested AT&T from its local network companies, separated long distance and local service, and drew a further line between regulated local service and competitive enhanced service. The 1986 Computer III decision attempted to open access to service suppliers by the technical means of Open Network Architecture (ONA).[10] Hence, the United States has a variety of regulatory divisions, all enacted so as to protect voice service.

Whereas in Britain a decision was taken to introduce competition into the voice market, and later to free data transmission and the resale of voice to third parties, these measures have not been generally adopted within the wider area of Europe. Instead, a demarcation line more on the lines of the FCC's Computer II decision of 1980, which freed value-added (enhanced) services for competition, has been adopted. Inevitably, given the wide variation of possibilities in what may be considered "basic" service, the demarcation line has become a political issue.

The introduction of competition into a network, and the questions of anticompetitive practices by dominant operators, depend crucially on the concept of "costs." By construing the network as consisting of a long-distance component and a local component, it is possible to argue that, since the local network is actually the most expensive to put in place, each subscriber should pay for these costs. In effect, this intellectual (and not technological) construction of the network cheapens long-distance services for business users. Cost-based pricing, which effectively transfers the cost of providing the local loop to individual subscribers, benefits the better-off consumer, and industry. Its design in the United States was political, in the sense that it was seen as a means of preventing bypass by large users. However, the allocation of costs of particular services has always been subject to debate, and this particular allocation of costs is gradually being challenged.[11]

The challenge comes from the alterations in the technology. It makes little sense to tariff in relation to time of day and distance when distance is of much less importance, and when the large capacity of digital switching and fiber optic cable mean that demand does not outstrip supply at peak loadings. The issue of costing has always been fudged, since prices charged have also depended on demand elasticities. It is possible to charge more for local calls because they are insensitive to price increases.[12] (See chapter 7.) Basically, the distribution of costs is a political decision, which has been subject to little public debate in Europe. Instead, what is perceived as the American practice has been followed.

In fact, in America, the full costs of the local network have not been transferred to the local consumer. AT&T bears much of the costs of "universal service." Even in Britain, which has been the most rigid in its espousal of cost-based tariffs, and where rebalancing has proceeded for eight years, several hundred million pounds of BT's revenue are transferred from highly profitable services, such as international calls, to access charges for residential subscribers. In 1990, BT unsuccessfully petitioned to be allowed to end this internal transfer. Although call areas vary, and London in particular has a huge local calling area, the result of British policy is that Britain has the highest local call charges in Europe. The disparity of policies on pricing also leads to massive differentials between internal and external call charges between European countries for the same distance.[13]

TECHNOLOGICAL ADVANCE

There have been a number of technological developments in telecommunications that have produced changes in the sector. The reduction in the costs of fixed investment has allowed large businesses to construct their own private networks at less cost than the continued usage of PTT long-distance networks. In addition, the differentiation of large users' needs has brought new service suppliers into the market. The integration of companies' communications networks into (computer-based) Local Area Networks (LAN) or (telecommunications-based) Managed Data Networks (MDN) has become a growth area of competition between PTTs and computer service companies.

Within the public telecommunications network, the emphasis in the major industrial countries has been on upgrading the network with digital switches and optic fiber, and the introduction of ISDN (see chapter 7). Long-distance communications in the United States, Britain, France, West Germany, and elsewhere have all been digitalized. The degree of digitalization of the networks within Europe varies considerably. By 1990, countries such as Greece, Spain, Italy, and Luxembourg had less than half their long-distance networks digitalized. By then, only in France and Ireland were the local switching networks more than half digital.[14] Where digital networks are overlaid onto existing networks, they cater to the existing hierarchy of demand.[15]

Network operators are increasingly concentrating on their major customers in order to maximize revenue and prevent bypass of the network. The PTTs' aim is to install intelligent networks, not only providing such features as toll-free dialing but giving flexibility, security, and trouble-free maintenance to their largest companies. Because this network development increasingly relies on software rather than hardware, computer companies such as IBM have become involved in the upgrading of exchanges. Nevertheless, PTTs are still engineering- rather than computing-dominated.

Telecommunications costs have become one element in the competition between countries for inward investment, and have even engendered competition between states within the United States. However, possible reductions in international tariffs must be weighed against their revenue support to telecommunications manufacturing industries. In France, West Germany, Belgium, and Italy, tariffs support equipment prices. American pressure is for liberalization of the resale of capacity on international leased lines to third parties. Because these resellers would not pay international accounting rates, they could undercut PTTs and have the effect of reducing international tariffs. However, given the position of the current stakeholders, immediate radical changes seem unlikely.[16]

Whereas the United States pressured originally for the opening of equipment markets, toward the end of the 1980s its efforts had become primarily directed to the liberalization of services. This redirection of international policy reflected the perception of services as the area in which the United States held a competitive advantage, as well as the alliance of information service suppliers with the U.S. Office of the Trade Representative. The liberalization of services was expected to yield dividends in associated equipment sales.[17] In 1988, the ITU's rules on the provision of international networks were liberalized, and the de facto position, that governments could reach bilateral agreements on the provision of such networks, was recognized.[18] However, the concept of sovereign control of telecommunications systems was also reaffirmed.

It is this sovereign control that is currently being challenged by the United States within GATT negotiations. However, at the time of this writing, the U.S. State Department is reported to be having difficulty selling its GATT liberalization proposals to American telecommunications stakeholders other than information service suppliers.[19] In particular, AT&T is reportedly opposing the entry of foreign companies into network operations.

ISSUES OF THE 1990s

By the beginning of 1990, a number of new trends had emerged, once more altering the balance of advantage within the trade-offs between economic interest groups. The growing overlap between television and telecommunications has brought into the market a further set of potential participants in broadcasting and cable TV companies.

Broadcasters compete with off-air data distribution to closed user groups, and satellite broadcasters can also utilize spare capacity for point-to-multipoint data distribution. Cable TV can transmit voice and data point-to-point communications, as well as point-to-multipoint broadcasts. In both the United States and Europe, these various interests have been engaged in conflict. For instance, the European Commission delayed its policy document on the opening of the satellite distribution market following opposition from PTTs, which have feared the bypass of their networks by larger users.

At the national level, the introduction of broadband communications via satellite or optic fiber allows the entry of telecommunications companies into television carriage, leading to demands in both the United States and Britain for liberalization of the regulation that prevents them from such carriage. Telecommunications operators argue that television carriage on the pay-per-view basis will allow the economic introduction of optic fiber into the home. The question has therefore arisen as to how far cable TV networks should be integrated with those of the PTT. While some governments have decided on a gradual integration, as in the Netherlands, or hybrid networks, as in Denmark, in Britain, cable TV is seen as a potential competitor, and therefore separate from the PTT.

In addition, radio-based technologies have arisen to challenge the fixed network. Cellular mobile radio based on analog technology has grown dramatically in the United States, where more than three million citizens subscribe to the service. In Europe, the Nordic countries and Britain have had the highest growth. In Norway in 1989, penetration was 36 per 1,000 population; in Sweden, 29 per 1,000; and in Britain, it was 9 per 1,000. In other countries in Europe, such as France and West Germany, demand has far outstripped supply, partly because of the use of nationally based technology. Penetration had reached less than 2 per 1,000. Incompatible analog systems throughout Europe has meant that digital cellular technology is needed for compatibility and to meet demand. While delayed in the United States, it is due to be installed in Europe in the early 1990s.[20] In turn, this introduction is leading to restructuring and liberalization of the market. West Germany, France, and Sweden are to allow competition in cellular radio services, while in Britain, new competitors, including BT's main competitor, Mercury, will provide the Personal Communications Network, based on digital cellular technology.

As these various technological solutions to the delivery of signals have emerged, the very process of the restructuring of telecommunications markets to introduce new competition has brought problems. A plethora of technologies can fragment the market. And while market segmentation may protect consumers through competition, economics may demand network integration and standardization. Vertical concentration once more raises the need for regulation to protect consumers and to allow access to the new services. Hence, among these "first-wave liberalizers," there is increased concern at the regulatory trade-offs between interests and in the market segmentation of the network.

During the 1980s, there was a period of company-led (rather than government-led) concentration. Companies took over competitors or entered into cross-national alliances, seeking penetration of equipment markets. For network operators, the economics of scale and scope in telecommunications seemed to require backwards and forwards integration. IBM, AT&T, and British Telecom all attempted to integrate in this way. All have pulled back to what they do best. IBM pulled back from telecommunications transmission and from telecommunications equipment manufacture to computers and systems integration, AT&T has retreated from the computer market and its head-on clash with IBM, and BT has withdrawn from manufacturing. Only the American Regional Bell Operating Companies (Bell Atlantic, Southwestern Bell, Nynex, Americatech, US West, Bell South, and Pacific Telesis), or RBOCs, constrained to the local network by regulation, are still pressing to be allowed to forward integrate into the provision of information services and to backwards integrate into manufacturing.

In the latter 1980s, the previous overseas alliances and investments in equipment manufacturers have been replaced by investments in similar businesses. Thus the RBOCs are investing in cable TV in Britain, while BT has bought the information services company Tymenet and is investing in cellular radio in the United States. Similarly, France Telecom is investing in British competitors to BT.

In addition, compared to the previous period when alliances with American or Japanese manufacturers were common, cross-European alliances in R&D are increasing.[21] What has not yet emerged are cross-national alliances between PTTs to provide global private networks. In Europe, agreement between 18 PTTs on Managed Data Networks fell apart. Moreover, in providing global coverage, companies are hampered by their national origins. Therefore, as major users demand integrated networks on an international, rather than national, level, more alliances of primarily American information-services suppliers and European network operators, such as that announced in 1990 between IBM and BT, can be expected.

The implications for industrial policy for liberalization of the equipment market were not fully appreciated at first in either the United States or Britain. In both countries, liberalization first of equipment and then of networks has had a dramatic impact on the balance of payments in telecommunications equipment. In turn, this failure in exports has reduced employment in telecommunications manufacture in both the United States and Britain. In the United States, employment in production fell by 30 percent between 1984 and 1987, while in Britain, manufacturing employment dropped by 48 percent between 1976 and 1986. In contrast, there was a drop of only 16 percent in France over the same period, and an increase of 11.4 percent in West Germany. In general, the EC tends to have a slight balance of trade in its favor with the United States, and a massive deficit with Japan.[22]

While the issue of Britain's trade imbalance in telecommunications has received little attention, and the British government has attempted to replace domestic manufacturing industry with foreign inward investment, the American populace and the U.S. Congress have not welcomed such investment. The major focus of policy, and virtually the only unifying theme within American communications, has been the emphasis on the liberalization of other national markets. While the FCC has sought to place pressure on European countries to liberalize procurement by monitoring the procurement by the RBOCs of foreign equipment, policy does not tackle the massive decrease (29.8 percent between 1978 and 1985) in exports to developing countries suffered by the United States.

In 1988, the U.S. Congress enacted a bill that demands reciprocity from countries running a telecommunications deficit with the United States. The bill is therefore primarily concerned with manufacturing industry and exports, and is particularly aimed at Japan. However, it is only subsequent to the changes in Eastern Europe that the issue of the modification of export controls has been broached, and even as recently as 1990, the building of an optic fiber highway through the Soviet Union was vetoed.[23]

With attention increasingly directed toward trade issues and the PTTs' largest customers, the fate of the average consumer has relied on the traditional undertaking of "universal service." In fact, despite national penetration levels predominantly at the same level or below the worst of the American states, the general perception in Europe has been that the market is saturated. Only the Nordic countries meet the 95 percent overall household penetration level of the United States. In Britain, the 1990 level of 85 percent is equivalent to that of Mississippi. Much lower household penetration (around 50 percent) is evident in Portugal, Spain, Italy, and Ireland.[24] The public service commitment of PTTs also differs markedly, with the French and West German PTT having perhaps the strongest culture, and with the privately owned Spanish PTT having the weakest.

COMPETITION IN THE NETWORK—THE UNITED STATES AND BRITAIN

In the United States, under the regulation of the Federal Communications Commission provided for in the 1934 Communications Act, AT&T operated a vertical monopoly over the network and equipment manufacture. Through its research laboratories, Bell Labs, it retained the monopoly on innovation in the network. This national system of telecommunications operated on a system of trade-offs, balanced one with the other within the regulatory framework. Inasmuch as the trade-offs had developed bit by bit, they were neither recognized nor legitimated by the political process, and inasmuch as new technology provided an alternative to the end-to-end fixed network, it also altered the balance of negotiating power between AT&T and the large users.

In a number of decisions from the 1950s onward, the FCC and the courts allowed AT&T's monopoly to be eaten away in the interests of large users, and the supply of customer premises equipment was decoupled from the supply of the network. As pointed out in chapter 7, this decoupling and the entry of a number of companies into equipment manufacture immediately created the demand for standard interfaces. The decoupling also increased innovation in the equipment sector, with numerous products being developed to allow users to utilize the network more cost effectively. As entry into network supply became cheaper, so AT&T's monopoly was opened to transmission by competitors. Nevertheless, the previous trade-offs were held in place by allowing this competition only in the transmission of data, while the predominant voice market remained protected.[25]

The challenge to this redistribution of wealth through the telecommunications network arose gradually as the underlying costs of the long-distance network reduced more quickly than AT&T reduced tariffs. The attainment of almost full penetration of the network produced virtual stagnation in revenues and a seeming failure to invest in new technology and services. Hence, liberalization of services responded to requirements for service specialization and network revenue.

Spurred by the general economic downturn of the early 1980s, AT&T's divestiture can be seen as a mechanism for the redistribution of economic benefits away from the individual consumer to the large business sector in particular. However, the market segmentation put in place by the divestiture ignored a variety of interests served by the previous organization of the market. It was not simply that a number of interests fared badly in the short term, such as the trade union members of AT&T who lost their jobs. It was also that the impact of the divestiture on the organization of manufacturing and on the efficient delivery of services through network integration was never considered. In other words, the technical regulatory function embodied in AT&T's monopoly was never fully appreciated, with the result that standardization has become difficult, leading to technical fragmentation.[26]

The divestiture of AT&T in the early 1980s was undertaken by the District Court of Columbia as a specific antitrust action in order to allow the entry of other vendors into the network on equal terms with AT&T. The divestiture was intended to replace the previous ineffective behavioral regulation of AT&T by the FCC with market segmentation, which would regulate behavior through competition. In contrast to this stated intention, the effect has been to replace regulation of one entity (AT&T) carried out by the FCC with regulation of numerous entities (the RBOCs, AT&T, and its competitors) by competing regulatory bodies: the district court, the FCC, and state regulators.[27] Bureaucratic competition has led to a policy vacuum that has been filled by congressional demands for the liberalization of overseas markets and the passage of Super 301 trade legislation, which allows the imposition of retaliatory tariffs on the goods of countries named by the U.S. International Trade Commission, for not allowing market entry.

By setting RBOCs against AT&T and into competition with each other, the divestiture has fragmented the network and cut the linkage between manufacture and procurement. At the same time it has made evident the previously hidden trade-offs between large-scale business and individual consumers, institutionalizing the defense of those interests in separate parts of the political system.

While the FCC represents the interests of AT&T and the RBOCs in cost cutting, it has been forced by congressional disapproval to institute mechanisms to protect the poorest consumers, thereby disadvantaging AT&T. State regulators were not involved in the original divestiture decisions. The effect of that divestiture has been to increase their involvement in the sector, and, because many are elected, they represent the interests of individual consumers. The RBOCs were initially successful in persuading state regulators that they were threatened with the bypass of their network by large users, but the figures they produced have been challenged subsequently. State regulators have become increasingly concerned about protecting their electoral base through retaining cross-subsidies to the local network. In 1990, the RBOCs reported falling profits due to the lowering of tariffs.[28] In sum, the FCC has become a less important political actor, and large users have become a less potent political force.

In Britain, the liberalization of the equipment market in 1982 was then regulated by the Department of Industry. Its failure to control BT was the prime reason for the establishment of the Office of Telecommunications (Oftel) to regulate the sector. Market segmentation was originally based on the liberalization of the equipment market, a duopoly of voice carriage between BT and Mercury, which is now wholly owned by Cable and Wireless, and the further liberalization of Value-Added Network services (VANs). Subsequently, however, because of difficulties in defining VANs, all data transmission was liberalized. Cellular mobile radio is divided between a BT company and Racal Vodaphone. Resale of voice transmission to third parties was liberalized in 1989, and the British government planned to sell its own data and voice network to Racal, thereby effectively licensing a third operator. The plan failed.

The original intention of liberalization was to effect structural rather than behavioral regulation, with the major limiting factor on the latter being the government's intention to sell British Telecom's shares with the subsequent aim of ensuring British Telecom and Mercury's profitability. Regulation of BT was instituted via a "light rein" leaving consumers at the mercy of BT. A failure by Oftel to address these problems for the average consumer, except on an individual basis, led, in 1987, to a public backlash. This response eventually instigated not only stricter behavioral regulation of BT but also a renewed emphasis on structural regulation.[29]

Denied the convergence of cable TV and telecommunications in the American market, American capital is entering Britain in the telecommunications market through holdings in cable TV companies. Cable TV companies can compete in telecommunications only if they ally themselves to either BT or Mercury. Since BT has no interest in competing with itself, the companies providing such local service are all linked to Mercury. American investment in cable operations now rings London, and operators are beginning to demand the ability to switch traffic between each other. The effect of these developments will be to regionalize competition in local service and to mirror the American system of local exchange carriers linking to long-distance carriers.

Meanwhile, BT would like to see its license altered so that it might carry television programs on its terrestrial network, thereby making the provision of optic fiber in the local loop an economic possibility.[30] Instead, the policy emphasis is on the separation of markets based on technology and the exclusion of BT from certain markets. The aim of the Conservative government is to introduce competition to BT at local level, through cable TV and through radio technologies such as telepoint (CT2) and personal communications networks that are based on digital cellular technology.

Unlike the United States, Britain has weak consumer groups and no political institutions that defend the individual consumer. Hence, rebalancing of BT's tariffs has been targeted at reducing prices over long distance, increasing them at the local level, and increasing charges for access.[31] The intention of government policy is to place all costs of the local network onto individual consumers. Despite a public outcry, there is no political mechanism to prevent this from happening.

SECOND-WAVE LIBERALIZERS

The second-wave liberalizers, such as France, West Germany, and the Netherlands, have benefited from a policy geared to the needs of major suppliers. West Germany has always been regarded as the Japan of Europe, formally espousing a liberal policy but in fact preventing foreign penetration of the market by the imposition of high domestic-equipment standards.[32] It has been slow to liberalize its network. The monopoly of the Deutsche Bundespost has been supported by a unified trade union with 550,000 civil servant employees, by its own financial autonomy, and by the legal backing for its monopoly of the West German Constitution contained in the Basic Law which was passed immediately after the end of World War II.[33] The provision of telecommunications has been influenced by the consensus that surrounds the concept of the social market economy (a free market economy serving the needs of the community). As Theodore Irmer has pointed out:

Under the provisions of the "social market economy" a state telecommunications monopoly is justified if it complies with the social objectives of this economic structure (i.e., provide telecommunication services to everybody and everywhere in the country and under equal conditions, at equal charges and of identical quality).[34]

The high long-distance tariffs within the country, the poor state of the network (90 percent electromechanical equipment at the start of the 1980s), and the determination of the Bundespost to claim a monopoly over all aspects of voice and data transmission have long been a source of contention to foreign companies in West Germany. The Bundespost relinquished its monopoly over modems only after being taken to the European Court of Justice. No less than five reports from government committees and agencies have suggested forms of liberalization since the 1970s. Nonetheless, the monopoly remained intact until the late 1980s, partly supported by the incorporation of IBM into equipment provision but mainly due to the social acceptance of the importance of Siemens and of the cross-subsidies to residential subscribers and the postal service. That postal service involved a politically sensitive loss-making parcel service to East Germany.

The political necessity of low local tariffs has in turn reduced the desire of the Bundespost to provide leased lines, which it feared would cut its revenues. Pressure for liberalization of its policy on leased lines in turn led to the introduction of volume-based rather than flat-rate pricing for those lines. The change provoked an outcry from multinationals who were faced with increased charges, but was justified by the Bundespost on the basis that it was a "second-best" policy. In view of its obligation to provide universal service and uniform tariffs, it argued that it could not afford the loss of revenue that would follow from a liberal policy and flat-rate pricing of leased lines. Since the Bundespost monopoly has also contributed large amounts to the federal budget, there was relatively little incentive to restructure.[35]

In West Germany, as perhaps nowhere else, the importance of the telecommunications monopoly to the federal government has been in its broadcasting policy. The control over infrastructure by the Bundespost allowed the Conservative government to introduce private commercial broadcasting, paid for by the PTT. Equally important has been the massive investment by the PTT during the 1980s in the modernization of the network.

By the latter 1980s, the interests of domestic stakeholders had begun to change. The United States pressured economic ministries through the

Organization for Economic Cooperation and Development (OECD), seeking to broaden the question of telecommunications liberalization to include domestic industrial competitiveness. The liberalization of the neighboring Netherlands network also threatened West Germany. With overseas acquisitions and threats of American action against it, Siemens's interests also began to alter away from purely domestic protection. Responding to these changes in domestic interests, in January 1989 the West German PTT was broken into posts and telecommunications operators, and a separate regulatory body was created for telecommunications. However, the social goals have been retained. Deutsche Bundespost Telekom (DBP Telekom) continues a monopoly over voice transmission, and will continue to cross-subsidize the postal service.[36]

Until the later 1980s, the PTT in the Netherlands exercised a traditional monopoly over the telecommunications network and associated equipment. In fact, its policy on matters such as leased lines, which allowed their usage only where there was excess capacity, was illiberal. Private networks were allowed only over short distances.[37] This monopoly came under attack from large users such as Shell and Unilever. Its largest domestic manufacturer, Philips, also called for liberalization.

A commission to consider the Dutch PTT monopoly, headed by Theodor Steenbergen, reported in 1985. Although its division of the PTT into a regulated entity for basic services and a separate subsidiary for competitive services on the lines of the U.S. FCC's Computer III decision was rejected, most of its proposals have become law. Posts and telecommunications have been split, and telecommunications has also been split between regulated and competitive services, with separate accounting procedures. Regulated services include telephony, telegraphy, telex, and basic packet switching. The PTT has become a private joint-stock company, but with all its shares owned by the government. This provision releases the PTT from annual financing by Parliament.[38]

In France, industrial policy has taken precedence. The French have a long tradition of state involvement in industry. At the same time, the heavy centralized control and the stocking of nationalized industries with civil servants has been seen as reducing competitiveness. Industry has been dependent on the public sector for finance and markets, and financial support has primarily gone to the largest firms. In addition, the centralized state has perpetuated the traditional conflicts between its various elite cadres. The PTT's corps of engineers competes with other corps as well as with the French Ministry of Industry, which controls the components and electronic goods sectors.[39]

Telecommunications has been a major instrument for the French industrial revitalization in telecommunications manufacturing and the squeezing out of the American company, ITT, from the French market. Massive investment in telecommunications took place from the mid-1970s to 1980, changing the French system from the most outdated to the most modern in the world. The Direction Générale des Télécommunications (DGT), the French PTT, which was part of the Ministry of Post, Télécommunications, and Télédiffusion, and therefore staffed by civil servants, acted as the spearhead for industrial policy. It used public procurement to build up CIT-Alcatel (Compagnie pour l'Informatique et les Techniques Electroniques) and Thomson as national champion companies, and was instrumental in CIT-Alcatel's success in exports of switching equipment.[40]

The government-backed Nora-Minc Report on the informatization of society, published in 1978, also served to increase the power and autonomy of the DGT.[41] Coming at the time when IBM was moving into satellite transmission with its Satellite Business Systems, the report emphasized the danger of global domination by American companies. In 1978, under the Giscard d'Estaing government and with the full backing of the president, a Plan Télématique was adopted. This plan aimed to develop a telecommunications satellite for business services, and to install a cheap terminal in every home for the provision of an on-line directory. It also aimed to stimulate the production of a cheap facsimile machine and a "smart card" for electronic payments, and began a large-scale experiment at Biarritz to develop interactive broadband services. The aim of the plan was to replicate the perceived strategy of the Japanese—using the home market to develop sufficient economies of scale to provide cheap exports of equipment. The target export market was the United States, where the Carter phone decision of 1978 had allowed the attachment of non-AT&T equipment to the network and had liberalized the equipment market. However, behind the plan lay bureaucratic competition—a means by which the DGT and its corps of Ingénieurs de Télécommunications could protect their newfound status that stemmed from their successful modernization of the network.[42]

Much went wrong with the plan, particularly in relation to manufacture. New companies introduced to equipment manufacture by the DGT, such as Matra and Saint Gobain, were not particularly successful. The facsimile machine did not materialize, and the intention to furnish each home with an electronic terminal had to be dropped following opposition from the newspapers and opposition politicians. The satellite *Telecom 1* was launched, but failed to work fully.

Many of the large-scale French industrial plans have foundered on the conservatism and autonomy of the existing large companies and their failure to cooperate with each other.[43] Bureaucratic competition is also endemic, even within the DGT. Thierry Vedel has pointed to the centrality to policymaking of conflict between telecommunications and posts. In addition, the DGT has had a tradition of conflicting relations with Télédiffusion de France (TDF).[44] This conflict within the ministry is intensified by the overlapping of sectors: for instance, TDF runs a paging service in competition to the DGT.

Coming into power in 1982, the Socialists viewed previous failures of profitability in the national champions as the result of their traditional isolation from each other. They nationalized Thomson and CIT-Alcatel, and restructured them on product lines. This amalgamation of its two major suppliers was opposed by the DGT, which had previously introduced competitive tendering, and it is indicative of the DGT's declining influence that it failed to impose its views. The Socialists' plan was seen as a victory for the Ministry of Industry.

The Socialist government jettisoned the previous support of national champions, and looked to linkages between sectors for their industrial strategy. The Program d'Action Filière Electronique linked telecommunications to the computer and components sector, and had as its aim to place the French electronics industry in the same league as the United States and Japan by 1990. The intention was to develop the weaker parts of the French information-technology industry, such as computers, integrated circuits, electronic office equipment, and robotics, by taking advantage of the strong parts that already existed. It placed the DGT in a less powerful position because it now had to contribute to the whole of the French information-technology industry through subsidies and contracts. In Dang Nguyen's words, telecommunications moved from being a "growth pole" to being a "milk cow" for the whole electronics sector.[45] In the mid-1980s, telecommunications was also required to make substantial contributions to the general budget.

Technology has a symbolic importance in French politics, and when the *filière électronique* failed to produce results quickly, the government looked for another technological symbol, and found it within the DGT's Plan Câble.[46] The Plan Câble had the advantage that it favored both cultural production and also decentralization, and could therefore be "sold" to the Socialists.[47] At the same time, it promised domestic production of optic fiber (for this purpose, two medium-sized producers were merged), and experience in running optic fiber systems. Moreover, it took the DGT into TDF territory. The history of the Plan Câble is described in chapter 5, but it too was overambitious. However, in the DGT's missionary zeal concerning ISDN in the 1990s, one can see a repetition of the history of the bureaucratic competition of the 1970s (see chapter 8).

The French PTT has had a commercial orientation since 1970. Partly because the administrative law that governs public authorities in France is so restrictive, the PTT has created its own subsidiaries, such as Transpac Company, which runs the packet-switched network. Such commercialization and profitability meant that telecommunications was a candidate for privatization by the returning 1985 Conservative government. This privatization effort was defeated by the trade unions, which were concerned at losing their civil service status, but given the place of the DGT in industrial policy, it always lacked legitimacy. Instead, in 1986 a regulatory agency, the Commission Nationale de la Communication et des Libertés, was created to regulate the broadcasting and telecommunications sector. This body replaced the Haute Autorité established by the socialists in 1982 to regulate the audio-visual sector. It was replaced by the Conseil Supérieure de L'Audiovisuel (CSA) in 1989 by the Rocard Socialist government. However, the CSA lost telecommunications regulation, which was absorbed into the ministry. Although regulation was separated from operation of the network and telecommunications separated from posts under a law passed in June 1990, the DGT has actually accrued more power. It has gained both in its influence over regulatory decisions and in its financial autonomy.[48]

In general, France and southern Europe line up against Britain and the Netherlands in opposition to privatization. While the French PTT has effected entry into the British telecommunications market, BT has not been allowed to enter the French market, and accuses France of protectionism. However, it has been the French who have attempted a European strategy of bilateral collaboration, with West Germany on videotex and with Britain on switching equipment. Both were unsuccessful. More recently, it has been the French who have pressed for a European technological community. In many respects, the interests of France in technological leadership marry with the interests of the European Commission.

The priority given to large, technological programs by the German telecommunications administration has been altered by reunification, however. The costly projects of previous years, such as the cabling program, must now be paid for in a more commercial environment. The network in East Germany is in a hazardous state with only two million connections and calls between the two networks very difficult. Together with its East German counterpart, Deutsche Post Telekom (DPT), West German DBP Telecom aims to increase connections to one million annually within the next two years. German reunification has not only raised the status of the DBP Telekom but has also given new opportunities to major companies such as Siemens. Although the cost of modernization of the East German network is estimated in the region of $42 billion by 1997, calls from industrialists for the privatization of DBP Telekom, in order to meet the required investment, are opposed by the Social Democratic Party and the trade unions and are no more likely to succeed than previous, similar, demands.[49]

CONCLUSION

The restructuring of the telecommunications markets has been ongoing in both the United States and Europe since the 1960s. In the United States, the concentrated manufacture, vertical integration, and large home market provided the historical basis for the economies of scale that governments attempted to achieve in Europe. These attempts to gain such economies of manufacturing scale were particularly evident in Britain and France, both of which had fragmented national industries. In Britain, when such efforts failed to increase exports, liberalization of the equipment market was introduced in an effort to create the innovatory environment of the United States. That liberalization, in turn, led to the decimation of the small domestic industry. In the United States the disruption of the relationship between the network operators and Western Electric, and the opening of the customer premises equipment market have created a balance-of-trade deficit.

In the two first-wave liberalizers, the restructuring of network operation and the delineation between voice and data were primarily of benefit to the large users of telecommunications. In the United States their political primacy has faded. The political power of the large users has been subverted by the AT&T divestiture, the increased power accrued by state regulators, and the political saliency of telecommunications tariffs, which have placed them on the congressional agenda. In addition, technology is itself removing their bargaining power. As AT&T and the RBOCs increase the intelligence within their networks, so the balance of economic advantage moves away from private networks and toward the public network. In 1990, large users were complaining that their interests were not being met by the RBOCs. In fact, a political consensus seems to have developed on the need to retain universal service in telecommunications.[50]

In Britain there is no such consensus, and the centralized political system does not facilitate public debate. Regulation has moved away from concern with BT's profitability, and toward concern with competition. As the individual household bears increasing costs of the modernization of the network, the question of the cost of access to telecommunications is hardly being raised. The British government's duopoly review of 1990 excludes those unable to afford a telephone as providing uneconomic connections. Meanwhile the government has proposed to introduce further competition into the network with an increase in the number of long-distance carriers as well as the licensing of cable television companies to carry telecommunications. It has also proposed that BT be prevented from carrying both television and telecommunications for a further seven years.[51]

Since 1984 it has been the privatized BT that has gained power. The government, through market restructuring and further liberalization, is seeking to control BT's market dominance rather than use the company to spearhead an industrial policy. The presence of previously government-owned Cable and Wireless; of Racal, with its close links to defense; and of American operators seeking to enter the market, has created pressure against BT's market power. Hence, the new competitive policy is also an industrial policy, backing those thought to be more likely winners than BT. Meanwhile, a small manufacturer such as Plessey, with its low equipment prices, has found itself taken over by Germany's Siemens, which is protected at home by high equipment prices.

In contrast, on continental Europe, restructuring is taking place as part of an industrial policy, where it suits the interests of manufacturers in France, West Germany, and the Netherlands. In both West Germany and France, public investment is used to support manufacture. In France, the ideas of technological leadership and bureaucratic competition continue to fuel the upgrading of the network and its extension into television carriage. Privatization was defeated in France, partly because of the importance of the DGT to industrial policy.

Industrial policy in the major West European countries aims to take advantage of economies of scale evident within the EC market. The losers in the restructuring of markets in Europe will be companies with small domestic markets, such as Italy. High international tariffs used to protect national manufacture are coming under attack both from multinationals and from the United States. Overall employment in the manufacturing sector can be expected to fall as liberalization throughout Europe, promoted by the European Commission, replaces the domestic supply of customer premises equipment (CPE) with that from the Far East.

The prime network liberalizers in Europe have been countries such as Britain and the Netherlands, which are dependent on trade and with small home markets. With unification and the need to upgrade East Germany's infrastructure, one can expect West Germany's recent espousal of tele-communications liberalization to be shortlived.

Trade unions have had a differential impact. In the United States and Britain, they have been relatively ineffective. In France and West Germany, they have successfully opposed privatization. However, privatization, whether existing as in Spain or the United States, or government-led as in Britain and the Netherlands, does not necessarily alter political control. Governments control the markets, and regulation creates alliances.

In Britain and the United States, an increased fragmentation of networks is evident. In both countries, such fragmentation is justified on the grounds of structural competition. However, whereas competition in the market was originally thought to replace behavioral regulation, it is now evident that this is not the case. In particular, the interests of individual consumers require protection. While the American political system allows for competing interests to be institutionally represented, the same is not true in Europe. In West Germany, despite formal liberalization, the social objectives embodied in the previous monopoly remain. However, as the European Community moves to cost-based pricing of telecommunications tariffs, and as ISDN and broadband are introduced, so the interests of individuals are sacrificed to those of PTTs. Hence, the experience of British citizens is likely to be replicated throughout Europe.

NOTES

1. Jill Hills, *Information Technology and Industrial Policy* (London: Croom Helm, 1984).

2. Jill Hills, "Neo-Conservative Regimes and Convergence in Tele-communications Policy," *European Journal of Political Research* 17 (1989): 95–113.

3. See International Telecommunications Unit, *CCITT Red Book*, Volume II, Fascicle II.1, *General Tariff Principles, Charging and Accounting in International Telecommunications Services* (Geneva: ITU, 1985), Recommendations D.100–D.155.

4. Eli Noam, "International Telecommunications in Transition," in *Changing the Rules: Technological Change, International Competition and Regulation in Telecommunications*, edited by Robert W. Crandall and Kenneth Flamm (Washington, D.C.: Brookings Institution, 1989), 257–97.

5. Jill Hills, "The Industrial Reorganisation Corporation: The Case of

the AEI/GEC and English Electric Mergers," *Public Administration* 59 (Spring 1981): 63–84; Godefroy Dang Nguyen, "France: Telecommunications—Intervention at the Crossroads," in *Handbook of Information Technology and Office Systems*, edited by A. E. Cawkell (Amsterdam: Elsevier, 1986), 519–38.

6. Hills, *Information Technology*, 83.

7. Michael Beesley, *Liberalisation of the Use of British Telecom's Network* (London: HMSO, 1981).

8. Kevin Morgan and Douglas Pitt, "Coping with Turbulence. Corporate Strategy, Regulatory Policies and Telematics in Post-Divestiture America," in *European Telecommunications Policy Research*, edited by N. Garnham (Amsterdam: IOS, 1989), 19–39.

9. In 1989–90, Oftel conducted investigations into the pricing of digital leased lines and the quality of service of cellular networks.

10. Robert Bruce, Jeffrey Cunard, and Mark D. Director, *From Telecommunications to Electronic Services* (London: Butterworths, 1986), 6–16.

11. Geoffrey Mulgan, "The Myth of Cost-Based Pricing," *Intermedia* 18, no. 1 (1990): 21–27.

12. Geoffrey Mulgan, "Costs and Prices in the ISDN and Broadband Networks: A Case of Whatever You Can Get Away With?" in Garnham, *European Telecommunications*, 217–42.

13. James Foreman Peck and Jurgen Müller, "The Changing European Telecommunications Systems," in *European Telecommunications Organisation,* edited by James Foreman Peck and Jurgen Muller (Baden Baden: Nomos Verlagsgesellschaft, 1988), 40–41.

14. D. Ypsilanti and R. Mansell, "Reforming Telecommunications Policy in OECD Countries," *OECD Observer* 5 (1987): 20, quoted in Paul Slaa, "A Dutch Perspective on ISDN" in *European Telecommunications Policy Research*, edited by N. Garnham (Amsterdam: IOS, 1986), 81.

15. Andrew Gillespie and Howard Williams, "A Small Firm's Perspective on the Liberalisation of Telecommunications Services" (Paper presented to the 3rd Communications Policy Research Conference, Windsor, June 1988).

16. CCITT's Recommendations D.1 and D.6 are intended to retain a monopoly of international traffic to PTTs; see Hugo Dixon, "Ringing the Changes for Telephone Cartel," *Financial Times*, 16 July 1990.

17. Jill Hills, "Dynamics of U.S. International Telecom Policy," *Transnational Data Report* 12 (February 1989): 14–21.

18. William Drake, "WATTC-88: Restructuring the International Tele-

communications Regulations," *Telecommunications Policy* 12, no. 3 (1988): 217–33; Russell G. Pipe, "WATTC Agrees on New Telecom Rules," *Telecommunications* 23 (January 1989): 19–21.

19. William Dullforce, "U.S. Raises Hurdle in Way of Pact on Services," *Financial Times*, 18 July 1990.

20. David Charles, Peter Monk, and Ed Sciberras, *Technology and Competition in the International Telecommunications Industry* (London: Pinter, 1989), 82–83; Economist Intelligence Unit, *Retail Business Special Market Survey* (London: EIU, 1989).

21. Godefroy Dang Nguyen, "Industrial Adjustment and the EEC Policy for Telecommunications," in *Telecommunications: National Policies in an International Context. CPR '86*, edited by N. Garnham (London: Polytechnic of Central London, 1986), 187–220; Charles Leadbeater, "Europe Feeds an Appetite for Acquisitions," *Financial Times*, 20 June 1990.

22. Werner Neu and Thomas Schnoring, "The Telecommunications Equipment Industry. Recent Changes in Its International Trade Pattern," *Telecommunications Policy* 13 (March 1989): 25–37.

23. Ian Davison and William Dawkins, "CoCom Liberalises Technology Sales to East," *Financial Times*, 8 June 1990.

24. Nicholas Garnham, "Universal Service in European Telecommunications," in Garnham, *Telecommunications*, 139.

25. There are many books on the AT&T breakup. See Robert Britt Horowitz, *The Irony of Regulatory Reform* (New York: Oxford University Press, 1989); Alan Stone, *Wrong Number. The Breakup of AT&T* (New York: Basic Books, 1989). For an assessment of the impact of divestiture on equipment, see Kenneth Flamm, "Technological Advance and Costs: Computers versus Communications," in *Changing the Rules: Technological Change, International Competition and Regulation in Communications*, edited by Robert Crandall and Kenneth Flamm (Washington, D.C.: Brookings Institution, 1989), 12–61.

26. See Gerald Faulhaber, *Telecommunications in Turmoil. Technology and Public Policy* (Cambridge, Mass.: Ballinger, 1987).

27. Jurgen Schmandt, Frederick Williams, and Robert H. Wilson, eds., *Telecommunications Policy and Economic Development* (New York: Praeger, 1989).

28. *Financial Times*, 20 July 1990.

29. See Michael Beesley and Bruce Laidlaw, *The Future of Telecommunications* (London: Institute of Economic Affairs, 1989).

30. British Telecom, *Preface to Memorandum of British Telecommuni-*

cations PLC, House of Commons Select Committee on Trade and Industry, 19 July 1989. The reader should write to BT to obtain a copy.

31. Jill Hills, "Universal Service: Liberalization and Privatization of Telecommunications," *Telecommunications Policy* 13 (June 1989): 129–44.

32. Alfred Haid and Jurgen Müller, "Telecommunications in the Federal Republic of Germany," in Foreman Peck and Muller, *European Telecommunications*, 155–79.

33. Edgar Grande, "The Influence of Party Politics and Government Strategies on Telecommunications Policy" (Paper presented to the Telecommunications Policy Workshop, Max-Planck Institut fur Gesellschaftsforschung, Cologne, December 1987).

34. Theodore Irmer, "Information and Telecommunications Policy in Germany," in Cawkell, *Handbook*, 541.

35. Douglas Webber, Martin Rhodes, J. J. Richardson, and Jeremy Moon, "Information Technology and Economic Recovery in Western Europe. The Role of the British, French and West German Governments," *Policy Sciences* 19 (October 1986): 319–46.

36. Deutsche Bundespost, *The Restructuring of the Telecommunications System in the Federal Republic of Germany* (Bonn: Deutsche Bundespost, 1989).

37. Bernhard Wieland, "Telecommunications in the Netherlands," in Foreman Peck and Müller, *European Telecommunications*, 203–19.

38. Peter Lablans, "Privatization of the Dutch PTT: New Telecommunications Opportunities," *Telecommunications Business* 1 (November 1989): 59–65.

39. Thierry Vedel, "La politique Française des télécommunications dans un contexte de déréglémentation" (Paper presented to the European Consortium of Political Research, Gotenborg, April 1986).

40. Martin Rhodes, "Industry and Modernisation. An Overview," in *France and Modernisation*, edited by John Gaffney (Aldershot, U.K.: Avebury, 1989), 72.

41. J. Nora and A. Mino, *The Computerisation of Society* (Cambridge, Mass.: MIT Press, 1980).

42. Dang Nguyen, "France," 519–37.

43. Rhodes, "Industry and Modernisation," 66–95.

44. Thierry Vedel, "La 'déréglémentation' des télécommunications en France: Politique et jeu politique," in *La déréglémentation des télécommunications et de l'audiovisuel* (Colloque International, Paris, May 1986).

45. Dang Nguyen, "France," 533.

46. John Peterson, "Eureka and the Symbolic Politics of High Technology," *Politics* 9 (April 1989):8–13.

47. Godefroy Dang Nguyen, "Telecommunications in France," in Foreman Peck and Müller, *European Telecommunications*, 131–54.

48. Jean Paul Simon, "Aftermath: Deregulation in France in the 1980's" (Paper presented to the 18th Telecommunications Policy Research Conference, Airlie House, September 30–October 2, 1990).

49. *Australian Communications*, September 1990, p. 16.

50. Ralph Nader, "U.S. Telecom Policy: A Consumer Perspective," *Telematics and Informatics* 7, no. 1 (1990): 53–62.

51. U.K. Department of Trade and Industry, *Competition and Choice: Telecommunications Policy for the 1990s—A Consultative Document* (London: HMSO, November 1990).

4

The Restructuring of
the Broadcasting Market

ECONOMICS AND MARKETS

Just as the monopoly system of telecommunications previously evident in the United States and Western Europe has given way to a more competitive structure, with new entrants competing with the previous stakeholders, so too with the broadcasting market. What has been evident is a shift away from a concern with broadcasting as culture to policy that regards broadcasting in terms of economics. That is not to say that the issue of cultural diversity has not been debated within Western Europe, but rather that this issue has taken a secondary place to the issues of restructuring and commercialization.

Although based on different structural models, broadcasting in both the United States and Europe has traditionally been regulated by the state in terms of access and content. Whereas in the United States, market restructuring in telecommunications has involved both structural separation and increased regulation of that structure, as well as of behavior, in broadcasting, the opposite trend has been evident. In the 1980s, the emphasis has moved to a loosening of structural separation, to regulation in favor of commercial interests and away from protection of the citizen. In broadcasting, there has ensued a concentration of ownership, and, based on arguments concerning the diversity of programming available, a demand for no regulation at all.[1]

In Europe, both telecommunications and broadcasting were formerly regarded as natural monopolies. Both were based on sovereign territories with little intra-European trade. The 1980s have seen a whittling away of these previous monopoly rights. In some cases, restructuring has allowed broadcasting competitors into the previous monopoly market. In other cases, the vertical integration of the monopoly over such matters as in-house programming has been loosened. Overall, in broadcasting as in telecommunications, there has been an emphasis on commercialization—on revenues and costs—in response to potential, if not actual, competition. In some cases, as in telecommunications, the entry of competition in broadcasting has entailed a movement toward independent regulation and away from the previous indirect control exercised by governments through public ownership.

However, while these trends are common to the two markets, there are also certain developments that are specific to broadcasting. These stem from the economics of audiovisual production and distribution, which are peculiar to the information industry. In the information industry, the costs of production are in the original prototypes, whether software or television programs. The costs of reproduction are negligible. Hence, where there are no barriers to distribution, it is possible to spread the original costs over a wide market.

Language being a barrier to audiovisual distribution, these economics give an advantage to languages that are spoken in a number of countries—English, Spanish, French, and German. Hence, the English-speaking market of the United States and Canada is supplemented by other previous British colonial territories and the more than 45 million households in Europe that are spread across nations that speak English. The Spanish market comprises the U.S. Spanish-speaking population, Latin America, and about 15 million households in Europe; while the French- and German-speaking markets in Europe cover about 38 million households each. These 1985 figures do not cover the newly democratizing countries of Eastern Europe. As the two Germanies unify, the importance of German as a programming language will increase.[2]

The significance of language markets within the European context is not merely that the English market allows from imports of TV programs from the United States. The transcendence of state boundaries by language provides the basis for cross-national broadcasting, for which satellites can provide the delivery systems. Despite the prevailing social organization of broadcasting on national grounds, language markets provide the potential within Europe for the internationalization of production and distribution.

The economics of television also give an advantage to those who produce material for distribution networks that they themselves control. The original product can be further exploited by its delivery through a variety of distribution methods. Utilizing the "cascade strategy," films can be delivered through movies, television, and video recordings. Television programs can be sold as books, their music can be sold as records, and promotions in one market can be timed to coincide with and reinforce sales in another. In turn, the growth of distribution outlets depends on the availability of reception equipment. Distribution networks, programming, and equipment are therefore interdependent; and there is an economic rationale to vertical integration between program production and distribution, between distribution and reception, and between adjacent markets, where distribution of a product can be effected at only marginal cost. Given these synergies, it has been rational for newspaper, book, and magazine publishers to move into a number of adjacent markets. Advertising in one market can promote sales or corporate interests in another, while investing in a sector that represents potential competition protects existing advertising revenue.[3]

Similarly, given that unit costs fall with additional sales, it makes sense for media corporations to expand overseas from positions of domination in a product or geographical market. The strategy may involve exports or acquisition. In turn, exports may have implications for the product. These may vary from the emphasis on action rather than dialogue of American feature films (cutting dubbing costs), to packaging programs into specific time slots for exports from Europe to the American market.[4] With successful products breeding similar ones, the economics of information reproduction creates trends toward homogeneity.

As markets within any one country become more pluralistic, and segmentation and product differentiation become necessary, it becomes possible to repackage programs made, say, for one age group in one market, to be sold in the same segment of another national market. Hence, the diversity within and between national markets is replaced by market segmentation and an internationalized homogeneity of the product for the various segments.[5]

These economic pressures are further exacerbated by advertiser pressure. Advertisers demand the largest reach possible for their advertising. According to Ben Bagdikian's study of the American newspaper market, the cycle of lower unit costs, together with the advertisers' requirement for access to the largest number of potential consumers, inexorably leads advertisers to turn to the dominant operator.[6] The operator, in turn, has an incentive to increase its circulation in order to charge more to the advertiser. In broadcasting, the circulation battle of the newspapers is replaced by the ratings war but the pressures are the same.

It is ironic, therefore, that criticism has arisen in Europe on the failure of some broadcasting monopolies to respond sufficiently to the increased diversity of taste among their publics. In these circumstances, competition might be expected to create diversity. However, this is not the case if competition for finance from advertisers increases, particularly if advertising revenue has to be shared by a growing number of distribution outlets and does not grow to meet the new demand for revenue. Static or falling revenue demands cutting costs, whether through less expensive programs (game shows rather than news or current affairs), or through the casualization of labor effected through independent production (where terms and conditions of employment are tenuous), or through imports of material. As the original cost of making prototypes increases as a proportion of revenue, it increases the attraction of the bought-in product, which will already have had its production costs met from its home sales. An American made program such as "Kojak," selling for $3,000 per episode competes with "home-grown" material costing $200,000.[7]

Nevertheless, the laws of supply and demand may well work against this solution. Unless audiovisual production is increased to keep pace with the number of new outlets, a program famine drives up the price. Programs that attract high ratings, such as films and major sports occasions, have become increasingly expensive in the latter 1980s due to competition for supply. Coproduction of programs between nationally based broadcasting organizations, and the presales of such programs, are cost-reducing alternatives. However, here again, the danger is that the requirements of the larger markets will dominate the smaller ones.

Three market trends are, therefore, spin-offs from the entry or threat of entry of new competitors into national broadcasting markets. The first is the internationalization of production and the reproduction of original creative material. A second trend is toward homogenization. The third is an increase in concentration of ownership in media markets at both the national and international levels.

Graham Murdoch characterizes multimedia conglomerates into three types: industrial, service, and communications. In the first category fall companies such as Fiat, which often invest in media companies for the return on assets that they give. In the second category are companies such as Silvio Berlusconi of Italy's Finivest, with a diverse range of interests over many countries. In the third category fall companies such as those controlled by Robert Maxwell and Rupert Murdoch, German publishing groups such as Bertelsmann, Burda, and Springer, and Compagnie Luxembourgeoise de Télédiffusion of Luxembourg.[8] These often join with each other in new ventures, leading to interlocking interests in multiple-media enterprises.[9]

In Europe, these holdings are split not only between markets but also between countries. Their concentration has extended beyond Western Europe. In Hungary in the summer of 1990, parliamentary conflict developed over the takeover of Hungarian newspapers by Robert Maxwell, Rupert Murdoch, and Axel Springer.[10]

Graham Murdoch has raised the question of the influence of these combines over the cultural content of the media. In the United States, the FCC concluded in 1970 that concentration of ownership had reduced diversity of content. Gareth Locksley has raised other concerns about the potential for monopoly through control of interfaces between production and reception.[11]

The new technologies of distribution have aided this process of competition, concentration, and homogeneity, but are not its prime causes. While satellite transmission is insensitive to distance and has therefore increased the incentives for expansion and cross-media ownership, the major obstacles to such trends were previously the national boundaries, cultural and linguistic differences, and national regulations governing broadcasting. In the 1980s, however, the restructuring of the broadcasting market in Western Europe and the lifting of much broadcasting regulation in the United States has given an impetus to such concentration. In turn, that concentration has implications for program diversity and the representation within broadcasting of the plurality of society.

The purpose of this chapter and the next is to discuss how the social organization of broadcasting has been changed by government policies and by the entry of the new distribution systems of cable and satellite.

THE TRADITIONAL SYSTEM IN EUROPE

Regulatory activity in Europe originated in the late nineteenth century from laws established to control the development of wireless telegraphy. Because one service could interfere with another, particularly in crowded Europe, some form of regulation was necessary. From this need to work in cooperation evolved the International Telecommunications Union, allocating frequencies to individual countries. Whereas the pre-1924 American system of a free-for-all in broadcasting brought chaos, the Europeans opted for national monopoly broadcasters. The United Kingdom was the first country to erect a monopoly, with the establishment of the British Broadcasting Corporation (the BBC) in 1922. Shortly afterwards, a similar model was adopted by European countries such as Italy (1924), Sweden (1925), and Ireland, Denmark, and Finland (1926). Most Western European states have established nationwide monopolies with one institution serving the whole nation, the exceptions being countries with linguistic and cultural differences such as Belgium and Switzerland. There, each linguistic community has its own public broadcasting service. Some countries subsequently also started regional broadcasting.[12]

In contrast to the American model, since the early days of radio, the West European model developed largely outside the market. Although in America in the 1920s there was significant support for the idea of regulating radio as a public utility, the fear that such a situation might lead to a centralization of monopoly power led American decision-makers to adopt a market model in the service of the public interest. To secure this interest, under the 1927 Radio Act, public service obligations were imposed on commercial broadcasters similar to those imposed in Western Europe on public-broadcasting monopolies, but these obligations were policed through license renewals. As a consequence, in the United States, public broadcasting has been marginalized in relation to the dominant ideology of the market.[13]

Until recently, the Western European broadcasting model was distinctly different from the U.S. model as well as from the postwar Eastern European model. The Western European model was not monolithic. It depended on the style of regulation of each country, which in turn reflected the significant differences of historical experience and regulatory culture among the Western European countries. In essence, "in its ideal typical form, the West European model consists of a nationwide public monopoly which, although controlled by the state in matters concerning organization and finances, is still fairly independent in its programming policy."[14]

In Europe, while there is no universally accepted definition of public service broadcasting, it is usually taken as axiomatic that the notion embraces a commitment to quality and the service of the public interest, two terms with broad interpretations. Nicholas Garnham has defined public service broadcasting as:

> a means of providing all citizens, whatever their wealth or geographical location, equal access to a wide range of high quality entertainment, information and education, and as a means of ensuring that the aim of the programme producer is the satisfaction of a range of audience tastes rather than only those tastes that show the largest profit.[15]

Indeed, broadcasting in Europe is predominantly seen in a cultural context. Building on the public service values of universal service and widespread cultural dialogue, broadcasting has reflected concerns with access on behalf of national, regional, language, class, and cultural divisions within a particular society. In essence, at its inception, the potential reflection of this variety of opinions and the fear that it could lead to the dissemination of subversive ideas was the main justification for government controls over broadcasting.[16]

Public control was also considered a prerequisite for the protection of freedom of information. The First Amendment of the U.S. Constitution guarantees this normative goal, and the same concern can be seen expressed in concern for the independence of the BBC's output. In West Germany, where television has been dominated by the two public networks ARD and ZDF, it has been these networks' responsibility to offer the West German public a diet of what is called "balanced pluralism."[17] This concept not only entails a balanced presentation of views on all the important issues of the day, but also extends beyond news and current affairs to include entertainment.[18]

Two models have evolved under these conditions: the state-controlled monopoly, and the duopoly system. In both systems, public service bodies play a predominant role, due either to consistent state intervention or a high degree of self-regulation. The Luxembourg system, under which a private company, the Compagnies Luxembourgeoise de Télédiffusion, became the single public broadcaster, was a unique case in Europe.[19]

In the state-controlled monopoly system, public service broadcasters enjoy a de jure monopoly, whereas in the duopoly system there is a competitive environment that includes private broadcasters. In general, monopoly rights have been restricted to transmission only, and do not cover the production or reception of the signal. The main source of finance is the license fee, and restrictions are made on financing through paid advertisements in an attempt to safeguard the monopoly's cultural functions and to protect the advertising market of the printed press.[20]

Control of the broadcaster has tended to be through the government appointment of personnel to supervisory boards. This power, in turn, has led to concern over political control. In both Italy and West Germany, party politics has been prevalent in the control of broadcasting. The French government has always been involved in developing those public utilities and industries directly effecting national life. Given the French history and traditions of *dirigisme* and étatism, it was inevitable that the broadcasting media should be brought under state control. French television has had a sort of double personality. It has had to be the "voice of France," objectively presenting events, yet has also been obliged to be a means of propaganda serving government interests. Thus, major conflict has centered on the impartiality of the news output.[21]

In Britain since the 1950s there has been a duopoly system whereby public and private broadcasters coexist in competition for audience and programming but are financed differently. Under this model, the private broadcasters are also under public service obligations with a regulatory agency established to oversee their franchises, thereby guaranteeing that broadcasting remained a factor in the functioning of public opinion rather than simply a means of commercial advertising. However, broadly speaking, the British system is characterized not only by heavy regulation and representation of the "middle ground" of opinion, but also by a centralized general output, chronic financial problems, and constant arguments concerning the objectivity and impartiality of news output.[22]

Both public service broadcasting models are undergoing a deregulatory change, and moving toward a generalized system in which the public broadcaster competes with its commercial counterparts for both programming and some advertising revenue. This relaxation of rules, widely called "deregulation," or "regulation with a light touch," relates more to structure and finance than to program content. Thus, while governments have pushed toward a market economy in the broadcasting sector, they have also increased regulation over the content of broadcast programs, particularly in relation to violence and pornography. Perhaps the most notable example was that of Margaret Thatcher of Britain. A paradox of the 1990s is that we see, on the one hand, governments limiting state intervention through the introduction of commercial approaches to broadcasting, and on the other hand, increased government intervention by the establishment of new bodies to act as their watchdogs.

In some countries (Denmark, for instance) the relaxation of rules has been gradual. In others, such as France and Spain, it has been swift. In the United Kingdom, after years of discussion and debate, the 1990 Broadcasting Act has introduced more competition, new channels, and a substantial relaxation of controls over commercial television. British broadcasting has entered the 1990s anticipating the end of its duopoly structure. Under the Broadcasting Act of 1990 more commercial channels will compete with the BBC.

PUBLIC SERVICE BROADCASTING UNDER ATTACK

During the 1980s public service broadcasting was under attack from a number of directions. In some countries, there was dissatisfaction with its output. Insulated from the market, with a consequent failure to reflect internally the increased pluralism of tastes and interests among their public, and limited by their statutes, broadcasters have often found it difficult to respond to the new cultural diversity.[23]

Pressure has also come from advertisers anxious for the television advertising market to be opened up in Europe. Whereas in the United States, in 1983, 1.5 percent of gross domestic product (GDP) was spent on advertising, with the exception of Britain, the rest of Europe spent less than 1 percent. Moreover, whereas in the United States, Britain, and Italy, more than 30 percent of that total went to television advertising, in countries such as West Germany and France, the proportions were down to 21 and 10 percent respectively; in countries such as Sweden and Denmark, there was no television advertising at all.[24]

At the same time, because the penetration of television reception equipment had reached the saturation level in Europe, the revenue generated by the license fee has no built-in growth. To increase revenue via this tax requires annual increases. Dependent for such increases on politicians, who are reluctant to incur further public expenditure or electoral disapproval, broadcasters have faced financial problems that have been exacerbated by inflation. Inflation provokes political dependence, thereby contradicting the initial concept of the independence of public service broadcasting from political control. During the 1970s and 1980s, the license fee became a focus of contention within European politics, further politicizing the issue of future broadcasting structure.[25]

Crucially, the development of new media technology has undermined the concept of spectrum scarcity as a rationale for regulation. While new cable and satellite technologies have provided an alternative means of communication, bypassing the use of the domestic electromagnetic spectrum, new technologies, such as microwave distribution, allow the use of previously unused portions of the spectrum.[26] The development of satellite television, with its overlapping footprints and ease of reception, also undermines the possibility of the very state regulation on which the public service broadcasting model has rested.

Most importantly, the political consensus that supported the monopolies has crumbled. Industrial policy has conflicted with cultural policy, and even where cultural diversity and identity have been retained in public debate, it has been in the context of economic and industrial thinking.

Thus, in countries which have had broadcast services strongly based on cultural considerations (in the widest sense) such as France and West Germany, cultural arguments (e.g., about encouraging production in the national language and resisting cultural "invasion") are now deployed because of their relevance to economic competition rather than their own sake.[27]

In this debate, public service broadcasting has come under attack from two opposing political groups: the neo-liberals and the radical left. While the neo-liberal strategy has sought the introduction of market forces and competition in broadcasting, the radical left has called for a wider range of opinions to be represented, demanding that views that are currently repressed, mediated, or ignored should be allowed media access. They have argued for increased democratic control of broadcasting institutions.[28] Although local broadcasting in radio and some decentralization of television has been introduced, of these two ideologies, the neo-liberal, free market approach has been the most influential. It has coincided with the rise of liberal-conservative governments in much of Europe, and with the desire for private investment.

According to the neo-liberal view, broadcasting via the public service model is overregulated at the hands of the state. It is, therefore, necessary to have more channels and fewer controls, creating greater variety and greater consumer control through competition. Much of the argument reiterates the views of the American Federal Communications Commission, under Mark Fowler, quoted in chapter 1, that the only criterion for judging program quality is how many people watch it. As an editorial in *The Times* of London put it, "We need a more open and less monolithic system of broadcasting in which customers can choose what qualities they want from their television sets."[29] One can see here that the argument in favor of liberalization of broadcasting is in theory the same as that evoked in other spheres of state ownership, but in fact, the liberalizers are concerned with liberalizing ownership, and not in increasing the plurality of content or with broadcasting's social role.[30] The interests of advertisers lie in having more outlets for television advertising in order to lead to a decrease in prices. Thus, the rhetoric of "light-touch" regulation and "more choice" actually represents the interests of advertisers and private media actors.

As a result of these pressures and of internal electoral considerations, regardless of their formal political ideologies, governments have allowed the entry of private actors and interests into their previously closed broadcasting systems. Even the French Socialists in 1985 allowed the establishment of private channels. To some extent, there has been a domino effect as with the liberalization of telecommunications, with the entry of competition in one market increasing pressure on its neighbors. Italy began the process in the 1970s, with private broadcasting firmly under the control of Silvio Berlusconi, now the Italian owner of La Cinq. To some extent, the process has arisen from fear—that if the government's friends were not installed as private operators, that after an election, the opposition's friends might take control. In this respect, the entry of private operators is little more than an extension of the previous tradition of state control and corporatism.[31]

THE IMPACT OF LIBERALIZATION

Despite the belief of the proponents of market liberalization that quality programs can be maintained along with competition, the combination of financial exigency and the need to retain viewers in order to attract advertisers provides its own momentum, which can override regulatory considerations. In the United States, the Reagan administration's faith in regulation by market forces determined new conditions for the functioning of American television. For example, radio and TV stations were freed from government-imposed limits on commercial time, from having to provide minimum amounts of news and public affairs programs, and from having to provide educational programs. Programming logs no longer need be kept for financial inspection, and annual financial reports are no longer required. In addition, barriers to cross-media holdings have been relaxed.[32] One outcome is that

> the violence long associated with action melodramas has elbowed its way into the common talk show. Where once the talk circuit fed on celebrity interviews and innocuous chit-chat, today it trades on confrontation and emotional explosion. They are the kind of programmes that can be expected when the competition heats up and regulation is abandoned.[33]

In Western Europe, the privatization of the television market has yet to produce measurable results, but there are already some indications of what may follow. In some countries there is intensified competition among four, five, or six channels in markets that had previously supported three. For instance, France now must accommodate the two state channels A2 and FR3, the privatized TF1, the pay-TV channel Canal Plus, and the two new private channels, La Cinq and Metropole 6. The French terrestrial non-satellite channels have shown huge losses. In 1987–1988, La Cinq's losses were reported to be about $134 million, while Metropole 6 lost about $64 million. Silvio Berlusconi has called this a "financial disaster."[34]

Quantitative indicators of the commercialization of European broadcasting are hard to obtain. Although advertising spending is notoriously prone to fluctuations in line with economic growth, one measure of commercialization can be obtained by analyzing the growth in advertising spending on television since 1980. In 1987, Denmark reported on television advertising for the first time. Advertising had increased by 400 percent in 1989 as the first Danish commercial channel went into operation. In West Germany, television advertising spending from 1980 to 1987 increased by 75 percent, but then increased again by 30 percent in 1989, reflecting the steady take-up of cable television during the mid-1980s. In Italy, spending had increased by almost 700 percent, but had begun to slow by the latter 1980s. In Spain and Belgium, new commercial channels increased spending by more than 300 percent in each country. However, television advertising spending in West Germany in 1989 still only amounted to $17 per capita; in the Netherlands, $17.4; and in Switzerland, $19.7; compared to the United Kingdom's $66 per capita.[35] These figures suggest that the pressure for commercialization has not ended.

Imports of television programs from the United States have increased. In 1985, America exported $410 million of television programs, which rose to $500 million in 1987, of which 63 percent went to Europe. In 1986 it appears that the United States exported $1.2 billion in films and television to Europe.[36]

According to one consultancy firm, out of $21 billion of the revenues of Western European broadcasters in 1988 (from license fees, advertising, and sales), approximately $10.6 billion was spent on producing and buying programs. In-house productions accounted for about $7 billion, co-financing, coproductions for $1.45 billion, and $2.15 billion was spent on acquisitions. It is evident, however, that the costs of importing programs are rising faster than revenue. CIT Research estimated that while revenue would rise by 9.5 percent in 1990, software costs would rise by 41.5 percent. These figures suggest that broadcasters will be unable to afford to continue importing at the current rate.[37]

However, the trend in the late 1980s for broadcasters to reduce costs by subcontracting some of their program production to independents may also be threatened by concentration. The potential pattern is of the public service broadcaster as a kind of "publisher-contractor," while the independent production sector, formerly populated by small companies, will be consolidated into a handful of large firms. There have already been signs of new entrants in Britain, and the current small independent companies may soon cease to exist. Instead, the independent sector may well follow that of distribution, with super-independents functioning at both the national and the international level, and with some programs subcontracted to small companies.

At a qualitative level, the new concern for audience share and commercialization has affected public service broadcasters. Facing a license fee renewal in 1991, even the flagship of European public service broadcasting, the British Broadcasting Corporation, prepared during the latter 1980s for competition from satellite and cable TV by sharpening its programming schedules, upgrading news and current affairs, and adopting a highly competitive profile. This new commercialism is necessary. For instance, in West Germany, RTL Plus and SAT1, the two big private channels, in 1989 took almost half the viewing share of the public channels.[38]

Indeed, the dilemma for public service broadcasters in Europe is determining the role they should play: Should they try to act as their charter states—for all people—or should they participate in the ratings war, hunting for audiences and beating the commercial broadcasters at their own game? Alternatively, should they concentrate on the areas where newcomers would never venture, such as reaching minority audiences, and thus reinforce their right to public funds, even if audience numbers sink?

The difficulty is compounded by the fact that public service broadcasters may be operating under rules more restrictive than those applicable to private operators. In Italy, which was the first European country with a multichannel radio and television system, the only rules that apply to commercial broadcasting are those established by existing regulation, such as laws governing pornography. As D. Sassoon noted: "A private television company can broadcast, if it so wishes, non-stop adult movies or cartoons or both. State television is of course subject to restrictions on all these matters and is therefore competing from an unequal position."[39] The public broadcaster RAI (Radiotelevisione Italiana) was the first public broadcaster in Western Europe to face determined competition from a commercial operator, Silvio Berlusconi, whose company, Finivest, owns the three major private Italian channels, Canale 5, Rete 4, and Halia 1. RAI became more commercial, going on the offensive with imported series and large movie packages, and reducing in-house production. However, ratings successes have tended to hide the ensuing financial problems.[40] While changes in content lost it the patronage of politicians,[41] the war with Berlusconi cost it financially and politically.

Nevertheless, European public service broadcasters are not wholly on the defensive. The attack on their monopoly position has forced a reassessment of their role. In general, they have readjusted their position in the competitive market, with fewer losses in both audiences and advertisers than were expected to occur. Their relative success, in combination with the fact that the new commercial channels have found it difficult to attract advertising, has produced a new pressure from private broadcasters, who now advocate banning all advertising revenue to public service broadcasters.

Indeed at the 1989 MIPCOM (Marche International des Programmes et Communications) annual television program market and conference, leading members of the recently formed ACT (Association of Commercial Television), the coordinating body of new private broadcasters in Europe, argued that advertising should be the sole domain of private broadcasters. As Silvio Berlusconi said, "Public money for public channels, private money for private channels." In addition, Rupert Murdoch has attacked public service broadcasters for their deep elitism and questioned their right to provide news, claiming that they are under state control and therefore biased.[42]

CONCLUSION

The economics of broadcasting produce economies of scale and scope; consequently, vertical and horizontal integration and international expansion are rational strategies for companies. However, if access is controlled and information all comes from the same commercial source, then diversity will be limited and information biased. Competition for advertising funds precludes minority programs and furthers homogeneity of product. Indeed, this trend may intensify as Europe opens its markets to foreign investors. According to one consultancy firm, European broadcasters may be replaced by an emerging new breed of super-conglomerate, often part of a larger commercial concern whose major interest in broadcasting is financial.[43]

Concentration, therefore, appears to pose a major danger for European broadcasters and their public. Already in Britain, Rupert Murdoch controls 35 percent of press readership and five satellite channels. As these channels become established, the intensified competition may further pressure public service broadcasters to increase their mass entertainment programming and further reduce their minority programs.

Despite its still predominantly national base in Europe, the growing international characteristics of broadcasting make it increasingly difficult for national governments to impose their own rules. As the following chapter demonstrates, national industrial policies have dominated the debate on cable and satellites. These broadcasting markets have also been seen as national. However, to recall the history of telecommunications in the United States, AT&T gained its monopoly status through control of the interlinkages (long lines) between separate local markets. Hence, if diversity of ownership and information are to be preserved within Europe, the international linkages of electronic distribution networks must be controlled.

The fundamental problem for both Europe and America is how to ensure that citizens are treated as more than consumers, and that they have access to information.[44] A trade-off exists between market and politics, and is currently being resolved in favor of private interests for the sake of perceived competitive advantage. The major questions surrounding the social organization of broadcasting involve citizens' rights to diversity, access, and accountability in their broadcasting organizations.[45]

NOTES

1. See U.S. Department of Commerce, National Telecommunications and Information Administration, *Telecom 2000* (Washington, D.C.: Government Printing Office, 1988), 149–62.

2. Gallup survey quoted in Raymond Snoddy, "European Satellite Battle Looms," *Financial Times*, 16 September 1985.

3. Much of this section relies on research by Marion Banks for an unpublished master's dissertation "Multi-Media Business and the Restructuring of Communications" (City University, London, 1988). See Richard Collins, Nicholas Garnham, and Gareth Locksley, *The Economics of Television. The UK Case* (London: Sage, 1988); Gareth Locksley, *TV Broadcasting in Europe and the New Technologies* (Brussels: CEC, 1988).

4. Collins, Garnham, and Locksley, *Economics of Television*, 68–70.

5. Office of Economic Cooperation and Development, *International Trade in Services. Audiovisual Works* (Paris: OECD, 1986), 15.

6. Ben Bagdikian, *The Media Monopoly* (Boston: Beacon Press, 1987).

7. Collins, Garnham, and Locksley, *Economics of Television*, 88; Locksley, *TV Broadcasting*, 214.

8. Graham Murdoch, "Redrawing the Map of the Communications Industries: Concentration and Ownership in the Era of Privatization," in *Public Communication. The New Imperatives*, edited by Marjorie Ferguson (London: Sage, 1990), 1–15.

9. Locksley, *TV Broadcasting*, 255–56.

10. Nicholas Denton, "Hungarian Press Sell-Off," *Financial Times*, 4 July 1990.

11. See Locksley, *TV Broadcasting*, 273.

12. See D. McQuail and K. Siune, eds., *New Media Politics* (London: Sage, 1986).

13. W. D. Rowland and M. Tracey, "The Breakdown of Public Service

Broadcasting," *Intermedia* 16 (Autumn 1986): 32–42; W. D. Rowland, "Continuing Crisis in Public Broadcasting. A History of Disenfranchisement," *Journal of Broadcasting and Electronic Media* 30, no. 3 (1986): 251–74.

14. McQuail and Siune, *New Media Politics*, 114.

15. Nicholas Garnham, "Public Service versus the Market," *Screen* 24, no. 1 (1983): 13–14.

16. S. Hood, "Broadcasting and the Public Interest: From Consensus to Crisis," in *Communicating Politics, Mass Communications and the Political Process*, edited by Peter Golding, Graham Murdoch, and Philip Schlesinger (Leicester: Leicester University Press, 1985), 68.

17. Arbeitisgemeinschaft der offentlich-rechtlichen Rundfunkanstatten der Bundesrepublik Deutschland (ARD); Zweiters Deutsches Fernsehen (ZDF).

18. V. Porter, "The Re-Regulation of Television: Pluralism, Constitutionality and the Free Market in the U.S.A., West Germany, France and the U.K.," *Media, Culture and Society* 11 (January 1989): 5–6.

19. For an overview of each country, see Hans J. Kleinsteuber, Denis McQuail, and Karen Siune, eds., *Electronic Media and Politics in Western Europe* (Frankfurt: Campus Verlag, 1986).

20. McQuail and Siune, *New Media Politics*, 117–21.

21. R. Kuhn, *The Politics of Broadcasting* (London: Croom Helm, 1985).

22. See C. Seymour-Ure, "Media Policy in Britain: Now You See It, Now You Don't," *European Journal of Communication* 2 (1987): 271; J. Tunstall, *The Media in Britain* (London: Constable, 1983).

23. Kuhn, *Politics of Broadcasting*, 4–5.

24. T. Sylvesten, "Public Service Television in the 'Information Age': Choices, Strategies and Prospects for the Future," *Nordicom Review*, no. 2 (1988): 47.

25. G. Richeri, "Television from Service to Business: European Tendencies and the Italian Case," in *Television in Transition*, edited by P. Drummond and P. Paterson (London: BFI, 1985), 21–36.

26. See "A Simple Guide to the Electromagnet Spectrum and Broadcasting," *Report of the Committee on Financing the BBC*, Cmnd. 9824 (London: HMSO, 1986), Appendix F.

27. McQuail and Siune, *New Media Politics*, 200.

28. James Curran, "The Different Approaches to Media Reform," in *Bending Reality: The State of the Media*, edited by James Curran, J. Eccleston, G. Oakley, and A. Richardson (London: Pluto Press, 1986), 89–148.

29. *The Times*, London, 15 January 1985.

30. Hood, "Broadcasting," 67–68.

31. Raymond Kuhn, "France and the New Media," in *Broadcasting and Politics in Western Europe*, edited by Raymond Kuhn (London: Frank Cass, 1985), 50–67.

32. Suzanne Douglas, "The Reagan Era: An Overview of U.S. Telecommunications Policy," *Telematics and Informatics* 7, no. 1 (1990): 63–70.

33. L. Brown, "Flowers of Deregulation," *Television Business International*, January 1989: 26.

34. *New Media Markets*, 20 July 1989, 15.

35. Carat International, *Carat International European Television Handbook 1990*, quoted in "Unequal Europe," *Cable and Satellite Europe*, June 1990, 24–25.

36. U.S. Department of Commerce, National Telecommunications and Information Administration, *Telecom 2000*, 599; U.S. Department of Commerce, *Industry in 1988* (Washington, D.C.: Government Printing Office, 1989), 66–68.

37. This section relies on research undertaken by Fritz Phillips for an unpublished paper at City University, June 1990. CIT Research, London, quoted in Jeanette Peasey, "Der Markt fur Fernsehprogramme in Westeuropa," *Media Perpiektiven*, August 1989, 481–89.

38. *Television Business International*, November/December 1988, 33.

39. D. Sassoon, "Political Market Forces in Italian Broadcasting," *West European Politics* 8 (Spring 1985): 67–68.

40. *Broadcast*, 24 November 1989, 8.

41. M. Wolf, "Italy: From Deregulation to a New Equilibrium," in *The European Experience*, edited by G. Noell-Smith (London: BFI, 1989), 51–65.

42. Raymond Snoddy, "Murdoch Forecasts Fast Growth in Cable and Satellite Audiences," *Financial Times* 27 (July 1988); Rupert Murdoch, Opening Speech, International Television Festival, Edinburgh, 28 August 1989.

43. J. Hughes, A. Mierzwa, and G. Morgan, *Strategic Partnerships as a Way Forward in European Broadcasting* (London: Booz, Allen and Hamilton, 1989).

44. N. Garnham, "The Media and the Public Sphere," *Intermedia* 14 (January 1986): 28–34.

45. P. Whitehead, "Reconstructing Broadcasting," in Curran, Eccleston, Oakley, and Richardson, *Bending Reality*, 149–56.

5

The Politics of Cable and Satellite

Telecommunications and broadcasting have traditionally been separate markets. The first intimations of their overlap came with the development of cable TV and satellite television. Then, the new technology of optic fiber cable appeared to alter the potential of these distribution technologies.

In the 1980s, the potential of cable television as the means to provide a wide range of interactive tele-services to the home was hyped by numerous governments. The hype outran the technology. Interactive video services needed fiber optics and a particular network architecture based on opto-electronics, and the optoelectronics were not ready. Moreover, governments relied on existing stakeholders for the introduction of this new technology, giving the opportunity to PTTs and cable television companies to reorder their priorities.

In the United States, short-term commercial exploitation of the new technology and of satellite distribution retarded technological innovation. In Europe, PTTs have acted to retain control, while the penetration of video recorders has competed with that of cable and satellite television. As of 1990, the optoelectronics necessary for interactive video are still too expensive for installation to the individual home for voice and data carriage alone, and too expensive for television alone. Hence, economics are forcing the integration of the three markets. The vision of a wired society, giving access to the new technologies to everyone, has been replaced by a vision of private provision only to those who can pay. This chapter documents the various political interests and conflicts that have brought that scenario into being in the 1990s.

Where markets have developed commercially, as in the United States, the television and telecommunications markets have developed separately. The cable TV market has utilized the cheapest technology—copper cable, and optic fiber has been installed by telecommunications operators on long-distance, high-usage routes. In contrast, where markets have been state-led, governments have attempted to impose optic fiber and switched-star technology on the cable TV industry. However, this long-term view has conflicted with other policy goals of establishing cable TV networks quickly and retaining the separation of the markets.

In satellite transmission, similar problems of overlapping markets have occurred. Believing that direct broadcasting to homes needed high-powered satellites, the ITU, in 1977, allocated specific orbital slots for high-powered DBS satellites. In fact, however, the first broadcasting to cable head-ends came in both the United States and Europe from outside those slots, from satellites with orbital slots in the "fixed" (namely, point-to-point) service. Moreover, within a short time it became evident that medium-powered satellites could be received on individual reception equipment, thereby throwing the economics of high-powered satellites into doubt.

Despite their similar beginnings, cable TV and satellite transmission have had different growth trajectories in the United States and Europe. Because of the improvement it gave to the reception of broadcast TV signals, cable TV evolved alongside conventional television during the 1950s on both continents. In the United States, it then took off with the advent of satellite broadcasting to cable head-ends. In contrast, both cable TV and satellite broadcasting in Europe have been pushed by governments for their industrial competitive advantage. At the same time, the commercial success of satellite broadcasting to cable TV in the United States, together with the opportunities provided by satellite broadcasting for synergy between publishing and broadcast programming, has attracted owners of mass-media conglomerates and public service broadcasters into the market.

CABLE TV AND SATELLITE BROADCASTING IN THE UNITED STATES

Under the 1934 U.S. Communications Act, all broadcasters, whether public or commercial, had a public interest obligation imposed on them. Although cable TV was not covered by the 1934 act, the U.S. Federal Communications Commission first treated it as "ancillary" to broadcasting, and then as a potential competitor. During the 1960s the FCC protected terrestrial broadcasters, banning the expansion of cable to new subscribers and limiting cable TV's ability to compete via the importation of distant signals.

Just as broadcasting was originally seen as a local service, so the FCC's Third Report and Order of 1972 aimed to build up cable TV as a local community medium as well as a carrier for the commercial networks. Rules included a "must carry" regulation of local broadcast signals. In similar fashion to the later actions of European governments, the FCC's first order also required operators in the top 100 TV markets to provide interactive services, as well as to produce their own programming.[1]

As regulation was relaxed, cable began to spread to upper-income suburbs and municipalities.[2] In the 1970s, the "superstation" (broadcast stations microwaving long-distance signals to cable systems) emerged. However, it was the advent of domestic commercial satellites that provided the technological impetus that the cable industry needed. Satellite technology had been developed primarily through contracts for Intelsat, the international telecommunications satellite consortium launched originally by the United States in the 1960s. Comsat (Communications Satellite Consortium), the American operator of this international satellite cooperative, made an application to the FCC for a satellite for domestic use in the 1960s. Following the FCC's 1972 Open Skies decision, the two initial domestic satellite operators expected their market to be in television broadcasts.[3] However, because existing broadcasters were already tied to AT&T, distribution to cable head-ends filled empty capacity. In 1975, Home Box Office (HBO), Time Inc.'s pay movie channel, offered its service to cable operators using the *Welstar* satellite, thus starting an explosion in cable TV companies over the next nine years. Notably, it was the synergy between the market pull of cinema films and the technological possibility of charging a premium for the channel that created the explosion.

The gradual "wiring" of big cities that ensued brought with it concentration into large media and industrial conglomerates. While the growth of cable TV was slower than expected, it became more than a simple extension of terrestrial television; rather it became a programming source financed by subscription and some advertising.[4] However, in the early 1980s, most cable companies met losses. Low subscription rates imposed by franchise bidding and city regulations could not meet increases in capital and construction costs.[5]

During the same period, responding to pressure from the cable industry, the FCC abolished most of its public service broadcasting requirements for cable operators.[6] The move reflected the general deregulatory climate in Washington.[7] Now, market structure was to act as the regulator of behavior, and success in the market was to be taken as service in the public interest.[8]

In 1984, Congress, through the 1984 Cable Policy Act, set out to "minimize unnecessary regulation that would impose an undue economic burden." It aimed to "increase diversity of services to the public," and to establish an orderly process for franchise renewals.[9] In effect, the act gave the cable industry most of what it wanted, removing rate regulation and local access requirements by the cities, and making franchise renewal almost certain. The act also imposed cross-ownership restrictions, forbidding ownership by a broadcast station owner (or telephone company) operating in the franchise area.[10]

However, the act did not sort out all the regulatory problems caused by the hybrid nature of cable TV. The cable industry was able to argue that it had more in common with the press than with broadcasting, and that as "electronic publishing," on the basis of the First Amendment it should be unregulated. Less than one year after its passage, the Federal Court of Appeals invalidated the FCC's "must carry" rules relating to local broadcasts.[11] As a result, the balance of advantage between the cable industry and the broadcast networks swung decisively to cable.[12]

After 1986, when rate controls were lifted, the cable industry was accused of monopoly profit. In 1989, cities, municipalities, and consumers' associations lobbied for a return to rate regulation. They claimed that basic cable TV subscription rates had risen by almost four times the inflation rate since 1984, that 30 percent of cable subscribers had experienced rate increases of more than 40 percent since December 1986—the date when basic cable prices were deregulated. Because cable TV continued to erode the broadcasting networks' audiences, lobbying by the coalition of public interest groups also had the strong backing of the broadcasters. In 1989, cable TV stations claimed responsibility for a 30 percent decline in network audiences.[13]

Cable television has challenged the control of distribution previously enjoyed both by the network broadcasters and by movie companies in Hollywood. In turn, the networks have responded with defensive investment in cable, and in the 1990s, collaboration between network broadcasters and cable and satellite operators is likely to increase the concentration further. Initially, cable operators enjoyed an advantage in their dealings with Hollywood.[14] Later, however, the "cascade" strategy, involving spaced releases to different distribution outlets, as well as the demand for films on video, forced cable and satellite operators to take financial interests in video outlets and to sign up for total output at high prices over a period of years. In effect, the advent of video recorders (which came late to the American market but which nonetheless had achieved a penetration of 68 percent of television households by 1989), coupled with the increase in demand for programming material, has had an impact on its cost. Cable operators claim that these higher costs are responsible for the higher prices to subscribers.

What seems likely for the 1990s is that because of increased concentration in the cable industry (which is now run by 15 to 20 multiple system operators, each owning some 100 local systems), the U.S. Congress may enact new legislation, reregulating basic cable rates, restoring mandatory signal carriage, and imposing limits on the number of cable subscribers that a cable company may serve. Telephone companies are also pushing to be allowed to become cable programmers (which is currently forbidden) on the grounds that only the provision of television will make optic fiber economically viable in the local network.[15]

In contrast to Europe, where direct-to-home broadcasts supplement cable TV penetration, the very success of cable television—in 1989, it could potentially reach more than 80 percent of households, and penetration had reached 54 percent—has meant there has been little room for direct-to-home satellite broadcasting to develop. The original intent of direct-to-home broadcasts was to cover the part of the market—then 35 percent—that was not cabled. However, television receive-only dishes (TVRO) were already being used to receive the signals of low-powered satellites and to pirate those that were unscrambled. In the early 1980s, the demand for direct-to-home broadcasts using small earth stations was minimal, while the cost of the higher powered Ku band satellites required was expensive. The subsequent introduction of other means of reception, such as satellite master antenna TV (SMATV) and multipoint distribution systems, which have plugged the gaps in cable TV coverage, also means that cheaper alternatives to direct broadcasting by satellite (DBS) are available.[16]

Commercial satellite broadcasting in the United States originally developed separate from U.S. government–backed R&D programs. Although the National Aeronautics and Space Administration (NASA) developed experimental DBS satellites in the 1960s, they were utilized for educational and other social programming, and they were not commercially exploited by the industry. This separation may have been possible simply because the research and development costs of the American satellite industry were predominantly met in the early years by the Intelsat consortium. Through these contracts, the risk-taking and funding of the American satellite industry was shared indirectly by a number of governments. Partly because of these contracts, partly because the explosion of cable TV assured a domestic market for C band, low-powered satellites, and partly because the country's larger land mass allows consumers outside cabled areas to install TVRO reception dishes for C band satellites, the industry did not have to look for markets.

It was only the potential business market in fixed satellites needing smaller reception equipment that provoked the commercial development of higher powered satellites. It was not until 1980 that IBM, Comsat, and Aetna Life Insurance first launched a Ku band satellite for business services. To some extent, one can argue that the United States benefited from the six-year delay between the 1977 World Administrative Radio Conference (WARC), when frequencies for DBS were allotted by the International Telecommunications Union to Europe, and the WARC of 1983, when DBS slots for the Western Hemisphere were allocated. During that time, it became evident that medium-powered telecommunications satellites in the fixed point-to-point service could also be used for DBS, with consequent savings. However, this discovery has also meant that the American satellite industry has missed out on developing DBS experience.

In 1983, United Satellite Communications, backed by Prudential Insurance, inaugurated America's first DBS service, United Satellite, using a Canadian satellite. Just one year later, having attracted only ten thousand customers rather than one million as forecast, the service was in financial trouble. Comsat, Columbia Broadcasting System (CBS), and Rupert Murdoch's News Service also pulled out of DBS in the early 1980s.

In its interim DBS regulations of June 1982, which established regulatory policies over satellite broadcasting, the FCC had allotted the nine applicants their own specific orbital positions, some of which were unpopular. By 1989, in an effort to rejuvenate the DBS project, the commission had decided to allow all nine applicants to cover the country from a single orbital location. Potential operators were allowed to find funding and sign contracts for the construction of satellites.[17]

Operators see potential in the areas that are still uncabled and in additional program channels. However, in competition with so many other means of delivery of home entertainment, it is unclear whether DBS can offer anything more to an already saturated U.S. communications market. Nevertheless, a DBS service is planned for 1993, utilizing multiple spot beams and digital compression techniques, which will combine 108 new channels and HDTV transmission. Backed by NBC, the network broadcaster, Rupert Murdoch, Cablevision, and Hughes, the satellite supplier owned by General Motors, the technology reflects NASA's involvement with DBS.[18]

As early as 1977, the U.S. National Academy of Engineering recommended that after a four-year hiatus, NASA should return to R&D in civilian space technology because industrial R&D into satellite communications was failing. NASA began exploring the Ku band of 12–14 gigahertz (GHz) and ultrahigh-frequency direct broadcast technology, a system already being built for the Japanese by General Electric. Despite the successful launch of the resultant experimental Japanese satellite in 1978, the NASA program seems to have run into opposition from the network broadcasters, who feared competition. It was not until 1980 that NASA began once again to direct attention to the Ka band as a result of a study finding that existing satellite capacity in the C and Ku bands would be full by the early 1990s. In 1980, it launched a program to open up the Ka band of 20–30 GHz. Congress voted $45 million for subsystem development, which included the development of such features as on-board processing and multiple spot beams. Unfortunately, the satellite was due for launch at the end of 1988, and so was delayed by the 1986 *Challenger* shuttle disaster. Meanwhile, the Japanese *Sakura* satellite, which utilized the Ka band, was launched in 1977. Its successor is being utilized for High-Definition Television (HDTV) pilot broadcasts. Inter alia, the reaction of the American government has been to attempt to pressure the Japanese to end their Ka band satellite development program.[19]

The overlap in usage that exists between fixed and DBS satellites—between satellites designed for point-to-point communications subsequently used for broadcasting and those designed for direct-to-home broadcasts subsequently used for data transmission—exists also at the terrestrial level. The ideas of a "wired city," which were prevalent in the 1970s have returned, albeit in a different form.

THE RETURN OF THE WIRED CITY

A wired city is one in which electronic communication highways provide a wide range of interactive services to households and business.[20] This concept of the wired city was initially developed in America in the context of President Lyndon Johnson's so-called Great Society program as one means to solve urban problems and inequities. In the 1970s, the concept of the wired city was related to the demand for more localism, diversity, and decentralism. The famous QUBE experiment in Columbus, Ohio, was largely associated with the optimism of the wired city and the expectation that cable TV would offer not only a greater variety of programs, but also more locally originated and interactive services.

QUBE was a 30-channel interactive cable system. Although it proved technically feasible and introduced innovative programming, including interactive and local programs, it lost money. Consumer demand for such programming was insufficient.[21] In 1984, when QUBE funding ended, it signified the end of enthusiasm for cable TV as an interactive system. As E. R. Meehan suggested, the QUBE experiment

> was shaped by economic constraints that limit cultural production under capitalism. The system's interactivity was designed as a means of product testing and format development, which translated into multiple revenues from a single service. . . . In short, QUBE is far removed from the vision of a "wired society."[22]

As W. Dutton, J. Blumler, and K. Kraemer have pointed out, cable TV began as a vision of future communications only to be discounted as a utopian scheme before the end of the decade.[23]

However, the 1990s are beginning to see the reemergence of this vision of an interactive infrastructure, carrying video, data, and voice, and based on the possibilities and decreasing costs of fiber optics. However, the copper wiring and tree-and-branch structure of most existing cable systems, which are necessary because of the economics of up-front investment, do not meet the new vision of an integration between telecommunications and broadcasting.

The major challenge for American cable operators comes from the local telephone companies. Under the U.S. Cable Act of 1984, telephone companies were forbidden cross-ownership in cable companies in their telephone service areas. This market segmentation was a trade-off for cable companies foregoing entry to data transmission. Since 1987, when the FCC opened a docket on the matter, telephone companies have been arguing that the cable industry is no longer an infant industry requiring protection. They claim that only the provision of television can justify the cost of installing optic fiber in the local network, thus allowing other interactive services. However, some concern has arisen from previous experience that the lifting of cross-ownership rules will lead to concentration, and that if companies were allowed to buy cable TV operations, they would simply close them down. Since telephone companies can lease cable television services to other companies in their areas, their pressure relates to control of programming rather than carriage, and raises the same issues of vertical integration as are raised in Europe by broadband ISDN (see chapter 7).

Armed with expertise, experience, and money, both cable companies and the RBOCs have begun to expand into European countries, principally Britain and France. Ironically, the lure for investment into Britain rests not in the market demand for programs, but in the political demand for cable TV to provide local voice and data transmission. Hence, while cable companies are fighting off the telephone company threat in the United States, they will actually be taking on the role of telephone companies in Britain.

EUROPEAN SATELLITE AND CABLE POLICY

In contrast to the United States, European satellite broadcasting has been a state-led market supporting the desire of the major European governments to rival the United States in satellite technology. One can argue that in the United States, the market actually failed to provide the incentive for technological upgrading and basic research in the satellite industry. In contrast, the European experience is of the market being pressed into service to fund the technological learning curve of satellite manufacturers and operators.

The intention of Europe to build up its own space industry was signaled in the 1960s. In 1965, the first French satellite, *Astrix*, was put into orbit. Just as the desire for technological autonomy fueled the policy of supporting an indigenous French computer manufacturer, so the intention in space resulted in similar autonomy linked to independent military capability.

Hence, during the negotiations to establish Intelsat, the international satellite consortium, the French government indicated that they favored a federation of regional satellites, allowing the possibility of non-American manufacture. At that time, the United States argued instead for one world system—Intelsat. The ensuing treaty compromised between the two positions, allowing regional satellites if they "avoided significant economic harm" to Intelsat.[24]

In the early 1970s, France played a large part in the establishment of the European Space Agency (ESA), and convinced its partners of the importance of developing a European launch facility, Ariane. Launchers, with their clear military linkages, were subsequently a predominantly French development.

In 1977, Interim Eutelsat, the European Telecommunications Satellite Consortium, came into being, established as a private company to make a profit for the European PTTs. The operating agreements were signed in 1982, making the European Space Agency responsible for building, launching, and operating Eutelsat's satellites. Of the 26 members of Eutelsat, 13 are also members of the ESA, but in 1985, the majority of the

ESA budget was provided by France, West Germany, Italy, and the United Kingdom, and it was these countries that gained the major industrial benefits.[25] The European Communications Satellites (ECS) were a joint Anglo-Franco-German development designed primarily for point-to-point transmission.

As in the United States, it was the fact that a communications satellite, launched in this case for telecommunications transmission, had spare capacity for television transmission that had the greatest impact on European broadcasting. Eutelsat's satellites provided the first transmissions to cable head-ends. As a result of its English programmers' testing of the market, and their seeming dissatisfaction with Eutelsat's bureaucracy, the privately owned satellite *Astra 1A*, targeting the United Kingdom, was launched in 1988. This satellite allowed private commercial broadcasting to be beamed into the largest advertising market, that of German speakers, which in turn impacted on the acceptance of commercial broadcasting in West Germany and the build-up of cable TV.

Astra 1A is owned by the Société Européene des Satellites (SES), a Luxembourg-based consortium of European financial institutions. In its early days, like its predecessor, the Luxembourg-based Coronet satellite project, *Astra* met hostility from the international community. In particular, because Coronet chose to use an American-made satellite, it was accused of being an "American Trojan Horse," bringing American technology into Europe. American participation in the equity of the company was taken as further evidence of the company's betrayal of European interests.[26]

To Eutelsat, both Coronet and Astra represented first attempts to break its monopoly as a carrier of European telecommunications and television. Eutelsat argued that Luxembourg was one of the signatories to the Eutelsat Convention (modeled on that of Intelsat), by which it had agreed not to launch satellites in competition with Eutelsat, and that both Coronet and Astra would cause it "significant economic harm." Under Article 14(d) of both the Intelsat and Eutelsat Treaties, signatories undertake to avoid such "significant economic harm" to the consortium.

While *Astra* was still trying to convince its critics of its European identity, British Telecom International announced that it would lease 11 of *Astra*'s 16 transponders, thereby giving the project the approval of both a major PTT and that of a further signatory to the Eutelsat treaty. As a result, in 1987 Eutelsat and SES announced their "principle of co-ordination," under which any existing or new channels leaving Eutelsat would first have to reach agreement with that organization, and any start-up channels booking onto *Astra* would have to be coordinated on the basis of opportunity costs lost to Eutelsat.

Rupert Murdoch gave the new satellite commercial credibility with the announcement that his Sky channel would switch from Eutelsat to *Astra*. Sky's use of *Astra* is important. Murdoch's commitment has attracted other entrepreneurs, so that *Astra* is the satellite with the most viable programs to be watched with one reception dish.

In 1990, *Astra*'s owners were preparing to launch a back-up satellite, *Astra 1B*. However *Astra* seems the most threatened of all the European satellites by the problem of excess capacity and the potential decreases in transponder income. It is the only satellite operator that is neither state-backed nor provides programs, thereby making it a satellite common carrier and financially dependent on transponder leases.

The real DBS systems are the West German, French, and British satellites: *TV SAT*, *TDF 1*, and *BSB*. Franco-German collaboration began in 1969, and a first experimental communications satellite, *Symphonie*, was launched in 1974. Following the Space WARC of 1977, when five channels were allocated to each individual European country, there developed national programs to launch DBS satellites. These supplemented existing programs. Consequently, in 1978, the technocratic Social Democratic government of West Germany brought together manufacturing firms with an interest in space to consider the possibility of an "export-oriented" broadcasting satellite in cooperation with the French.[27]

It is this program that has resulted in two DBS satellites, *TV SAT* for West Germany, and *TDF 1* for France. The space segments came from the Eurosatellite consortium. Both satellites have four high-powered TV transponders aimed at their respective language markets. Because both projects are government-backed, domestic political considerations have threatened their demise on several occasions. One might call them "politico-industrial" satellites. It was to combat this venture that Britain decided to build its own satellite, *Unisat*, and other European countries, such as Italy and Sweden, have also gone ahead with their own launches.

The first "bird" to be launched was the German *TVSAT 1*, but this failed to be deployed in orbit after its 1988 launch. The French *TDF 1* was, therefore, the first operational DBS system in Europe. The 1986 disasters of NASA's space shuttle and the European Space Agency's *Ariane* launcher have had an impact on satellite broadcasting, both direct, in failed launches, and indirect, in increased insurance costs. A shortage of launchers has restricted the numbers of commercial satellites placed in orbit.

CABLE AND SATELLITE TV IN EUROPE

Cable development in Europe, at least in the larger countries, has been very slow. In the 1970s, most European countries, with the exception of Austria, Belgium, Luxembourg, and Switzerland, allowed the construction of cable systems to rest with their telecommunications administrations (PTTs). The PTTs construct, install, and are responsible for the network's maintenance. This perception of cable TV as a public utility is evident in the 1960 Council of Europe agreement, the *European Agreement on the Protection of Television Broadcasts*, which gives states the right to authorize or prohibit cable TV distribution within their borders. Despite carrying some foreign channels, cable TV is essentially a national affair, over which, prior to the advent of satellite broadcasting, governments held control.

Within Western Europe, one can see three levels of cable penetration. In some countries, such as the southern European nations (Italy, Spain, Portugal, and Greece), cable TV is virtually nonexistent. Here, compared to the Benelux countries (Belgium, the Netherlands, and Luxembourg), there is little spill-over of foreign broadcasts and no policy on cable TV.

Second, in the smaller European countries (Belgium, the Netherlands, Luxembourg, and Switzerland) there is high cable TV penetration. Between 60 and 90 percent of television-owning households use cable TV. The early cable success in these countries, particularly in the Benelux countries, has resulted from the amount of high-quality programming, coming free of charge, from their larger neighboring countries. In addition most of the population is multilingual.

Third, in the larger European countries, West Germany, France, and Britain, cable TV policy has been a matter of state-led industrial policy.[28]

West Germany

Of the three major West European industrialized countries, cable TV in West Germany has been most successful. While in 1985, only 129,000 households were connected, by April 1989, 5 million homes were connected to PTT cable, representing 20 percent of all West German households.[29] However, because the system was built by the Bundespost, it utilizes the old technology of tree-and-branch which cannot be interactive and therefore poses no threat to the telecommunications network.

The project has also been financed at enormous cost to the government. Although the industrial policy of satellite building was launched by the Social Democrats, that party was predominantly against commercial broadcasting. Because broadcasting is cultural policy for which, under the Basic Law, the *Länder* (states) have responsibility, and because those *Länder*, which are controlled by the Social Democrats, steadfastly held out against commercial broadcasting, the Christian Democrat federal government, which entered power in 1983, utilized the telecommunications monopoly of the Bundespost and the hybrid nature of cable TV to intervene in the broadcasting field. The cable program was allocated 1,000 million deutsche marks per annum, rising to 1,500 million in 1986. At the same time, and linked to the policy of cabling, the federal Minister for Posts and Telecommunications announced that in addition to the four transponders to be allocated on *TVSAT*, two further channels would be rented by the Bundespost on Eutelsat satellites, and six on an Intelsat satellite.[30]

By this time, Sky channel had already begun broadcasting on Eutelsat's *ECS1* satellite to German households, raising the possibility of foreign investment leading German investment. Taken together, the two policies of cabling and satellite broadcasting can be seen as a means of providing German households with German-controlled broadcasting, emanating from private interests favorable to the party in government. However, since cabling has been slow, the Bundespost opened up the SMATV market in 1985 to allow the reception of programs by other households, helping satellite programmers with penetration and the equipment industry with sales. It also took the financial burden of converting cable head-ends for reception of the European standard, MAC (Multiplexed Analogue Component), transmissions (see chapter 8). Finally, when the introduction of MAC standards for DBS threatened to slow down its penetration, low-powered local commercial television stations were allowed to re-broadcast signals. One can therefore argue that by taking all the financial risks, the Bundespost, supported by the federal government, was effectively delivering consumers to advertisers and programmers.

However, because of the ideological split between *Länder*, the allocation of transponders proved difficult, and satellite channels were slow to fill the available capacity. The first German channel started on the *ECS1* satellite. In 1984, Radio Télévision Luxembourg-Plus (RTL-Plus), which was majority-owned by the West German Bertelsmann multimedia conglomerate, and the Westdeutsche Allgemeine Zeitung (WAZ) newspaper group (both of which were considered ideologically liberal), began beaming into West Germany from outside. The following year, a rival grouping of publishers, headed by the Springer Press (which was ideologically conservative), began broadcasting its channel, SAT1, from *ECS1*. Similarly, 3 SAT, a joint venture between the public service broadcaster, ZDF and its counterparts in Austria and Switzerland, began broadcasting to the German speaking populations of those countries. As Peter Humphreys has pointed out, this public service broadcast channel is highly significant as a cultural channel for the Germanaphone area of Central, including Eastern, Europe.[31]

The federal structure of West Germany meant that decisions on the allocation of the four transponders had to be made in trade-offs between the *Länder*. As a result, TVSAT is divided between the 11 states according to their population. This structure has given rise to an alignment of three groups of states, each with a full transponder, and a fourth transponder reserved to the state broadcaster, ARD, for its satellite channel, Eins Plus. The three state groupings were largely determined by political affilia-tions.[32] The resulting allocation gave transponders to SAT1, RTL-Plus, and SAT3.

While the competition between the commercial channels SAT1 and RTL-Plus has been fierce, the main result has been the politicization of satellite development in Western Germany. The commercial prospects of *TVSAT* have been overshadowed by political considerations. And, in fact, by 1990, the German private broadcasters had decided to move to *Astra* rather than *TVSAT*, which had become little more than experimental.

France

In contrast to West Germany, where the conservative central govern-ment has been intent on promoting the commercialization of broadcasting through satellites and cable has been a tool for its corporatist relations with the programmers, in France there has been considerable distrust of DBS and the fact that governments cannot control it. However, in France also, state-led cable policy has been supplemented by state-led satellite broad-casting policy.

The Plan Câble was initiated by the Socialist government in 1982. It aimed to build up an integrated network of fiber optic cable, providing interactive systems that would eventually make France a major interna-tional hardware provider. At the same time, it was intended to protect French culture against foreign companies and programs and to transform France into an "Information Society." The project was so ambitious that it promoted fierce criticism and ran into problems with both the supply of optic fiber and the investment cost.[33]

Although the Plan Câble was to reflect a partnership between the state and local operators (the so-called Sociétés Locales de l'Exploitation Commerciale), the state was to provide the bulk of funds needed for the construction of the fiber optic networks. The municipalities were to provide 30 percent of the capital costs, and were to be responsible for financing the local production of programs. Private or other public actors were expected to raise a further $100 million.

Although the French government pushed for short-term, fast cable development, manufacturers and program suppliers were reluctant to commit themselves while the municipalities had doubts about the profitability of the exercise. Following a debate between the ministries of the Interior and Finance, a compromise was reached whereby the DGT would initially assist in financing the build-up of the network. The DGT also encouraged the municipalities to join together in financial partnerships, negotiating the terms of agreement on a case-by-case basis. Nevertheless, the municipalities remained skeptical, arguing that the risk was enormous and wanting programming control.

Further problems arose between the DGT and Télédistribution Française (TDF), the body responsible for the transmissions. DGT argued that its less expensive and technically less complicated communications satellites, such as *Télécom 1A*, could transmit programs to head-end operators, who would then distribute them to subscribers. In contrast, TDF supported direct-to-home broadcasting, utilizing its high-powered satellites.

In 1984 Jean Dondeux, the DGT's director general, publicly announced his support for cabling with optic fiber, and expressed his fears that electoral considerations and lack of funds threatened the cable project. Because regulation was possible over cable but not over DBS satellites, he also recommended that the government abandon high-powered in favor of medium-powered satellites.

Behind these arguments lay the DGT's anxiety at losing its monopoly status as a telecommunications carrier. Before 1984, because of cable's potential challenge to its monopoly, it is not certain how much the DGT wanted cable to succeed. After 1984, when the DGT was required by the government to raise prices to aid the general budget, it could not afford the financial burden. By 1989, against Plan Câble's forecast of 7 million households cabled, only 81,971 households subscribed to cable, of which 23,000 were in Paris. Nevertheless, the plan has provided the basis for cabled "islands," which, when connected together, will provide a nationwide broadband infrastructure. Because of its commitment to ISDN, by 1990 France Télécom had begun to invest in cable TV, and penetration was on the increase (see chapter 7).[34]

The original TDF satellite venture was initiated by the Giscard d'Estaing government of 1974–1981. However, the incoming Socialist Mitterand administration of 1981–1986 was unsure whether to proceed.

DBS was seen as a technology that could destabilize national sovereignty and disrupt culture, two extremely sensitive issues for France. Although the *TDF1* project seemed dead, especially after the 1984 report to the government by M. Gerard Thery, the former DGT telecommunications chief, which characterized high-powered satellites as obsolete technology, in 1985, a year before legislative elections, the government revised its approach to satellite broadcasting. While sustaining the project, it decided that *TDF1* should take on a more commercial and European dimension so that it might become more attractive to programmers and advertisers, and therefore more profitable. Cynics have pointed out the fact that, knowing they would lose the upcoming election, the Socialists were attempting to retain some influence in the mass media through alliances with private satellite programmers.[35]

Despite initial hostility to the venture, the Conservative Chirac government, which came to power in 1986, succumbed to industry pressures. However, the contracts signed between the Socialists and private programming channels were revoked.[36] Political interference dogged *TDF1* and prevented each attempt to finalize the programming lineup for the satellite. Eventually, following its launch, transponder allocations were determined by the new regulatory body, the Conseil Supérieure de l'Audiovisuel, in a more impartial manner.[37] Despite the fact that only a French cultural public service channel, La Sept, transmits on the satellite, the backup to *TDF1* was put in orbit in 1990. By 1989, only 20,000 reception dishes had been bought, and Canal Plus, which was awarded two transponders on *TDF1*, considered utilizing *Astra* instead. Few analysts believe that *TDF1* can be commercially successful. However, because it and West German's *TVSAT* help to secure the future of MAC and High Definition TV standards and also keep the European satellite industry in business, a political-industrial alliance keeps *TFD1* alive (see chapter 8).

Britain

Cable TV in Britain has also had a *dirigiste* component, but rather with the state attempting to use private capital to fund a national broadband infrastructure. The Thatcher government behaved somewhat like the French in demanding that cable operators should utilize the expensive, futuristic, optic fiber technology while at the same time refusing to fund cable TV development. Its market- and entertainment-led policy has had a similar outcome to that of the French. The high penetration of videocassette recorders (VCRs), the better quality reception of broadcast TV compared to U.S. broadcasts, and the higher quality of broadcast programs meant that private investors perceived poor commercial prospects for cable and were reluctant to fund the high capital up-front investment that was needed. A major blow to the hopes of the cable TV entrepreneurs was the government announcement, in the April 1984 budget, of the end of capital allowances against tax in relation to machinery, buildings, and the laying of cables. According to Tom Forester, this decision meant that the average break-even point on a consortium's investment was extended from seven to nine years.[38] In this situation, investment was led by British Telecom (the privatized PTT), which by 1989 had interests in the Aberdeen, Westminster, Swindon, and Coventry cable companies, amounting to 1.3 percent of TV households.[39]

The British DBS system had a similar parentage to cable TV—a strong state attempting to utilize private enterprise to fulfill its ends. The government first planned to match the opportunities given to French and German aerospace and consumer electronics industries by using the DBS project to back the British satellite industry. Hence, at first its aim was to support British technology by the formation of the Unisat consortium, which was to launch a British-made satellite. Originally the BBC was to provide programming. When the BBC withdrew, another group, the so-called Club 21, consisting of broadcasters and manufacturers, was to operate the satellite. Unfortunately, this mixture of free market and state *dirigisme*, involving the specification of technology to private entrepreneurs, proved unsustainable. Due to the high risks and huge investment required, the private parties pulled out of the project.

Reviewing its plans, the government then turned its attention away from the satellite industry to the provision of a strong base for British TV program makers. In 1986 it proposed a 15-year programming license, and withdrew its specification of a British satellite system. By so doing, it enticed several companies to bid for the right to beam the four channels allocated to the United Kingdom by the WARC 1977 regulations. The winner of this competition was British Satellite Broadcasting (BSB), a consortium made up of a number of seeming blue chip companies. These included commercial television companies; Granada Television, an independent TV company; Richard Branson's Virgin PLC (Public Limited Company); the Pearson Group, owners of the *Financial Times*; Anglia Television; and Bond Corporation owned by Alan Bond, the Australian media magnate. However, technical problems with its receiving equipment postponed the 1989 launch of BSB until 1990.

By 1990, following massive advertisements and some free distribution of reception dishes, Sky television had 1,363,297 subscribers in Britain.[40] It continued to operate at a loss ($280 million in 1989), cross-subsidized by the newspaper interests of the Murdoch group. As in West Germany, satellite broadcasting in Britain has permitted the concentration of cross-media ownership. Because Rupert Murdoch used *Astra*, which does not broadcast on a British DBS slot, he bypassed cross-media ownership regulations.

The Peacock Committee Report on the financing of the BBC (1986), undertaken for the government, largely recognized the failure of cable TV. It recommended that British Telecom (or another company such as Mercury) should become a common carrier of cable TV, thereby making it economical to replace local circuits with fiber optics.[41] However, the 1988 government White Paper, *Broadcasting in the 90's*, rejected this recommendation on the grounds that it would inhibit the growth of competitive telecommunications networks. At the same time, the White Paper threatened to divorce the provision of carriage from programming.[42]

Once more the government rejected a recommendation that it invest in a fiber optic network, preferring instead that the market should decide which technology would survive. Despite the fact that such a development would fit with the European Commission's plans for broadband cable, BT's request that it be allowed to carry both television and telecommunications signals along fiber optics to the home has met with hostility to the potential extension of its market dominance.

Although in the latter 1980s increased investment in cable TV has come from overseas, particularly American companies, the government's priorities are with satellites and the satellite programmers. At one time it publicly suggested that two of the existing terrestrial channels be put on satellite. Moreover, like the West German government, it liberalized SMATV, thereby undermining the market prospects for cable TV. However, unlike West Germany, by the device of choosing an unpopular part of the radio spectrum, it backtracked on its stated intention to liberalize microwave local television distribution, which would have competed with satellite distribution. By 1989, despite increasing investment by American telecommunications operators in cable TV in the hope of further liberalization of the voice transmission market, the government had seemingly jettisoned cable TV as a possible local telecommunications competitor to BT in favor of Personal Communications Networks based on digital cellular radio technology.[43] In 1990, British cable TV policy was neither wholly broadcasting policy nor telecommunications policy.

The concept of public service broadcasting has been evident in British regulation of cable TV with a new watchdog, the Cable Authority, established in 1984. In 1990, this authority merged with the Independent Broadcasting Authority, the regulatory authority for commercial terrestrial television, to form the Independent Television Commission. Given the Thatcher government's policy of centralized state power, there was no question of the involvement of municipal authorities in cable TV, as in France. The editorial and advertising content of cable programs has been given a wider latitude than has been allowed existing broadcasters. The 1990 *Broadcasting Act* has abolished the requirement for cable networks to carry the four existing terrestrial channels, and no restrictions on foreign material are imposed. In contrast, France has specified that foreign channels may not take up more than 30 percent of a system's total capacity, 15 percent of that capacity must be locally made, 60 percent of feature films must be EC-made, and 50 percent must come from Francophone nations. The problem for all cable operators, however, is that with high up-front investment, the revenue available for local programming is limited.[44] The French have found that content regulation increases subscription rates, which in turn impacts on penetration.

A COMPARISON OF POLICIES

In the United States, both the cable and the satellite markets have developed outside an R&D policy for the hardware or programming industry. Liberalization and deregulation of both market structure and content have been the only industrial policies, pursued both domestically and internationally. Given the up-front costs, cable and satellite companies have provided cheap technology to meet current demand. Basic R&D has been derogated to NASA.

In contrast, cable and satellite television development in Europe has been strongly linked to gaining a competitive advantage in international markets for hardware and program manufacturers. Faced with these problems, governments have adopted contradictory policies, backing all the possibilities (cable, satellite, and deregulated terrestrial television) via optic fiber, coaxial cable, and high-, medium-, and low-powered satellites.

The proliferation of actors, both public and private, together with financial and technical problems, create policy conflict. Where technology is changing fast, bureaucratic alliances do not necessarily reflect these changes. One part of the bureaucracy may well have an established linkage with one technology whose development would serve its own interests, as well as corporatist relations with its producers. In France, there were public clashes between the DGT, backing cable TV and low-powered satellites, and Télédistribution Française, backing DBS. In Britain there was private conflict between the Department of Trade and Industry and the Home Office over territory. In West Germany, audiovisual policy was utilized by the federal government in its attempts to erode the autonomous media policy of the *Länder*. Finally, in the United States, the audiovisual industry has been only one of the territories occasioning dispute between states and federal-level regulation, and between the FCC and Congress.

However, where governments have backed all technical options, the policy seems unrealistic. In Western Europe, commercialization of terrestrial television has increased the difficulties for the potential profitability of satellite and cable television channels. In addition, the costs of the new technologies of distribution have been underestimated.

The American scenario of cable TV inextricably linked to the marketplace and commercial activity has been followed in none of the major West European countries. In state-centric Britain and France, direction has come from the government to private industry. In Europe, cable's development has also been more closely related to telecommunications than in the United States. In France and West Germany, powerful PTTs were asked to carry the financial burden of cable's development, and its potential as a tool of liberalization has consequently been circumscribed by political design. In Britain, it is being utilized as a potential private competitor to the telecommunications local monopoly. Within Europe in general, politics rather than technology has played the predominant role in the development of cable TV.

Satellite television has similar problems. All systems represent colossal investments. *TDF1* and *TVSAT* cost $800 million each. British Satellite Broadcasting committed $700 million and had to raise another $600 million following the satellite launch, and *Astra*'s first satellite cost $200 million to build and launch.[45] The anticipated arrival of Eutelsat's second generation of satellites with 80 transponders will lead to overcapacity and a reduction in transponder leasing prices. By 1992 it is expected that there will be more than 160 transponders available on high- and medium-powered satellites in Europe. This additional capacity will exacerbate the financial difficulties of the satellite operators and benefit program providers. However, because transponder leases are only a small part of setting up an attractive channel ($6.4 million in 1989 compared to $48 million for programs), the decrease in transponder leases may not be sufficient to attract new programmers.

In a large geographical area such as the United States, DBS satellites make a lot of sense. One or two satellites can cover three thousand miles of continental spread at a significantly lower cost than either terrestrial transmitters or cable. Europe, however, is different. The existence of national, linguistic, and cultural barriers every few hundred miles pose difficulties from a commercial point of view. Moreover, even though

Europe imports more than $350 million of American programming each year, there is as yet no homogeneous trans-European culture. Hence, Eutelsat is thinking carefully about the feasibility of a pan-European satellite.

It seems that only the collaboration of cable and satellite TV can help offset some of the commercial problems. However, as in the United States, such a collaboration raises problems of concentration and bottlenecks to access in local markets. In Europe, the regulation of such concentration is made more difficult by the cross-national nature of satellite broadcasting. Even on a national basis, the financial problems faced by satellite operators also tend to pressure governments into allowing such concentration. In Britain, in 1990, the decision to allow the merger of Sky and BSB into one company, brought about by the financial disaster that each faced, has placed Rupert Murdoch in effective control of five channels of the only satellite operating company, as well as in control of one third of newspaper readership.

Differences between the United States and Europe are likely to remain. In the United States privately owned cable television is replacing privately owned network broadcasting. In Europe it is in competition not only with such private commercial broadcasters but also with public service broadcasting. Its commercial future must then, to a certain extent, depend on how far governments are prepared to allow public service broadcasting to be eroded, or how far they will financially support the distribution of public service broadcasting via satellite.

During the 1980s, the argument for more consumer choice, a liberal market concept of freedom, was the principal rationale for the introduction of the new technologies of distribution. However, in reality, consumer demand has been given little attention. Greater priority has been given to economic and industrial factors. The consumer was thought of as a commodity, one ready to purchase products (programs) as well as other consumable items (advertising). Hence, the new media represent the individuation of a mass public. Just as the original introduction of radio allowed the extension of advertising into the home and commercial broadcasting linked audience profiles for certain programs to advertising, so the new media allow the further differentiation of consumers as advertising targets.

In this process it is governments that have facilitated private capital, and not consumers who have chosen it. Ironically, it seems that the immediate future of cable may be dependent not on its entertainment aspect but on the original concept of its provision of a wide range of services. However, in the long term, this interrelationship may prove its downfall. As optoelectronic components become cheaper, the PTTs will modernize the local network and broadcasting will become yet another value-added service. The political battle of the 1990s is already set to be the conflict surrounding the convergence of telecommunications and broadcasting. Because of this convergence, through HDTV, governments, including the U.S. government, are in the process of intervening in the current divorce between the broadcasting transmission market and its mass equipment applications.

NOTES

1. J. Tunstall, *Communications Deregulation* (Oxford: Basil Blackwell, 1986), 122–27.

2. B. L. Sherman, *Telecommunications Management: The Broadcast and Cable Industries* (New York: McGraw-Hill, 1987), 8.

3. Robert Magnant, *Domestic Satellite, an FCC Giant Step:Toward Competitive Communications Policy* (Boulder, Colo.: Westview Press, 1977); J. C. Hsiung, "Direct Broadcasting by Satellite in the U.S.A.," *Telecommunications Policy* 9 (March 1985): 49–61.

4. J. Tydeman and E. Kelm, *New Media in Europe* (London: McGraw-Hill, 1986), 120–35.

5. Tom Forester, *High Tech Society* (Oxford: Basil Blackwell, 1987), 104–5; *Financial Times*, 6 April 1982.

6. U.S. Congress, Office of Technology Assessment, *Critical Connections: Communication for the Future* (Washington, D.C.: Government Printing Office, 1989), 81–83.

7. W. R. Cooke, "Broadcast and Cable Deregulation in the United States" (Paper presented at *La Déréglémentation des Télécommunications et de l'Audiovisuel*, Colloque International, Paris, May 1986).

8. T. Streeter, "Policy Discourse and Broadcast Practice: The F.C.C., the U.S. Broadcast Networks and the Discourse of the Marketplace," *Media, Culture and Society* 5 (July 1983): 256.

9. Cable Communications Policy Act, 1984, Public Law 98-549.

10. Exceptions were made in remote rural areas, where a local newspaper was allowed to cross-own a local cable company.

11. Tunstall, *Communications Deregulation*, 139.

12. NBC (National Broadcasting Company) in April 1989 launched a 24-hour consumer and business news cable channel; NBC and Capital Cities, together with ABC (American Broadcasting Company) and Hearst Corporation (the media conglomerate company), each own one-third of the Arts and Entertainment Network, a cable network; and ABC owns one-third of Lifeline, a health and family cable network, together with

80 percent of the Entertainment and Sports Programming Network, a 24-hour sports channel.

13. According to A. C. Nielsen, in November 1989, 52,564,000 homes were cabled out of the total U.S. TV universe of 92,100,000 households, an increase of 8.1 percent over 1988 (*Cable and Satellite Europe*, January 1990, 9).

14. Tunstall, *Communications Deregulation*, 170.

15. *Telecommunications Reports*, 20 July 1987, 24 August 1987, 4 April 1988; Wilson P. Dizard, "Conference Quotes," *Intermedia* 17 (December 1989): 40.

16. Satellite Master Antenna Television is a master antenna television system (MATV) with a receiving dish for picking up and distributing satellite television signals. An MATV is a cable system confined to a small housing development served by a common aerial, whereas Community Antenna TV (CATV) covers a whole community, such as a town.

17. Constantinos Sfiktos, *A Review of the U.S. Cable Television Industry* (Unpublished master's dissertation, City University, London, 1989).

18. Heather Hudson, "Satellite Broadcasting in the United States," in *Satellite Broadcasting*, edited by R. Negrine (London: Routledge, 1988), 216–33; Alan Friedman, "Network the Right Stuff and Reach for the Sky," *Financial Times*, 23 February 1990.

19. *Electronics*, 28 February 1980, 14 July 1983.

20. James Martin, *The Wired Society* (Englewood Cliffs, N.J.: Prentice-Hall, 1978), 1–22; R. L. Smith, "The Birth of a Wired Nation," in *Readings in Mass Communications, Concepts and Issues in the Mass Media*, edited by H. Emery and T. C. Smythe (Dubuque, Iowa: W. M. C. Brown Publishers, 1983), 247–58.

21. W. Dutton, J. Blumler, and K. Kraemer, eds., *Wired Cities: Shaping the Future of Communications* (London: Casel, 1987), 1–40.

22. E. R. Meehan, "Technical Capability versus Corporate Imperatives: Toward a Political Economy of Cable Television and Information Diversity," in *The Political Economy of Information*, edited by V. Mosco and J.Walso (Madison: University of Wisconsin Press, 1988), 184–85.

23. Blumler and Kraemer, *Wired Cities*, 53–138.

24. On "economic harm" and Intelsat, see J. Hills, *Deregulating Telecoms. Competition and Control in the U.S., Japan and Britain* (London: Frances Pinter, 1986), 164–79.

25. Chatham House, Royal Institute of International Affairs, *Europe's Future in Space. A Joint Report*, Chatham House Special Paper (London: Routledge for RIIA, 1988), 197.

26. M. Hirsch, "The Doldrums of Europe's TV Landscape: Coronet as

Catalyst," in *Tracing New Orbits*, edited by D. A. Demac (New York: Columbia University Press, 1986), 114–30.

27. Electronics companies were AEG (Allgenzeine Elektrizitagesell Schaft)/Telefunken (West Germany) and Thomson-CSF (Compagnie Telegraphique Sans Fils) (France). Aerospace companies were Messerschmidt Boelkow Blohm (West Germany) and Aerospatiale (France).

28. Compare T. Hollins, *Beyond Broadcasting: Into the Cable Age* (London: BFI, 1984); J. Miller, "Cable Policy in Europe: The Role of Transponder Broadcasting and Its Effects on CATV," *Telecommunications Policy* 11 (September 1987): 259–68.

29. B. Novotny, "Germany: The Slow March of Cable," in *The European Experience*, edited by G. Noell-Smith (London: BFI, 1989); H. J. Kleinsteuber, "Federal Republic of Germany," in *Electronic Media and Politics in Western Europe*, edited by H. J. Kleinsteuber, D. McQuail and K. Siune, Euromedia Research Group Handbook of National Systems (Frankfurt: Campus Verlag, 1986), 44–86.

30. Peter Humphreys, "New Media Policy Dilemmas in West Germany: From Ideological Polarisation to Regional Economic Competition," in *Broadcasting and New Media Policies in Western Europe*, edited by K. Dyson and P. Humphreys (London: Routledge, 1988), 185–222.

31. Peter Humphreys, "Satellite Broadcasting Policy in West Germany—Political Conflict and Competition in a Decentralised System," in *Satellite Broadcasting*, edited by R. Negrine (London: Routledge, 1988), 126.

32. K. Dyson and P. Humphreys, "The Political Implications of Broadcasting from Outer Space: The German Dimension" (Paper presented to the European Consortium Planning Sessions, Barcelona, 25–30 March 1985).

33. Claude Sorbet and Michael Palmer, "France" in Kleinsteuber, McQuail, and Siune, *Electronic Media*, 87–109.

34. For a survey of TV in Europe, see *Cable and Satellite Europe*, June 1990, 24–26.

35. *Financial Times*, 5 February 1987.

36. Just before the 1986 elections, the Socialists allocated one transponder each to Silvio Berlusconi for La Cinq; to Robert Maxwell (U.K. publisher); to Canal Un—a joint venture of the public service broadcasting channels; and to a new ad hoc consortium, European Satellite Television Broadcasting, whose owners included Berlusconi and Maxwell.

37. The Conseil Supérieure de l'Audiovisuel was inaugurated 1989 by the Rocard Socialist Government.

38. Forester, *High Tech Society*, 126.

39. Saatchi and Saatchi, *European Market and Media Fact* (1989), 167.

40. *The Guardian*, 19 April 1990.

41. Peacock Committee, *Report of the Committee on Financing the BBC*, Cmnd. 9824 (London: HMSO, 1986), 144.

42. *Broadcasting in the 90's: Competition, Choice and Quality*, Cmnd. 517 (London: HMSO, 1988), para. 6.43.

43. Advisory Council on Science and Technology, *Optoelectronics* (London: HMSO, 1988); Communication Steering Group, *The Infrastructure for Tomorrow* (London: HMSO, 1988); Department of Trade and Industry, *Phones on the Move* (London: DTI, 1989).

44. *Screen Digest*, April 1984, 67.

45. *Broadcast*, 22 December 1989, 15; *Broadcasting Abroad*, September 1984, 4.

6

A European Broadcasting and Telecommunications Community?

This chapter discusses the attempts of the European Commission to regulate broadcasting and telecommunications. Technologically, the two traditionally separate market sectors are increasingly being seen as related. The commission conceptualizes broadcasting as a "tele-service"—a service that may be delivered over a telecommunications network—and justifies its intervention on economic grounds. The technological push within the European Community (EC) is to provide the infrastructure of the future via a broadband highway, along which will be delivered television as well as other services. However, as this chapter demonstrates, the integration of regulation at the European level falls far short of this technological aspiration.

Within the EC, tensions have arisen over the pace and extent of the economic and political integration that should take place, and over its ability to integrate such Southern European states as Greece, Spain, and Portugal, which joined it in the 1980s, and the potential integration of countries from the Eastern bloc. In particular, the British government of Margaret Thatcher was reluctant to cede sovereign rights over policy to the European Community. The conflict between those with a vision of Europe as an integrated federal entity with power skewed toward the center (Brussels) and those who see Europe's future as a federation of sovereign states with minimal harmonization at the center permeates policy-making.

In turn, these competing perspectives reflect the wider theories of neo-functional integration and consociational democracy.[1] Neo-functional theorists argue that the integration of nation states can be pursued in steps.

From one function that becomes the subject of consensus, and in which states are prepared to concede their sovereignty, will arise others, so that states will gradually become enmeshed. As this process continues, aided by central policy-making institutions, so identity will be transferred from the nation state to the center. Eventually, full political integration will stem from the built-in dynamism of spill-over. Each action will demand another action in order to make it effective, eventually bringing about de facto political union. From this perspective, the integration of telecommunications and broadcasting national systems into a European system will aid in fuller political and cultural as well as economic integration. This model of integration was espoused by the founders of the EC and was prevalent in the 1960s and early 1970s, until it became evident that the nationally based EC Council of Ministers, not the European Commission, was the preeminent institution. Lack of progress toward integration within Europe then called the theory into question. However, it retains currency among EC personnel.[2]

The model of consociational democracy, first developed by Arend Liphart in relation to the Netherlands, analyzed a society that was elitist and divided into groups more concerned with themselves than each other. Each of the groups was then represented in proportion to its numbers within the various state organs and layers of elites. Decision making took place through a cartel of elites in which interests were traded off against each until consensus was reached. Further, in order to deliver its portion of the trade-offs, the retention of stability of the political system demanded the control of each of the subsegments by its elite.[3]

For the theme of this chapter, Paul Taylor's brilliant extension of the concept of consociationalism to Europe can be used to explain developments in telecommunications and broadcasting. He has argued:

> Integration in the sense of strengthening the regional functional systems may help to sharpen rather than to soften the cleavages in the existing society of nations. . . . Members of the cartel of elites . . . will have an interest in increasing the size of the cake, and the share obtained by their own segment, whilst at the same time protecting the distinctiveness of their segments in comparison with others, since they serve as each member's constituency and power base.[4]

Tension arises between the economic, social, and cultural links needed to foster economic growth in the region, on the one hand, and the power base of the elite, on the other. The interests of the elite of any one segment are not necessarily the interests of the general population. Moreover, as integration proceeds, the "theory suggests that elites will become more determined to strengthen controls over their own segments." Thus, regional integration "helps to reinforce the anti-democratic tendencies of elites."[5]

The theory of consociationalism helps to explain why there was so much resistance from national governments, and particularly from that of Britain, to EC entry into the cultural broadcasting field. It also helps to explain the seeming contradiction of increased regulatory controls exerted by the British government over national broadcasting. Finally, it helps to clarify why there is a fundamental lack of concern at the EC level for the societal implications of the technologies.

The contrasting theories of neo-functional integration and consociational democracy also reflect the varied conceptualizations of networks that have already been discussed in this book. The former reflects the internationalization of capital in that it conceptualizes communication networks as going from company A to company B, and taking no notice of the political boundaries determined by nation states. The latter conceptualizes networks as based on the billiard-ball model of nation states joined at the peripheries into an international network. In the former, control is passed to the private actor, while in the latter, control remains with the nation state.

This chapter suggests that while the major feature of European Community negotiations is still that of consociational democracy—of competing national alliances of state bureaucratic and business elites—the mechanisms by which the European Commission seeks to move power to the center undermine the national sovereignty on which that model is based and result in the failure of regulation. At the same time, the member states, by seeking to retain national control, both ignore the realities of the internationalization of the sectors and preclude solutions that would diffuse access. Hence, the major beneficiary of European integration is international private capital, and the major loser is the individual citizen.

THE EUROPEAN POLITICAL CONTEXT

There are a number of competing institutions that impact on policy-making at the European level. In the area of trade, within Western Europe there are two groups of countries operating free trade agreements between themselves: the European Free Trade Association (EFTA), consisting of the Nordic countries, Switzerland, and Austria, and the European Community, which began in 1957 with 5 countries and by 1990 comprised 12. In 1990, the two trading blocs were negotiating to come together into one

"European Economic Space" (EES), based on common decision making. The intention is that the EES should come into being in parallel with the EC's open market of 1992.[6] In telecommunications, CEPT—the European Conference of Postal and Telecommunications Administrations—consists of 26 members. The Council of Europe, an intergovernmental body primarily concerned with culture, consists of 20 countries, of which all members of the European Community are also members. The European Broadcasting Union, which primarily promotes program exchange between public service broadcasters, has 40 members in 33 states. Economic policies of the EC aimed at integrating a European-wide market must take account of these potential institutional competitors as well as the wide disparity of economic performance and social and cultural traditions within member countries.

Further competition to the European Community has come through the Eureka project. Eureka was initiated by the French Mitterand Government in 1985, partly for domestic electoral reasons, but also as a European counterbalance to the American Star Wars research program. It is an industry-led program of cross-national collaborative research projects aimed at improving industrial performance through the application of science. At first there was considerable tension between its officials and those of the EC, who saw it as competing with EC research programs. It includes 19 European nations, including the 12 EC countries, 5 EFTA countries, and Turkey and Finland, and has companies, academic institutions, governments and the EC as participants.

However, since the European Community contains the largest and most economically powerful countries in Western Europe (particularly Germany and France), it is the community that now leads the attempt to counter the traditional national fragmentation of Western Europe. Measured in terms of such factors as trade, mail, and travel, the level of structural integration of the EC remained on a plateau for a decade after its inauguration.[7] From existing as a marginal institution of the 1960s and 1970s, the EC has gained a momentum toward integration due to the shared experience of recession in the 1980s together with the prospect of American and Japanese economic dominance. In 1985, the EC governments committed their countries to the establishment of a Single European Market by December 1992. Embodied formally in the Single European Act of June 1987, the aim was defined as "an area without internal frontiers in which the free movement of goods, persons, services and capital is ensured."[8]

In essence, the elimination of all physical, technical, and fiscal obstacles in the EC has become the most important method of achieving a single internal market. Underlying that proposal is the belief that the small home markets of the community do not have the necessary size to benefit from economies of scale. The implication of this economic analysis is that the industries of America and Japan are successful primarily because of their size rather than large due to their success.

The validity of this underlying economic model, which gives centrality to size and scale and to capital concentration, has been challenged by some economists as inappropriate to much of the manufacturing and service industries in the 1990s.[9] Although in some products such scale economies are possible—for instance in telecommunications, switching markets, and computers—these occur primarily in products and services where nationally based public procurement or standardization has reduced competition. In other markets, the primary result of reduced barriers to internal trade will be wider product ranges within domestic markets. John Kay has therefore contended that the European market will be no more homogenous after 1992 than before, and that diversity will remain because liberalization of trade affects supply, not demand. Moreover, demand is structured by differences in "preferences, habits, language, culture, climate, incomes."[10] Hence, the trend toward Euro-mergers and a European industrial policy targeting large groups is counterproductive.

With the exception of these siren voices, the approach to 1992 has been dominated by the EC's vision of a unified, homogenous market, reduced costs for community producers, and scale economies. Implicit within the proposal is the idea of a European economic and political bloc within the international economic system. Within this internal market, digital telecommunications are intended to provide the electronic infrastructure, which in turn is intended to increase the productivity and competitiveness of European manufacturing and retailing.

However, telecommunications is also of particular importance because it is the only industry within the information-technology sector where Europe showed a positive balance of trade in the 1980s. In total, telecommunications is currently estimated to account for 2 percent of GNP within the EC, with an estimated increase to 7 percent per annum by the year 2000.[11] Taken together, the revenue of the network operators in the three major countries (France, West Germany, and Britain) was twice that of AT&T and a third more than that of Japan's Nippon Telegraph and Telephone (NTT).[12] With the linkage between the growth of services and equipment, in conjunction with standardization, telecommunications has represented a potential "growth pole."

Similarly, in the broadcasting field a linkage exists between information, services, and equipment. The European Commission justified its

1986 Draft Directive on services as being complementary to its actions to unify standards for reception equipment and to aid the program-producing sector. The expansion of European program production was needed to support the new satellite and cable channels (the annual demand for programming is expected to rise to 300,000–500,000 hours).[13] In turn, the new channels, financed by advertising, would support the European satellite industry (see chapter 8). There is more than a hint of the French *filière electronique*, with its forward and backward linkages, in the commission's proposals.

Although some consensus seemed to surround the commission's 1987 proposals for harmonization of telecommunications regulations, by 1990 they had run into problems of acceptance from member states. The technological fix that the commission had substituted for political consensus could not hold. Similarly, the proposals on broadcasting met with determined resistance from a wide range of EC, public, private, and international actors. This chapter, then, concerns the attempts by the European Commission to foster economic and political integration through technology. On the one hand, it is about the permeability of sovereignty, and on the other, it is about the resistance of states to that erosion.

THE ENTRY OF THE EC INTO BROADCASTING AND TELECOMMUNICATIONS

The founding document of the European Community, the Treaty of Rome, was signed in 1957 by six nations—Belgium, France, the Federal Republic of Germany, Italy, Luxembourg, and the Netherlands. This membership was expanded in 1972 with the addition of Denmark, Ireland, and the United Kingdom; and was further expanded in the 1980s with the addition of Greece, Spain, and Portugal. The Treaty of Rome is founded on a liberal market philosophy, which previously had found expression in the General Agreement on Trade and Tariffs (GATT). Among the earliest of the actions of the commission in relation to the communications and information industries was its 1976 public-sector purchasing restrictions on contracts above a certain size. This directive made it more difficult for member countries to pursue the policy of favoring "national champion" computer companies, such as ICL (International Computer Limited) in Britain, and actually opened the market to American companies. The EC also took antidumping action against Japan through the imposition of tariff barriers on integrated circuits which protected the weak European industry. The commission has accrued power through international trade-related actions and its position as mouthpiece for its members in bilateral negotiations with Japan and the United States, and in such fora as GATT.

Technological advance has also tended to open the way for the commission to take on additional importance as a regional coordinator of national provision in telecommunications. Satellites broadcasting across national boundaries, the need for networks to work together, and the technological, economic, and political problems associated with ISDN and HDTV have produced the political environment for a unified response from Europe on behalf of European manufacturers. European standardization is of the utmost importance in defining a European as opposed to a Japanese or American market, and in combating fragmentation.

While the commission acts as an umpire between the interests of member states and as the administrative arm of the Council of Ministers, it also regards itself as a policy initiator.[14] References to the role of the commission in bringing proposals forward are contained over 80 times in the 248 articles of the Treaty of Rome.[15] Inevitably, given the many actors at the regional, national, and subnational levels—manufacturers, operators, and users—policy-making is a lengthy process, with much of the work being done by the permanent group of officials (civil servants from each country, who are based in Brussels). The main objective is to bring together contrasting views and to gradually "harmonize" national policies.[16] In this respect, the commission's major levers are located in existing trends in the international and regional economy. However, in addition, a community-wide movement toward liberalization undermines member government regulation and enhances the power of the commission.

A commission proposal such as the Directive on Broadcasting becomes legislation or regulation only when the council has approved it, an often lengthy process. In practice, the commission proposes, the European Parliament makes some amendments, and the Council of Ministers approves or disapproves a directive.[17]

When a directive becomes EC law (or a so-called *aquis communautaire*), member states must incorporate it into their domestic legislation. In cases where national legislation conflicts with EC law, European law takes precedence. The European Court of Justice, the community's court, also has the power to either reject acts of the commission as being outside its competence or to enforce compliance by member states.

Implementation tends to be slow. For example, of the 279 planned Community Directives aimed at the completion of the Single Market, by 1990 only 130 had been approved by the Council of Ministers, and only 6 had been implemented. Disagreements arise between the commission and the permanent officials as to who should have the power of implementation, the commission or member states.[18]

In the telecommunications sector, the commission justifies its competence on the grounds of the Single Market. In fact, the commission's Green Paper on telecommunications is not formally connected with the 1985 White Paper on the Single Market, and is not cited within it. However, the Green Paper has also set a completion date of 1992, and its aims and scope parallel closely those of the White Paper. The commission holds the view that telecommunications are directly related to the economic goals of the Single Market. In particular, tele-carried services play a decisive role in the process of more closely linking production, services, and final consumption in the economy. Among these services it includes television.

However, the commission's entry into the broadcasting sector has caused considerable political conflict. Some member states were unwilling to see the commission extend its authority, especially into "culture," while public service broadcasters reacted against potential market liberalization. The Council of Europe (CoE), with its more diverse membership, and the European Broadcasting Union (EBU), the coordinating body of Western European broadcasters, were put forward as preferable coordinating bodies.[19] The justification given was that these bodies represented the cultural interests of broadcasting versus the economic bias of the EC. However, the real political interests concerned the latter two groups' institutional weakness and lack of enforcement power.

However, the European Court of Justice has interpreted transfrontier broadcasting as a "service" within the meaning of the EC Treaty, thereby bringing it within the scope of the Common Market. In light of this ruling, the argument that broadcasting is culture and not part of the economy has been defeated. Nevertheless, one can see how in broadcasting, as in telecommunications, the commission can move only with the already established international market trends. By the time of the final agreement to the Commission's Directive on broadcasting in 1989, satellites were in orbit, private broadcasters were operating, and the economic importance of television had already been demonstrated.

By examining individual cases concerning the community's competence and clashes of national policy with community law, the European Court of Justice plays a significant role in both telecommunications and broadcasting. Cases such as those between the Dutch Advertising Company, the Bond van Adverteeders, versus the Netherlands over the degree to which satellite channels might carry advertising,[20] and that of the French government versus the commission concerning French liberalization of the telecommunications terminal equipment market,[21] are examples of the European Court's policy-making capacity.

However, as has been demonstrated in the United States, the law is not necessarily the best arena for decisions on technology to be made. Because of the time dimension and the difficulty of reaching political compromises through the legal process, it seems likely that the commission's role as a de facto regulator will gradually be enhanced as markets become regionally rather than nationally based.

BROADCASTING—THE POLICY PROCESS

The commission's intervention in the broadcasting market began in 1982 with a request from the European Parliament for a report on legal problems in broadcasting. This request followed two decisions by the European Court that allowed national regulations on advertising and copyright to apply until community rules were harmonized. The commission's 1983 report, *Realities and Tendencies in European Television*, was drawn up in response to that request and recommended support for the European Broadcasting Union's plans for a European public service channel.[22] This report was followed by a Green Paper of 1984, *Television without Frontiers (TWF)*.[23]

The *TWF* Green Paper justified community intervention on the basis of broadcasting's effect on European integration which, it stated, was "not only economic in character, but also social, cultural and political." It argued:

> In exercising their democratic rights and fulfilling their responsibilities, Community citizens must be able to draw upon a range of information, ideas and opinion that reflects the variety of the Community itself. . . . To this end, cross-frontier broadcasting, particularly of television, offers the most potentially effective means of guaranteeing that the traditional pluralism of our political systems develops a healthy Community dimension.[24]

In seeking this plurality of information, the commission invited discussion with member states on how broadcasting and copyright laws might be harmonized. It identified four areas of national regulation requiring harmonization: advertising, the protection of children and young persons, the right of reply, and copyright.

The following year, the European Parliament adopted a resolution calling for a regulatory framework for an EC media policy, and subsequently, the commission issued its Draft Directive.[25] The principal aim of the directive was to establish a free flow of television programs within the community, and to "sweep away" national regulatory obstacles to the free market. While protecting consumers by ensuring that programs respected certain standards of taste and decency, the intention was to enable viewers to receive programs from any other EC country. The directive also aimed to provide an agreed regulatory regime on the amount, frequency, and ethics of advertising, not simply for cross-national broadcasts but for national markets as well.

Because of the commission's desire to justify its competence in relation to broadcasting and to liberalize monopoly sectors, the emphasis, as in the *TWF* Green Paper, is on private sector broadcasting rather than on public service broadcasting. Indeed, it stated, "to complement the action taken as regards the equipment manufacturing industry, a framework for decision making is to be established for the benefit of operators, including cable distribution enterprises, and the receiving public."[26] Trade in goods and services was to be promoted via advertising. The commission argued that this economic emphasis had to be taken in the context of its overall approach to the audiovisual sector, which included support for the creation of a European television channel and also a community aid scheme for program production.

The audiovisual program, now renamed Media '92, aims to strengthen national audiovisual industries and coproduction on the basis of cofinancing between programmers and the commission. Proposed in 1985, some of its projects had still not begun by 1989, indicating a lack of enthusiasm among program makers. There was some dissension about the program, with Britain and Denmark opposed. France wanted the program but not under the EC, and in 1989 an audiovisual Eureka program was established.[27]

The Draft Directive ran into determined opposition from member states, who objected to the EC's extension of authority; from advertisers, rejecting limitations on advertising and sponsorship; from public service broadcasters, concerned at the invasion of their territory; from newspaper owners, concerned at advertising loss; and from small countries, concerned about cultural identity. It was redrafted several times. During this period, and mainly backed by Britain, Denmark, and Luxembourg, the CoE initiated its own proposals for a European television regime. Its document *Transfrontier Broadcasting* did not entail a dramatically more liberal approach than those in the Commission's Draft Directive, but contained no clauses concerning a quota of European-made programs.[28] Eventually, in preference to some members signing the CoE convention, the Council of Ministers agreed on an amended EC directive on October 3,

1989. The member states must incorporate it within two years. Portugal and Greece (being recent entrants to the EC, and the poorest countries) have three years for implementation.

EC BROADCASTING REGULATION

Based on its policy of a free flow of programs in its *TWF* Green Paper, the commission took the view that since EC member states had different content rules regarding advertising, broadcasters might find it impossible to produce programs for community-wide broadcast. Thus, the commission proposed (1) more airtime for commercials, (2) a ban on advertising tobacco products, (3) special rules for alcohol advertisements, and (4) rules to ensure that TV programs were legally received in all member states. These proposals aroused disagreement because of different advertising policies in the member countries. Some countries, such as Denmark, did not allow advertising, while others such as the United Kingdom and Luxembourg favored its expansion.

The Directive (Article 13) imposes a 15 percent ceiling on advertising airtime (20 percent in peak time), but restricts commercial breaks to no more than one in every 45 minutes during films shown in the cinema or on television. This proposal, which follows the exact CoE wording, was a compromise between the 20 percent of airtime proposed by the British and 10 percent proposed by the Italians. It leaves states able to impose additional regulation within the maximums.

A similar approach is taken in the case of sponsorship. Article 12 of the directive suggests that responsibility for programs rests with the broadcasters, and that their editorial judgment should remain free from the sponsors' influence. However, whereas the 1986 draft directive contains specific limitations on sponsors' ability to control programs and the linkage of advertising to program content, following pressure from advertisers, in the 1989 directive, the detailed administration of this provision is left to the member states. The provisions are actually weaker than those of the CoE.

Some provisions have been targeted on moral welfare grounds in order to protect young people from broadcasts that are pornographic and violent (Articles 15 and 16). The member states are responsible for enacting effective measures to ensure compliance. Except in Britain, where they were opposed as beyond the commission's competence, in general these provisions elicited little reaction.

The right to reply was discussed in some detail in the *TWF*, but then disappeared in the first version of the directive. This was interpreted as another compromise due to the difficulties arising from different national approaches (for instance, Britain accepts no right of reply). With the reappearance of the issue as a result of the demands of the European Parliament, Article 20 of the final directive states that anyone, regardless of nationality, shall have a right of reply or comparable remedies. This right exists in relation to all broadcasters under the jurisdiction of a member state. According to Article 20 the member state must "adopt the measures needed to establish the right to reply and determine the procedure for the exercise thereof."

Compromise between the issuing of the *TWF* Green Paper and the directive is evident on the issue of copyright. In *TWF*, the commission argued for a statutory license for the retransmission of programs via cable in other EC countries. It argued that existing contractual agreements between copyright holders and cable operators were impractical because of the time they took and the fact that agreement was sometimes never reached. It therefore proposed that the copyright holders exchange their right to forbid broadcasts for the right to adequate remuneration. This provision was modified in the draft directive, where the commission proposed a statutory agreement only if a contractual agreement in the first place proved impossible. However, this proposal was itself attacked, and in the final directive all mention of copyright was omitted.[29]

The proposals on program quotas caused the major controversy. The Directive (Articles 2, 3, and 4) originally proposed that channels transmit a minimum amount of European-made programs, with an initial quota of 30 percent, rising to 60 percent three years later. These programs would not include news, sports, game shows, or advertising. In Article 3, the commission also requested broadcasters to commit 5 percent of their budgets (rising later to 10 percent) to the purchase and showing of works by independent producers from EC countries.

Following sustained objections from some members to a fixed quota of European-made programs, the final Directive now utilizes the wording of the CoE's milder provision on the issue. Broadcasters are to reserve a majority proportion of their transmission time for European works "where it is practicable." In terms of politics, this compromise was seen as a victory for the anti-quota countries (such as the United Kingdom, West Germany, the Netherlands, and Denmark) and a defeat for the pro-quota countries (such as France, Italy, Spain, Greece, and Portugal). It also reflected considerable American pressure, on France in particular.

Moreover, in their October 1989 meeting, the Council of Ministers followed West Germany's continued opposition, and decided that this provision is only politically, not legally, binding. In other words, a diplomatic way was found to obliterate the quota. Noncompliance with a political commitment would not be sufficient for the commission to bring member states to the European Court.

In general, one can see in the EC's broadcasting policy the tensions not only between internal directorates of the commission—between the directorate in charge of internal markets and competition and that concerned with culture and communication—but also the tensions between the legal systems, government ideologies, and cultural concerns of member states. For instance, the Directive's original provisions on Euro-content mirrored much of French media law, but clashed with the less legalistic framework of British regulation of broadcasting. Hence, it was not simply the provisions themselves, although some of the targets were considered unrealistic, but their being written into a law that increased the power at the center that caused so much concern.

In general, as the issue continued to be debated, the powers of member states became increasingly retained in relation to the center. In terms of implementation, on most provisions the directive allows member states the latitude to introduce their own regulations within parameters stated by the directive. Advertising, sponsorship, and the moral welfare of children are examples of this form of implementation. Only in the area of the right to reply do member states have little room for maneuver. While the original directive, using detailed implementation mechanisms, took the view that regulation should come from the center, the final directive takes the position that what is aimed at is the harmonization of minimum standards and the mutual recognition by sovereign states of each other's standards.

The result is that the final Directive is biased toward giving broadcasters who were previously impeded by national regulations the freedom to broadcast across borders. Since responsibility for regulation rests with the up-link country, nations with the most liberal forms of content regulation can overrule those with more restrictive regulation. The solution of such clashes is left to bilateral negotiations. There is no right to block transmissions, whether from EC or non-EC countries. Nor does the final Directive say anything on the question of multimedia ownership, foreign ownership, or concentration, although these issues were raised early on by the European Parliament.

As a result of the outcomes of specific national objections to particular clauses, the final European Directive bows to the concept of European broadcasting as a billiard ball model. Nevertheless, it actually undermines the sovereignty of states. While they keep their national forms of regulation, they are powerless to prevent the reception of broadcasts that might offend against those same regulations. The outcome is that regulation can neither be imposed at the center nor by the states.

TELECOMMUNICATIONS

Although the most publicly evident feature of the commission's tele-communications policy was the 1987 publication of the Green Paper, *On the Development of the Common Market for Telecommunications Services and Equipment*, in fact, the commission's policy on telecommunications goes back to the 1970s.[30] At that time, telecommunications in the member states was firmly under the control of the national monopolies, which pursued policies that were more or less autonomous from member governments. Manufacturers and operators were satisfied with the status quo, and there was no political constituency supporting change. The most politically salient issue was the technology gap between the community and both the United States and Japan in the computer and microelectronics sectors. Hence, the commission's policy on telecommunications was first linked to areas such as data processing (1974) and computer design. The concern with telecommunications came after the revitalization of the French sector and the 1979 Nora-Minc report, which emphasized the development of an information society.[31] From within the commission, the movement into the computing and telecommunications sectors was spearheaded by the Directorate of Industry, DGIII, and in particular by two men, Vicomte D'Avignon and Christopher Layton.

Although the commission first began in 1973 to attempt to generate interest among the European PTTs on the standardization of equipment and the opening of markets, the hostility from the PTTs and the telecom-munications sector's exclusion from GATT provisions caused telecom-munications to be omitted from the 1976 directive on the liberalization of large-scale public procurement contracts.[32] It was only in the mid-1980s that the commission achieved progress on liberalization, after the divest-iture of AT&T and after Margaret Thatcher's electoral victories in Britain.

Consistent attempts during this period were made by the commission, first to enter competition with the PTTs through the establishment of its own computer-based information network, Euronet,[33] and then to link policy on telecommunications networks to the more politically salient market of information-technology products. Consequently, in September 1980, the commission proposed parallel actions in information technology and telecommunications, suggesting the harmonization of networks and services, and the opening up of 10 percent of national telecommunications markets to purchasing from other nations.[34] Again because of opposition from within the member governments, several of which supported "national champion" telecommunications manufacturers, these proposals were not agreed on until October 1984, and in 1990 had still not been fully implemented.

The majority of the commission's effort went into the fields of micro-electronics and computing, where member governments were more pre-pared to recognize the weakness of European industry. However, even here the member states were unwilling to cede authority to the community. The commission began to work with the companies themselves, and it was out of discussions with a grouping of the leading European component companies, set up in 1976, that a commission proposal arose in 1980 for a council regulation in the field of microelectronics technology in order "to achieve . . . the strategic leap forward in technological capability that is now necessary and possible."[35] Once more, it proved difficult to gain agreement from member states.

Eventually, in 1982, out of round-table discussion between the heads of European manufacturing companies and the commission, who had been galvanized by the Fifth-Generation Computer Program of Japan, came the concept of the European Strategic Programme for Research in Information Technology (ESPRIT). This collaborative program for European firms in precompetitive R&D was agreed to in 1983–1984, and scheduled to cost $5.4 billion over five years. Simultaneously, in 1983, the EC Task Force in Information Technology and Telecommunications became the focal point of community policy-making in a sector gradually gaining in eco-nomic importance to member governments.

Reflecting this new concern, a similar program to ESPRIT was estab-lished in the telecommunications sector. Called RACE (Research in Advanced Communications in Europe), and costing $380 million, it was agreed to by the council in 1984, but subsequently ran foul of British and West German concern about the EC budget. A small amount of funding was allocated, but it was not until 1987 that the council agreed to the full expenditure for the program, which had also been broadened to extend beyond manufacturing to include network operators.[36]

The commission's policy has had two major aspects: technological push through such programs as ESPRIT and RACE, and market liberalization. There has also been a small element of public procurement by the com-munity itself. These differing strands of policy have been reflected in the division of responsibility within the commission. In 1986, the Task Force on Information Technology was merged into the Directorate General for Telecommunications, Information Industries and Innovation, DGXIII, which is mainly responsible for technology push, while competition policy has remained with DGIV, the commission's competition directorate.

The technology-push programs have all suffered from political conflict, mainly because smaller states have wanted a redistributive effect from the funding while the larger states have wished to operate independents.[37] However, these programs still have been easier to initiate than those demanding more open markets. France and West Germany agreed in 1984 that they would procure 10 percent of their telecommunications procurement from each other, but nothing happened. An agreement between the two countries on radiotelephones also fell apart, and French approaches to British Telecom on the reciprocal purchases of public exchanges were rebuffed.[38]

Despite this lack of movement in the opening of markets, and the previous lack of political support, in November 1984 the commission managed, by emphasizing the importance of telecommunications to other industries, to gain agreement from the council to its five-pronged policy proposal, designed to:

1. Create a community market for telecommunications equipment and terminals via standardization, mutual recognition of type approvals (where apparatus standards approved by one are approved by all), and the opening of access to public contracts;

2. Improve the development of advanced telecommunications services and networks (ISDN);

3. Launch a development program for the technology required for future broadband networks, and implement infrastructure projects of common interest (RACE);

4. Promote the introduction and development of advanced services in the less favored regions of the Community (STAR); and

5. Coordinate negotiating positions with regard to international bodies dealing with telecommunications.

These five action lines constitute the framework of the European Telecommunications Policy. In 1986 alone, the council agreed on proposals from the commission on six major measures concerning the standardization of telecommunications terminal equipment; the adoption of the Multiplexed Analogue Components (MAC) family of standards for DBS; increased standardization in the field of information technology and telecommunications; the introduction of community-wide ISDN; and the institution of a community program, termed STAR, to improve access to advanced telecommunications services in the less favored regions of the community.

These latter two programs can be seen as paralleling each other, and also as allowing a trade-off between the various interests of member states. In the words of Herbert Ungerer,

> An accelerated programme of investment in digitized, and later broadband technologies, as foreseen by the STAR programme, could turn the potential danger to the development of the periphery posed by the informatics society into a unique opportunity to overcome the handicap of geographic isolation.[39]

The focus of the STAR program is primarily on business users, with special emphasis on small- and medium-sized enterprises. The intention is both to develop the infrastructure itself and also to develop the demand for services among businesses in these areas. Approximately 60 percent, 780 million ECU (European Currency Unit), of the total funding comes from the community budget, with matching funding from the member countries concerned.

In the telecommunications sector, one can see the various trade-offs made between countries with national manufacturers, those with software industries, those with liberal national regimes, those with large numbers of multinational users, and those with a weak infrastructure. Although French and West German industry may well be the primary beneficiaries of the community policy, potential benefit for other countries and industries is visible. In contrast, it is difficult to see any such trade-offs within the broadcasting sector, where the major beneficiaries are the private broadcasters, satellite operators, program makers, and the consumer-electronics and advertising industries. Major electronics companies benefiting from broadcasting policy are located in France, West Germany, and the Netherlands, while program makers are located in the United Kingdom. It may be the lack of trade-offs possible with the smaller or poorer countries, as much as the break with the European tradition of public service broadcasting, that has so politicized this sector.[40]

TELECOMMUNICATIONS POLICY-MAKING

In its policy on broadcasting, the commission entered entirely new fields, but in telecommunications, much of its policy-making has relied on the twin models of American and British liberalization experience. Its

R&D policy has built on the model previously developed in ESPRIT for information technology. In contrast to the broadcasting sector, the telecommunications sector in Europe has not seen the entry of massive numbers of new competitors.

In general, both large users and small consumers have been conspicuous by their absence in the policy-making arena at European level. The major players have been governments and PTTs, and manufacturers. To a large extent policy on infrastructure has utilized the technologies preferred by PTTs, those of terrestrial rather than satellite transmission. It is notable that, while the *TWF* Green Paper on broadcasting waxes lyrical about potential data-service carriage by satellites, no European market opening for such satellite transmission had transpired by 1990. By extending its technology push from manufacturers to operators, by focusing on infrastructure enhancement via ISDN, on R&D into new technologies and broadband, and on standardization of terminal equipment, the EC program became nonthreatening to PTTs. Moreover, while governments might have preferred to retain their national champions, the research consortia promoted by the commission broke down the nationally based boundaries of manufacturers and reinforced the trends of the international market toward inter-firm collaboration to meet the need for product specialization. Hence, by the time national sovereignty over domestic markets became threatened through the regulatory changes put forward by the Green Paper, recalcitrant national governments had to a large extent already been outflanked.

Just as in broadcasting, it might have been possible for members to utilize existing institutions to compete with the commission. The European Conference of Postal and Telecommunications Administrations (CEPT) was founded in 1959, and comprises membership from the PTTs of 26 European countries, including EC and EFTA (European Free Trade Association) states. However, staffed by PTTs, and able to claim some autonomy through technical expertise, CEPT was concerned with service provision and technical matters such as standardization and tariffs, rather than with overall regulatory matters. Moreover, as early as 1984, the commission entered an agreement with both CEPT and CEN-Cenelec (the European Committees for Standardization and Electrotechnical Standardization) and enhanced their influence by giving the standards on which they agreed an immediate impact. To a large extent, by 1987 these bodies had been co-opted into the commission.

Cooperation with the standardization bodies was essential to allow the introduction of European standards for the type approval of equipment and the interworking of infrastructure. Hence, the standards bodies produce standards and specifications for the commission. The intention was to go beyond mutual recognition of standards, which would open trade but would not unify infrastructure, yet to stop short of total harmonization, which might slow progress. The result has been that both CEPT and CEN-Cenelec significantly increased their activities, and it was they who began the process of determining European standards. It was only following the Memorandum of Understanding on the introduction of ISDN in 1987, agreed on by 18 European PTTs, that it became evident that CEPT could not cope with the standards workload. The commission then established its own standardization organization, ETSI (European Telecommunications Standards Institute), which brought together operators, manufacturers, and users, and the European Workshop for Open Systems, in which all the major organizations with an interest in Open Systems Interconnection (OSI) standards are represented.

Until 1987, the commission's major focus of policy was on the provision of infrastructure, its standardization, and the R&D necessary for its future provision. In 1986, the council issued a Recommendation for the coordinated introduction of ISDN. The Recommendation defined two penetration objectives for ISDN, one in terms of numbers of lines and the other in terms of geographical penetration. Thus, by 1993 member states were to have 5 percent of lines (five million) and enough territorial coverage to give 80 percent of the population access to ISDN. The Recommendation not only specified the tariff principles that should be adopted, moving toward tariffs less dependent on distance, but also the services that should be provided. However, as Loretta Anania has pointed out, the implementation and coordination required for this task go beyond any such coordination previously known.[41]

While the introduction of ISDN followed through on the existing plans for digitalization of the PTTs, the commission in 1988 also issued a directive on the movement toward a broadband telecommunications network based on optical fiber and satellites. The network was to form the "electronic highway of 1992." It is the potential for broadband that has motivated the commission's RACE program. The objective of RACE is "community-wide introduction of Integrated Broadband Communications by 1995, taking into account the evolving ISDN and national introduction strategies." About 40 percent of the commission's total R&D expenditure goes to RACE and its sister program in information technology, ESPRIT. Less than 6 percent goes to the overall improvement of science and technology cooperation and the diffusion of research.[42]

Other infrastructural actions included a 1987 Directive on pan-European mobile communications to replace the fragmented standards then in operation with second-generation digital mobile communications. This service would be needed to replace the saturation of frequency bands anticipated to occur by 1991. The intention of a unitary digital standard had to be supplemented by the reservation of radio spectrum for the service. Since the commission does not have control over the allocation of the spectrum, which rests with member states, members were instructed to reserve the 890–915 and 935–960 megahertz (MHz) frequency bands for that purpose.

It was not until 1987 that the commission made another attempt to deal with market-opening issues. The commission's Green Paper on telecommunications was issued in 1987, its purpose being to raise debate on the future regulation of telecommunications. The Green Paper proposed the liberalization of both terminal equipment and services. In setting out its proposals for a regulatory division between regulated and competitive services, the Green Paper explicitly referred to the experience in the United States. Attempting to avert the problems of boundary definition between basic and enhanced services, the commission drew the line between the "reserved" service of voice telephony and all other services, which would be regarded as competitive. However, PTTs were to be allowed to compete with other suppliers. Moreover, since such competitive services needed access on equal terms to the infrastructure, the commission proposed a solution, termed Open Network Provision (ONP).

Similarly, the commission's concern with such access also led it to argue for the separation of PTT regulatory and operational functions within each member state. However, the commission took no position on either the liberalization of facilities provision, or the privatization of PTTs, stating that those were matters that would depend on the geographical size of the country, its political and social perceptions, and the potential competitors. It anticipated that reserved services would continue to be provided by PTT monopolies. Nevertheless, it argued for the ending of cross-subsidies between reserved and competitive services and a clear cost orientation in tariff policy. Hence, the heavy cross-subsidies between international, long-distance and local calls would have to be phased out. Since no discussion took place within the Green Paper on different methods of costing, and only a cursory mention was made of the distributionary effects of such a policy, the emphasis can only be described as paradoxically both conservative and liberal.

Neither is there any recognition within the Green Paper of the regulatory functions that the commission was accruing to itself while at the same time continuing to make policy. The very strictures it applied elsewhere were also applicable to itself.

The implementation of the commission's policies have not proceeded without difficulty, even on the seemingly easy tasks. The commission's use of Article 90 of the Single European Act, which allows it to short-circuit the lengthy policy process and act against state monopolies in order to hasten the opening of equipment markets, provoked the French into an application to the European Court. It was not that the French objected to the opening of the terminal market—theirs was open already. Rather, they objected to the commission's extension of power. In a 1990 opinion, the advocat general advised the court in favor of the French. If this advice is followed by the court, then the commission will be required to follow a lengthy policy-making process.

In 1989 a compromise agreement was reached on what constituted a competitive service. The transmission of data in packets (packet switching) was exempted until 1993. The French objected to the division between voice and "other services," in which the latter category, the transmission of data, was included. Having built up their packet data network to be the most modern and efficient in Europe, the DGT had no wish to hand the benefit over to others. Moreover, the commission also agreed to allow national governments to regulate Open Network Provisions rather than imposing regulation from the center.[43]

In this compromise, as in others, one can see national governments defending their corners. Nor have governments been prepared to cede autonomy to the EC in the international negotiations regarding telecommunications. Consequently, in the ITU's 1988 meeting (termed WATTC 88), which was called to update international regulation of telecommunications, and where the commission was represented at an ITU meeting for the first time, not only did the EC fail to speak for the member states, but member states fought publicly among themselves. At times, the commission's competition directorate, DGIV, had to publicly remind member states of the relevance of the Treaty of Rome to their proposals. Ironically, the entry of the question of liberalizing telecommunications services in GATT, where the EC is already the accepted trade spokesperson of member states, gives the commission the autonomy it lacked in the ITU and legitimacy in fostering liberalization based on the Treaty of Rome and its harmonization with GATT principles.

CONCLUSION

It is possible to argue that the community's actions are the result of increasing trade, communications, and personal flows between community members as part of an international trend leading to closer political relationships. Underlying EC actions are those of multinational companies within the community. These companies are both economic and political actors, and their interests lie in the unimpeded flow of information. These interests are not linked to the boundaries of the community, but rather embrace EFTA and Eastern Europe as well. They are coupled with the desire for private entry to the provision of information services and the liberalization of networks. For these companies, the community's actions are salient and they retain active European-wide associations at the community level and in member states. At times they may be supporters of the community against the nation-states, while at other times, the community may defend the nation-states against them, as when multinationals attempt to play off one country against another for investment incentives. Accordingly, one can argue that it is the actions of these actors, and not of the commission, that create the reality of the community. Moreover, inasmuch as these alliances are with companies in the United States and Japan, one might argue that community attempts to revitalize European industry are irrelevant.

As long as this form of market integration proceeds, neither the economic nor the political assumptions of the current sectoral approach to European integration will prove wholly correct. The expectations aroused by this model have not been matched by the reality. Looking at the case of telecommunications, it is clear that the commission in particular expects some transfer of sovereignty from member states, and an accrual of power to itself necessitated by the integrated nature of new networks. Similarly, there has been some spillover from one sector to another. The commission justified its intervention in broadcast services based on its involvement in satellite standards and equipment. It linked broadcasting to the field of telecommunications through its definition of tele-services, and telecommunications to information technology. As a result, some aspects of the neo-functional model fit the case of the EC.

However, member states have resisted conceding their sovereignty to community institutions. Hence, while the commission may have been looking at a European-wide interest, its member states have seen the community as a means of expression of national interests. In the case of broadcasting and telecommunications, member states have been able to impede the development of community-wide programs and proposals. For instance, some member states tried to escape the legally binding nature of community Directives in broadcasting when, during the 1970s, they ignored attempts by the commission to introduce a telecommunications policy that worked against the interest of national monopolies. The RACE program was delayed by the West Germans, possibly because it would support manufacturers in competition with Siemens; and STAR was the outcome of bargaining regarding the entrance of Spain and Portugal in 1985. Moreover, even within the international arena, at WATTC 88, the community was unable to unite.

According to the consociational model, the community is simply the product of trade-offs between national interests. Its positions are then those on which some consensus can be reached: where the ensuing package can be sold to each nation by its leaders. The model also fits within the representation of interests in community policy-making. Dominated by European business and state elites, it excludes from its political agenda concern for the individual person or the social impact of technology. While the Social Charter represents the general interests of workers, only the European Parliament has raised such issues as the right of reply and cross-media ownership.

However, the consociationist model does not fully describe the reality. EC actions also favor the EC itself. By conceptualizing broadcasting as a tele-service, it has extended its influence into new areas. And it has enhanced its autonomy from its member states by its linkage to large corporations and to subnational peripheral regions. The contradiction is that in order to establish its autonomy from member states, the EC has utilized alliances with private economic actors to undermine political sovereignty. However, because national governments are unwilling to cede authority in a formal manner and conflict over the prospect of a federal Europe, the EC as a regional actor lacks both the mechanisms to regulate infrastructural investment and the control of a wider democratic accountability. Nonetheless, as will be detailed in the final chapter, if television and broadcasting are to converge, the mechanisms of their distribution need coherent regulation in the interests of universality of access and accountability.

NOTES

1. A. J. R. Groom and Paul Taylor, eds., *Frameworks for International Co-Operation* (London: Pinter, 1990), 139–49.

2. J. Pelkmans, "Economic Theories of Integration Revisited," *Journal of Common Market Studies* 18 (June 1980): 335–54; Carole Webb, "Theoretical Perspectives and Problems," in *Policymaking in the European Community*, edited by H. Wallace et al. (London: J. Wiley, 1983), 1–42.

3. Paul Taylor, "Consociationalism and Federalism," in Groom and Taylor, *Frameworks*, 172–84.

4. Ibid., 176.

5. Ibid.

6. David Buchan and Robert Taylor, "Talks with EC Will Mean All Change at Efta," *Financial Times*, 11 June 1990.

7. Karl Deutch, *The Analysis of International Relations*, 3rd ed. (Englewood Cliffs, N.J.: Prentice-Hall, 1988), 256.

8. Article 8A of the Single European Act, as agreed December 1985 and effective 1 July 1987.

9. See Paolo Cecchini, *The European Challenge, 1992. The Benefits of the Single Market* (Aldershot, U.K.: Wildwood House, 1988).

10. J. A. Kay, "Myths and Realities," in *Myths and Realities*, edited by Centre for Business Strategy (London: London Business School, 1989), 2.

11. See H. Ungerer with N. Costello, *Telecommunications in Europe* (Luxembourg: CEC, 1988).

12. Eurostrategies, *The European Telecommunications Industry*, Report to the Commission of the European Communities, June 1989 (Brussels: CEC, 1989).

13. European Parliament, de Vries Report, *Report on the Economic Aspects of the Common Market for Broadcasting*, Com. (84) 300 Final, Document A 2 102/85, Brussels, 30 September 1985.

14. P. Taylor, *The Limits of European Integration* (Worcester: Croom Helm, 1983).

15. F. Vibert, *Europe's Constitutional Deficit* (London: Institute of Economic Affairs, Inquiry 27, November 1989).

16. S. Papathanassopoulos, "Broadcasting and the European Community," in *International Political Economy of the Communications Policies*, edited by K. Dyson and P. Humphreys (London: Routledge, in press); S. Papathanassopoulos, "Beyond the Directive," *Cable and Satellite Europe*, February 1990, 38.

17. Following the Single European Act (1987), directives can be approved by majority voting in the Council of Ministers, which is weighted by size of country.

18. Karlheinz Neunreither, "Application of the Single European Act: Emergence of a New Institutional Triangle" (Paper presented to the 14th World Congress of the International Political Science Association, Washington, D.C., 1988).

19. The EBU was established in 1950. It has 40 members, principally West European public broadcasters in 33 states. Its concerns are program exchange, coproduction, legal issues (for example, copyright), and transmission standards.

20. The European Court decided that satellite channels transmitting to Dutch cable networks could carry advertising.

21. France's dispute concerns the commission's right to take action under Article 90 of the Single European Act in relation to the liberalization of the terminal equipment market.

22. The Eurikon experiment, a collaborative venture between four public service broadcasters, began transmission as Europa TV in 1985, but had lost approximately $30 million by 1986. European Parliament, *Realities and Tendencies in European Television: Perspectives and Options*, Com (83) 229 Final, 25 June 1983.

23. Commission of the European Communities, *Television without Frontiers, Green Paper on the Establishment of a Common Market for Broadcasting, Especially by Satellite and Cable*, Communication from the Commission to the Council, COM (84) 30, Final, Brussels, 14 June 1984.

24. Commission of the European Communities, *Television Without Frontiers*, Summary, COM (84) Final/2, 14 June 1984, para. 8.

25. Com (86) 146, Final, Brussels, 29 April 1986. Amended Final Version, Com (88) 154 Final; *Official Journal of the European Communities*, 24 November 1989.

26. Com (86) 146 Final/2, Revised Version, 6 June 1986, para. 6.

27. Media 92 has ten main projects. Distribution projects include a cooperative for distributing low-budget films, a fund for multilingual productions, and a fund to help independent producers.

28. Council of Europe, Steering Committee on the Mass Media, *Draft European Convention on Transfrontier Television*, Strasbourg, 30 June 1988.

29. See Vincent Porter, "The EC: Broadcasting, Competition Policies and National Sovereignty," *Intermedia* 18, no. 3 (June–July 1990): 22–26.

30. Commission of the European Communities, *Towards a Dynamic European Economy: On the Development of the Common Market for Telecommunications Services and Equipment*, Green Paper, Com (87) 290, Brussels, 10 June 1987.

31. S. Nora and A. Minc, *L'informatisation de la société* (Paris: La Documentation Française, 1979).

32. Directive 77/62/EEC, OJ L 13, 15 January 1977.

33. G. Dang Nguyen, "The European Telecommunications Policy or, the Awakening of a Sleeping Beauty" (Paper presented to the European Consortium of Political Research, Amsterdam, April 1987).

34. Com (80) 422 Final.

35. Com (80) 421 Final, 5.

36. Jill Hills, "Europe, Telecommunications and Information Policies

of Competition, Crisis and Confusion" in *Information Technology and Office Systems*, edited by A. E. Cawkell (Netherlands: Elsevier-N. Holland, 1986), 497–517.

37. Dang Nguyen, "Sleeping Beauty," 1987.

38. Hills, "Europe, Telecommunications," 506.

39. Ungerer and Costello, *Telecommunications in Europe*, 158.

40. D. McQuail and K. Siune, *New Media Politics* (London: Sage, 1986), 205.

41. Loretta Anania, "The Protean Complex: Are Open Networks Common Markets?" (Paper presented to the Eighth Annual International Telecommunication Society, Venice, April 1990); Council Recommendation 86/659/EEC, 22 December 1986.

42. Ungerer and Costello, *Telecommunications in Europe*, 174.

43. Hugo Dixon, "Untangling Europe's Telecommunications Networks," *Financial Times*, 11 December 1989.

7

The Politics of Standards:
Integrated Services Digital Networks

The politicization of standards is not something recent. Rather, national standards for all kinds of products from agricultural produce to manufactured goods have been used for many years by national industries attempting to protect their domestic markets. However, inasmuch as other forms of protection against changes in the international economic structure have become less effective as a means of dealing with import penetration, national standards have become a primary nontariff barrier to trade. Standards may be used to integrate a domestic industry; for instance, in the 1970s, by determining a specific software language for its public-sector computing purchases, the French government "dragged" its country's software houses from an infant industry into the strongest software sector in Europe.

Alternatively, the adoption of another country's standard for a piece of equipment can increase imports. Consequently, for instance, in the mid-1980s, the British government adopted American standards for cellular mobile radio, thereby opening the domestic market to American firms. Uniform international standards increase the size of a market, while national standards fragment it.

The benefits of standardization are many. From the manufacturers' point of view, they allow economies of scale in production. Providing these are performance rather than design standards, they also allow some product differentiation, although competition tends to be shifted to quality and price, and away from specific features. Standards also save on learning costs for users, and reduce the risks in buying from small companies.

There is also a trade-off between standardization and innovation. The premature adoption of a standard can "freeze" the technology, yet too late adoption may mean that a large installed base of noncompatible equipment will exist, which users will not wish to replace. Existing investment may then slow the adoption of compatible technology.

Because of standardization's impact on trade, because it often involves regulatory issues broaching on national sovereignty, and because of its importance to national industries, governments have become increasingly involved in this process. In general, this involvement takes the form of backing national delegations in international forums. Some governments also lead domestic cooperative talks between those involved: manufacturers, operators and customers. Thus, for instance, the British Department of Industry has fostered cooperation in the implementation of OSI standards.

However, standards are not always determined by governments. Despite European efforts to promote Philips's alternative, the Japanese gained a de facto world standard in video recorders, achieved by licensing the VCR and Betamax technology. Until the 1980s, the computer industry was dominated by the de facto world standard of IBM, achieved through market dominance. When computers were stand-alone models, the lack of standards and their incompatibility, even between different models of the same manufacturer was irritating and financially expensive for those wishing to change their suppliers or upgrade their system. However, as users moved from stand-alones to distributed processing and wanted increasingly specialized equipment, it became more difficult for one manufacturer to produce a complete range. Instead, firms had to buy in from other manufacturers, and the need for interworking and compatibility between computers became increasingly evident.

Until the late 1970s, IBM was precluded from entering the transmission market in the United States through its antitrust agreement with the U.S. Department of Justice. It was also late to move into smaller computers, an area where a number of fast-growing companies had already entered the market. Once IBM was released from the regulation of its activities, it became evident the company could use transmission markets and its own proprietary standards to limit interconnection of personal computers and thereby extend its domination of the mainframe market into others. While IBM adopted its own Systems Network Architecture (SNA) as a standard, other computer manufacturers backed by governments created the Open Systems Interconnection Standard, which was intended to allow the products of a number of manufacturers to interconnect. The intention was simply to deny IBM the advantage of its existing customer base.

However, the length of time that it takes to specify international standards can act to the detriment of an industry that is growing fast. Because SNA (Systems Network Architecture) was already specified by the 1980s, and OSI standards have taken many years to specify, the two have existed side by side. Despite the competition, OSI standards have continued to exist, buoyed by the demand created by the commitment of European governments.

When there is no clear market leader, and when government is not involved, the process of reaching a consensus on a standard may be more difficult. Thus, for instance, in the United States in the latter 1980s, disparate attempts by the Bell Operating Companies to define Open Network Architecture led to calls for more effective leadership on the part of the FCC. Moreover, in the European Community, while leaving the definition of Open Network Provision to national governments, the commission has reserved the right to intervene if necessary.

It is sometimes thought that standardization in the communications and information industries refers mainly to hardware and is primarily technical, dealing with such matters as interfaces. But standardization across markets is often as much a matter of agreement on definitions of services or on methods of costing and pricing as it is an agreement on hardware. For instance, the development of digital cellular radio in Europe demands not only compatible equipment but also agreement between countries to reserve a certain portion of the radio spectrum for the service. Standardization is an activity that involves technology, economics, politics, and law.

Increasingly, as the necessary standardization has moved to the multilateral arena and the numbers of interests involved have increased, so it has become more difficult to reach consensus. Sometimes no agreement is reached. Thus, for instance, the videotex market has seen efforts by the Canadian, Japanese, and British governments to promote their national standard as a world standard. Chapter 8 discusses exactly how that situation has also arisen with High Definition Television standards. Global standards are not necessary if sufficient economies of scale can be reached through a regional standard.[1]

Sometimes large users have been heavily involved in pushing for standardization. However, while users may want agreed-upon standards, manufacturers, who may be adversely affected by the new technology, can delay their implementation. For instance, proprietary standards for intrafirm equipment such as private exchanges may delay the widespread adoption of the Integrated Services Digital Network (ISDN). Moreover, the decision of the FCC to enforce an interface between the ISDN and customers equipment different from that in the rest of the world is said to have resulted from pressure by modem manufacturers, whose market would have otherwise disappeared.[2]

Proprietary standards are anathema to the telecommunications industry. The European sector in particular has traditionally seen telecommunications as tied to national security, and therefore its standards have been a matter of national decision. Domestic markets have been viewed as the province of domestic companies and publicly owned PTTs. Where companies managed to break into domestic markets, it was through local production that they met those particular requirements of PTTs.

However, this emphasis on PTT-led standardization of equipment has had disadvantages. At first, the system was designed to save PTTs the costs of installation and maintenance on a variety of equipment, and to ensure a good supply. PTTs, therefore, developed close relationships with their national suppliers. In the case of the United States, this vertical interdependence between manufacturers and network operators resulted in AT&T's undertaking R&D at Bell Labs while conducting manufacture through Western Electric. While AT&T was the standard setter in the United States, providing necessary information to its suppliers, the vertical integration was also said to have allowed AT&T to escape regulation.[3]

In Western Europe and Japan, standardization involved the PTT in retaining a corporate relationship with its suppliers. The result was often the overspecification of standards, high prices, and a gold-plating of technology which, while suitable for a non–profit-making organization, was unsuitable for commercial exploitation elsewhere. In addition, possible economies of scale in such markets as telecommunications switches were not realized.

Where competition has been introduced into the network, this relationship between operators and manufacturers has been disturbed. Manufacturers compete with each other to provide equipment to the operator. Such competition on price may be effective where products are mature, but where research and development is involved and the penetration of network services depends on the equipment available to customers, new forms of cooperation between supplier and customer have had to be established. Such has been the case with ISDN.

Equally as important as the standardization of equipment is the standardization of network interlinkages. In the telecommunications sector, standards involve users, manufacturers, network operators (mainly PTTs but also Recognized Private Operating Agencies, such as AT&T), and standards institutions. The demand by large users for networks with end-to-end service has been a driving force in the international standardization process, which now consumes the industry. Their demands are not simply for international interconnectivity and compatibility of technology, but also for standardization of regulation and tariffs. In particular, multinationals wish to be able to establish their own networks wherever they need them and to run them without having to deal with numerous different national regulations or different tariffing systems.

Whereas previously the major standardization effort was at the national level and international standardization only concerned the linkage of one national system to another, today the globalization of companies and markets has brought about an increasing emphasis of international standardization which impacts on the domestic markets of governments. Power has passed from the national institutions to international institutions such as the International Telecommunications Union. This accrual of authority on the part of the international standards–making bodies has been primarily the result of the introduction of the concept of global ISDN.

WHAT IS ISDN?

The original concept of ISDN was of a worldwide network along which data, video, and voice could be transmitted, and that could be accessed by users through one identical plug. In 1984 the Consultative Committee on International Telegraph and Telephone (CCITT) defined ISDN as

> a network in general evolving from a telephony integrated digital network (IDN) that provides end-to-end digital connectivity to support a wide range of services, including voice and non-voice services, to which users have access by a limited set of standard multipurpose customer interfaces.[4]

The advantage of ISDN over separate networks is that it allows voice, data, and images to be transmitted simultaneously, and that the same equipment can access a variety of services. The service will provide

> transmission of voice, interactive and bulk data, facsimile, compressed and full-motion video, efficient and clean channels for continuous and bursty traffic, high message delivery rates, allocation of bandwidths tailored to specific voice/data/video needs, low bit error rates, varying security levels[,] . . . improved performance, enhanced services, more efficient use of equipment, [and] standardized and portable terminals.[5]

Technologically, ISDN comes out of the digitalization of switching.

However, this technological potential has been allied with specific economic problems for PTTs emanating from the increased demand for specialized services.

Data transmission over telephone lines began in the 1970s, but at that time the traditional method of using modems to send text, data, and graphics over the telephone network was "bumping up against inherent limits of speed and quality."[6] As demand moved from voice transmission to data transmission of different speeds and formats, PTTs found themselves providing separate networks for each service. In Japan, a data packet-switched network began in 1980, a facsimile network in 1981, and a videotex service in 1984.

These separate networks not only increased costs but also increased the potential risks of providing these services. Consequently, for instance, in the 1970s, PTTs undertook the costly provision of videotex services, which were expected to gain a mass market, only to find that the market did not materialize. PTTs were anxious to develop such mass markets because of the slowdown in the growth of network usage and the virtually complete penetration of households in industrialized countries. At the same time, as the network was maturing, private companies increasingly demanded the flexibility of leased lines that were tariffed on a flat-rate, or set up their own private networks, thereby reducing the income of the PTTs. However, in order to meet the demand for network modernization, PTTs had to increase their income and reduce costs.

Originally put forward in the early 1970s, the concept of ISDN married with the concern at that point with the future "information society" and countries' desires not to be left behind in its development. One of its initial proponents in Japan, Yasusada Kitahara, saw it as a means toward the democratization of an information society, with interactive services available to all individuals. Field experiments with the technology in Japan reflected these initial concerns.[7]

The concept also satisfied several other interests. It provided the raison d'être for increased investment in telecommunications at a time when the saturation point for telephones had been reached in most industrial countries. Standard interfaces and digital switching provided the possibility of growth in customer equipment markets. And ISDN could also be used to cut out the private networks of large users, thereby increasing PTT revenues. Hence, in the decision to adopt its implementation as an international goal, it became a technology designed primarily to cut PTT costs, to improve the quality of transmission, and to reintegrate the network. As such, it became an engineering-led development and was largely independent of the market.

The genesis of ISDN has also impacted on its technical development. It evolved out of work done during the 1970s on a system of data transmission known as Common Channelling Signal No. 7, in which the signal controlling the transmission is separated from that carrying the speech. In order to achieve global standardization, the practical limit available over pairs of copper wires of a bit rate of 144 kilobits per second (kbs) was then divided between two channels that would carry voice and data and one channel that would control the signals. The basic rate service was defined as two B (Bearer) channels of 64k each, over which voice and high-speed data will be carried, and one D (Delta) channel of 16 kps, for network-management signaling information, which could also be used for low-speed data such as facsimile and videotex. For heavy business use, a "primary" rate access would be available of 23 B channels capable of transmitting data at 64 kilobits per second and one D channel (23B+D) of 64 kps in the United States and 30B+2D in Europe, giving a bit rate of either 1.5 Megabits or 2 Megabits. Within this primary ISDN, access operators could offer high-speed H channels (the equivalent of six or more B channels) or a mixture of B and H channels.

The genesis of narrow-band ISDN has led to criticisms of its hierarchical architecture. With the reductions in costs of optic fiber and the requirements on the part of large users for larger bandwidths, narrow-band ISDN has evolved into broadband ISDN (B-ISDN). It has been argued, however, that the hierarchical engineering architecture evident in narrow-band ISDN is unsuitable to broadband; that telecommunications networks are, in fact, data processing networks; and that the nonhierarchical concepts of computing architecture should influence their development.[8] Similar criticisms of narrowband ISDN were made by satellite operators (see below). These criticisms arise from the predominant role in standardization played by the national network operators, and from the exclusion of such bodies as Intelsat, user groups, and, to a lesser extent, manufacturers.

As ISDN has evolved, the major emphases have become clearer: the more effective use of a greater number of media, the faster transmission and processing of a greater volume of data, and greater intelligence located in the network, allowing users more control of their transmissions.[9] The use of the network will be less predictable than in the past, with customers utilizing variable bandwidths, with logical rather than physical connections, on demand. Hence, ISDN itself has become a moving target, with narrowband ISDN likely to be overtaken by broadband before it has even been installed.

STANDARDIZATION BODIES

The main actors involved in developing the necessary worldwide standards have been the Consultative Committee on International Telegraph and Telephone (CCITT) of the International Telecommunications Union (ITU) and the International Standards Organization (ISO), which was responsible for the development of Open Systems Interconnection (OSI) standards. ISO was established after World War II to promote global standards. Unlike the ITU, it is the forum for computer companies, not government organizations.

Early in its discussions, the CCITT decided to adopt OSI standards for ISDN equipment, making the work of the two organizations complementary as well as bringing about problems of overlap. Together with their regional and national counterparts, these two bodies have been responsible for negotiating global standards for the introduction of ISDN. The ITU and CCITT are dominated by state-owned PTTs. Hence, ISDN is predominantly a PTT-led policy, but one in which the CCITT has considerably more power over domestic standards and systems than had previously been the case.

The increased work load on the CCITT demanded by ISDN standardization has also impacted on the work of the ITU, leading to a backlash from developing countries which have seen that organization's main concerns divorced from their desire simply to achieve full penetration of the basic telephone.[10] ISDN standardization has primarily been carried out by the industrialized countries, but these countries have also displayed dissatisfaction with the slow process of standard setting within CCITT. Although in 1988 the CCITT Plenary Assembly took steps to lessen the length of time for standard setting from four years to six months, during the course of the development of ISDN it has become evident that regional standards bodies have increased in importance.[11]

Three regional standards bodies, the T1 Committee in the United States, the European Telecommunications Standards Institute (ETSI) in Europe, and the Telecommunications Technology Committee in Japan, have begun to cooperate. Beginning first with observer status at each others' meetings, the intention is to feed the workings of the committees into the CCITT, but since the three regional groupings provide the input into the CCITT, their future cooperation may bypass that organization, thereby disadvantaging the newly industrializing countries, such as South Korea and Singapore.

To some extent, the ITU's fears of this development have been allayed by an interregional summit held in 1990, at which the ITU's committees and the regional standards organizations were represented. These bodies agreed to cooperate with national standards bodies to help the standardization committees of the ITU identify key priority areas. What seems to be developing is an alternative method of establishing an agenda at the ITU. Whereas previously, PTTs specified four years in advance the issues they wanted considered, this new method of working takes as its basis the existing work plans of national and regional bodies. From these, "a subset of key activities will be identified by the parties, defining the plan objectives, scope and timescale." Then, "these plans will be compared with the work program of the ITU's standardization committees and used to strengthen their priorities reflecting the market priorities of the participating groups."[12] Given American hostility to the ITU, there must be a suspicion that the intention is, if not to bypass that body, then to alter its agenda in accord with American interests.

The CCITT has not attempted to impose detailed component ISDN services onto member countries. Nevertheless, American industry and the U.S. government have regarded ISDN with suspicion, as a means whereby European PTTs could reestablish control of the network and prevent the spread of private networks. Additionally, American interests have been loathe to concede sovereignty over domestic standards to an international organization dominated by other countries.

This increase in international dependence has given rise to considerable anxiety in the United States. The problem is that the original purpose of ISDN is not easily compatible with liberalization and the provision of competitive facilities on the basis of local versus long distance, or with the traditional American concepts of basic and enhanced service as carried over from the older technology. ISDN services are divided into "bearer services," which include both packet-switched data and circuit-switched data, and "tele-services," which include terminal-to-terminal services such as facsimile, videotex, and teletex, as well as specific services such as user-to-user signaling and private metering. The ISDN division is dependent on the amount of standardization needed in terms of the various layers of the seven-layered OSI model, whereas the regulatory models are designed to allow competition while protecting voice transmission. Crucially, ISDN is an end-to-end transmission system, and allows that transmission between data, voice, and images. All services become enhanced, and the division between them becomes even more arbitrary than in the past.

The FCC's first report on ISDN was mainly concerned with raising such points related to competition. It demanded, for instance, that the ISDN numbering plan should allow users to choose a vendor and, on the grounds that "enhanced" services should be open to competition, that the CCITT should take into account the American distinction between basic and enhanced services.[13] Even if that distinction between basic and enhanced is perpetuated, it will be in the interests of the PTTs to define basic ISDN in relation to bearer services. Recognizing this logic, the FCC redefined the RBOC's data services as "basic," partly because of ISDN.

The problems of ISDN in a liberalized environment were further indicated by the FCC's Computer II decision, which defined the termination point of the network within customer premises as part of the customer's equipment, and therefore to be provided by the equipment manufacturer not network operator. This decision went against both the expert advice it received and the CCITT decision on the consumer premises equipment (CPE) interface, which included the network termination point within the network.[14] Clearly, the more intelligence in the network, the less opportunity for product differentiation and innovation among suppliers of customer premises equipment. The FCC has defended its decision in terms of potential innovation. For a time, this difference in termination points between the United States and the rest of the world caused friction. However, the two sides have gone their own ways, with the Americans finding it extremely difficult to gain consensus on the standardization of this interface. In effect, numbers of manufacturers are responsible for deciding on standards for equipment that will drive the network provided by local exchange companies.

Furthermore, as the major producer of satellites, America was concerned that ISDN and its broadband successor were biased toward land-based rather than satellite-based systems. Intelsat shared this concern. In 1987, Joseph Pelton, then director of Intelsat Policy, argued

> that the majority of people involved in defining how ISDN will be implemented tend to . . . perceive fiber optic cables as more controllable and "ownable" since cables are basically only a point to point medium. Major planners also view ISDN as a means of tying the end-user more closely to their products and services. They view ISDN as evolving from telephony IDN, and thus see the network in terrestrial terms. Also ISDN planners are tending to build from the city and region up to national networks, and international networks are seen as just a further and least important extension of the network.[15]

Intelsat also argued that the conception of ISDN as a terrestrial, hierarchical system ignored the Third World, which could not afford the relevant terrestrial investment.

To some extent these fears have been allayed by developments in Europe, where satellite transmission may be opened to competition, thereby giving an incentive to PTTs to utilize the medium. In 1990 in West Germany, the PTT is beginning to utilize its own satellite, *Kopernicus*, for ISDN transmissions to major cities.[16]

There was also some difference between the United States and Europe on the question of channel capacity. U.S. companies were anxious to see the introduction of an intermediate version of ISDN with a 56kps B channel rather than 64kps, with which the AT&T standard transmission format could not cope.[17] However, the CCITT has continued to retain 64kbs as the building block for ISDN.

Finally, in the early 1980s, large American companies were particularly concerned about the potential loss of leased lines within ISDN. In its historical context, the issue arose at the same time that the West Germans were moving to a bit-rate tariff on their leased lines on the justification of preparing for ISDN. Logically, there is no place within ISDN for leased lines, only for virtual tie-lines. However, as PTTs have moved toward increasing intelligence within the network and with it, flexibility of usage, this fear seems to have subsided. In general, the use of leased lines and private networks requires the use of a highly skilled, specialist staff by the user, whereas virtual private networks place the burden on the network operator. Since specialist staffpersons are in short supply and expensive, the balance of advantage has gradually shifted to the network operator. Virtual private networks are said to be growing in the United States by 60 percent per annum.[18] Nevertheless, there are a number of outstanding issues and concerns about the practicality of ISDN.

ISSUES

Cutting Costs to PTTs?

During its evolution, it became evident that the original idea of service to residential households was not likely to be economical. At the same time, with the change in the economic climate of the 1980s, large users of communications began to pressure PTTs on the cost of services. As these companies exerted their influence on PTTs, so the liberalization of the networks in America, Britain, and Japan changed the regard that all PTTs held for their largest customers. ISDN began to be marketed as a replacement for private networks and as an innovation that would reduce costs and increase the large users' control over their communications. In turn, this marketing has tended to rebound on the PTTs, which actually need more than the transfer of existing data transmission to ISDN, and which, because they are aware of this fact, have been unwilling to supply packet-switched services within ISDN. PTTs need increased revenue from new services.

According to one consultancy firm, network operators will find their costs not reduced but rather increased by the implementation of ISDN, primarily because customers will require a mix of ISDN and non-ISDN technology.[19] In order to gain increased usage, PTTs will need to find new applications.

New Applications for PTTs

Both small and large users were absent from the debate on the establishment of ISDN. Only when PTTs found that they needed new applications in order to sell the technology were users wooed. In the United States in the first field trials, users were given the technology either free or at low cost. The French PTT was one of the first to enter into cooperative contracts with customers for the development of new applications. The West Germans followed in 1990, and the British government has sponsored projects to establish the potential use of ISDN among smaller businesses.

In one sense, these cooperation contracts are a reversion to the traditional mold of micro-corporatism of telecommunications network operators and suppliers, but today it is a corporatism between the PTT as network operator, its manufacturing suppliers, and a variety of customers.

One argument is that PTTs should concentrate on enabling companies first to use the technology internally, then consider its usage among the extended community of companies plus suppliers, and only later concern itself with wider penetration. Bill Bauer has argued that the "most likely scenario is one in which ISDN will provide sophisticated facilities to the small- and medium-size sites of large companies, for which dedicated data networks cannot be economically justified."[20] He has suggested that companies should start from the simplest kind of information flow—conversation between two sites—and then see how "telephony-plus"—the addition of ISDN's ability to transfer data, image, and voice simultaneously—could be utilized to enhance that communication. Finally, once individual functions had been satisfied, cross-organizational functions could be met.

Others have argued that diffusion depends on aggressive marketing by the PTT, and will ultimately depend on the rate at which ISDN is installed. Without a national network, usage will not spread. France and West Germany are taking this national network route with the fast installation of ISDN service nationwide. In other countries, such as Britain, the network operators have been unenthusiastic and have done little marketing.

The question of applications is linked with that of regulation. Both in the United States, where Open Network Architecture has been instigated by the FCC, and in the European Community, the intention has been to open access to the network to service suppliers. In 1990, it is still unclear exactly how ISDN and regulatory provisions will work.[21]

Compatible Equipment

Prior to the release of the CCITT Q series of standards for ISDN equipment in 1988, there was a lack of standardization of both networks and equipment in Europe. In this situation, unless national standards are imposed, it is possible for equipment manufacturers to retain their market share through proprietary standards that are incompatible with the new technology. The April 1989 Memorandum of Understanding between 18 PTTs in Europe, which was designed to introduce common interfaces and services, has been followed by a speeding up of the regional standards process. Whereas manufacturers and users were previously barred from standard setting in CEPT, they do take part in ETSI, which intends to have all the relevant standards complete by the end of 1990.

In contrast, despite the efforts at coordination from Bellcore (the research labs of the RBOCs), ISDN equipment in the United States is unlikely to be compatible between the different ISDN services of RBOCs, and may also be internationally incompatible. In particular, while primary-rate access equipment is being developed for 1.5 Mbps, it may not be able to cope with the European 2Mbps. Network operators (RBOCs) are having to work with manufacturers to determine standards for equipment, but these are not compatible between the regions. Hence, customers need to go for their equipment to the particular companies that work with their network suppliers.

Tariffs

It is not at all clear that customers will take up the new services unless ISDN offers a rebate on current leased-line tariffs. In particular, large users with private networks may have invested too much to wish to migrate to the public network. However, PTTs argue that ISDN represents an increase in quality and flexibility for customers. The argument goes that, despite having higher tariffs than leased lines, ISDN will allow large users to save money in configuring their networks.

To a large extent, tariffs still follow the old voice-tariffing structure, with PTTs setting a tariff on value to the user—basically, what the market will stand—and pricing leased lines, telephone, and data services so as to drive users on to ISDN. While the CCITT has recommended that tariffs should be in line with costs, the existing difficulties of distributing costs are magnified by ISDN. In general, ISDN tariffs have been priced at about two or three times the cost of telephone tariffs.[22]

One possibility originally favored by West Germany was for a tariff by bits of information passed. This tariff has the disadvantage that although the customer will pay only for the number of bits passed along the network, these will also include the systems management information required to set up the call. This is currently included within call costs. Such charging will favor those modes of communication with lower bit rates—telex and facsimile versus voice—which may well prove unpopular, as well as increase business costs.

An alternative mode of charging on the basis of access has been put forward as a means for PTTs to stabilize income. The difficulty with ISDN is that as control of networks is passed to customers, the revenue of PTTs becomes unstable. However, in order to invest in the modernization of the network, the PTTs need capital.[23]

COMPARISON OF POLICY

The major driving force for the introduction of ISDN in the United States by the Bell Operating Companies is the threat of bypass, but state public utility commissioners have varied in their enthusiasm for the technology, which the average residential consumer will not use but may end up paying for. In particular, the California Public Utilities Commission (PUC) blocked a six-billion-dollar network modernization scheme by Pacific Bell in 1986. In other words, ISDN is by no means universal.

According to a 1990 survey, the seven RBOCs vary in the number of ISDN lines from 57,000 at Bell Atlantic and 22,000 at Southwestern Bell down to 1,700 at Pacific Telesis. Equally they vary in the proportion of lines accessed by customers rather than the RBOC and its suppliers. The proportion of customer access lines is highest in Bell Atlantic, with 92 percent, and lowest at BellSouth and Ameritech with 30 percent each.[24]

In the U.S. context, the competitive and fragmented nature of the communications infrastructure is likely to complicate ISDN. As early as

1985 it was pointed out that because one long distance telephone call involves two local telephone companies, one interstate carrier, and two sets of CPE, "there is no single driving force for new public network services on a national level."[25] In 1990, the position was still fragmented, with unconnected "islands" of ISDN.

In Europe, despite agreement within the EC that 5 percent of lines should carry ISDN by 1995, a similar diversity in the provision of ISDN is evident. Some PTTs have begun with basic access, and others with primary rate access. Some have marketed primarily to small- and medium-sized businesses, and others to large business users. Paul Slaa has characterized two approaches: the "technical" approach taken by West Germany, where specifications were being worked out prior to commercial service, and the "market" approach taken by BT, where specifications were worked out only when necessary. Writing in 1987, he questioned whether such diversity of timetables, standards, and tariffs could ever be harmonized.[26] Three years later, Loretta Anania raised similar questions about the real potential for European integration of ISDN.[27]

The cost of establishing a nationwide service is huge. In West Germany, estimates of cost varied from $590 million prior to 1988 to $2.4 billion annually thereafter.[28] However, West Germany previously had a primarily electromechanical network, so the introduction of ISDN has also coincided with digitalization. By 1990, ISDN had been implemented in 39 cities and had an installed base of 20,000 basic and primary-rate access lines. Full nationwide service is expected by 1993. Deutsche Bundespost Telekom (the liberalized PTT) also expected to introduce broadband ISDN services early in the 1990s.

In France, an experimental service began in 1983 and has gradually expanded from Brittany to the Paris area. With France's already modernized network, nationwide coverage is expected by 1990 with 150,000 access lines by 1992, and between 500,000 and 700,000 by 1995. France Telecom has taken the most aggressive stance on marketing ISDN by signing cooperation agreements with computer manufacturers and more than 30 partnership contracts with customers and service suppliers.[29]

In Britain, British Telecom began an integrated digital access network in 1985, but this had to be upgraded to CCITT specifications in 1988. Britain has been slow to market services. Mercury's ISDN service covers only nine cities.

Although ISDN is currently put forward as a market-led innovation, its introduction in Europe seems to have more to do with industrial policy and the provision of a home market for domestic companies. By retaining the network termination point within the network, the main European market has been differentiated from the American market, while regional standards may favor European companies. However, there is no guarantee that the Japanese, with whom the EC has a 210 million ECU trade deficit on telecommunications equipment, will not be the major beneficiaries. There may be little room for smaller European manufacturers.

Although standards for narrow-band ISDN are not yet complete, thoughts are turning to broadband. The continued steep decreases in the cost of optical fiber have in turn led to the question of whether fiber can replace copper in the telecommunications network, and how quickly to upgrade the network to broadband technology. At the same time, the increasing use of broadband communications within companies for data exchange in Local Area Networks (LANs) has produced pressure toward extended broadband networking (B-ISDN). Its introduction in the local network depends on whether fiber is cheaper than cable and under what conditions, and crucially, it depends on regulation.

Despite these uncertainties, it seems likely that PTTs will increasingly opt to put fiber into the network, both because of increased bandwidth and because it is cheaper to maintain than copper. Additionally, the cost of electro-optical components is dropping fast. Hence, fiber may be placed in the network passively at first, taking narrow-band services, and then upgraded later, utilizing wavelength division multiplexing.[30]

At the international level, standards have been agreed on an optical interface with the current network.[31] Full B-ISDN will allow circuit switching, but the major difference between the broadband and narrow-band ISDN is that broadband will be based on packet-switching/cell technology using the Asynchronous Transfer Mode (ATM). This technology will make the fiber equivalent to a road with different-sized "vehicles" (cars, trucks, and so forth) directed to different destinations. Greater control will be handed to the user.

The CCITT has been working on broadband standards since the mid-1980s. It has listed as potential broadband services: high-quality broadband videotelephony, high-quality broadband videoconferencing, existing quality TV distribution, and high-definition TV distribution, as well as existing ISDN bearer services. The width of the proposed broadband channels can go up to 132–138.4 Mbps, which would be needed for high-definition TV.[32] B-ISDN foreshadows the overlapping of point-to-point telecommunications with point-to-multipoint broadcasting, interactive with distributional services.

The European Community has also adopted a plan to move from ISDN to broadband.[33] Broadband infrastructure is seen as the means to provide the market pull that will bring European industry level with the American and Japanese.[34] Again, the debate has primarily been in terms of industrial policy.

Movement toward B-ISDN depends as much on regulation as on technology. In Britain, BT has overlayed its Flexible Access system, direct to major customers, and is advocating an evolutionary migration to broadband. This strategy is due to the government's refusal to help finance the introduction of fiber into the network, but BT may well use overlay techniques to introduce fiber into the local network as a response to competition from radio-based technologies. In the United States, such overlay techniques are being utilized in the local network with the renting out of spare capacity to cable TV companies (an option not currently available in Britain). A second approach is that adopted in West Germany, where additional bandwidth is being provided for certain services such as videoconferencing, but cable TV is being provided independently. A further approach is evident in the United States, where "islands" of cable TV or local area networks are being interlinked. A similar approach is evident in the French *Plan Câble*, where 500,000 subscribers are now connected to multimode, switched star local fiber networks for CATV and some interactive telecommunications services.[35]

The problems broadband brings are in the convergence of broadcasting and telecommunications on the regulatory front, in the potential invasion of privacy, and in particular, if the technology is to be introduced piecemeal, in how interim regulations will affect different stakeholders. The major questions of how the fixed costs of the network should be distributed, how it will be regulated, whether residential users will have to pay for services they do not use, and what will be its societal impact all tend to be bypassed. As Paul Slaa has pointed out, because decisions have been made in technical fora, in the CCITT, in ETSI, and in the European Commission, "on the EC-level politicians can be faced with established facts, with no room for choice left. The technical lead the ISDN has taken in the past might be reinforced at the cost of national, and even European, policymaking."[36]

This technology push and elite policy-making is nowhere more evident than in the question of tariffs. The RACE project has suggested tariffs based on access costs four times that of voice telephony.[37] As with narrow-band ISDN, the difficulty of establishing costs and of tariffing a multitude of different bandwidths from the PTT point of view lends itself to one access charge. However, if B-ISDN is to be the universal pipeline carrying voice traffic and television, the recommendations of RACE take no account of the social implications of such charging. In terms of universal service of telecommunications and universal access to sources of information through broadcasting, high up-front access charges contradict traditional tariffing tenets.

CONCLUSION

What seems evident is that narrow-band ISDN, while sold by technologists and PTTs as the transport medium of the future, was devised without consideration of usage or who would pay. Although this fact is hidden at the moment by the imposition of tariffs based on current voice carriage, ISDN implies a system where there can be no cross-subsidies between long-distance and local service, between business and residential. It also implies a system where there is no division between basic and enhanced services. While the EC presses for cost-based tariffs, the implication is that the costs of the predetermined technology then determine policy rather than vice versa.[38]

Most important, ISDN has been decided upon with no public debate. Its major beneficiaries are likely to be the equipment and component manufacturers, while the social implications of its introduction have been ignored. The following chapters look at the linkage of ISDN to high-definition television.

NOTES

1. Lee McKnight, "Technical Standards and International Telecommunications Regimes" (Paper presented to the 29th International Studies Association, Washington, D.C., September 1987).

2. Megumi Komiya, "Integrated Services Digital Networks in the U.S. and Japan: A Comparative Analysis of National Telecommunications Policies," *Pacific Telecommunications Council '86 Proceedings* (Honolulu: PTC, 1987).

3. Alan Stone, *Wrong Number. The Breakup of AT&T* (New York: Basic Books, 1989), 59–82.

4. International Telecommunications Union, *CCITT Red Book*, Fascicle III.5, Rec. I-ISDN (Geneva: ITU, 1984).

5. Ralph Miller, "Integrated Services Digital Network. Telecommunications in the Future," *Online* 11, March 1987, 27.

6. T. Murakami, "ISDN: Advancing towards the 21st Century" (Paper presented to Asia Telecom, Singapore, April 1989).

7. Yasusada Kitahara, *Information Network System* (London: Heinemann Educational Books, 1983).

8. Loretta Anania and Richard Solomon, "User Arbitrage and ISDN," *Intermedia* 16 (January/February 1988): 25–31.

9. Thomas Lundmark, "CCITT No. 7 Signalling Opens the Door to ISDN," *Telephone Engineer and Management*, 1 April 1986, 74–80; Murakami, "ISDN."

10. Jill Hills, "Telecommunications Rich and Poor," *Third World Quarterly* 12 (April 1990): 71–90.

11. "The ITU Plenipot: Renewal without Reform," Special Report, *Transnational Data Report* 12, August/September 1989, 7.

12. N. Budwey, "Interregional Summit on Telecommunications Standards," *Telecommunications* 24 (April 1990): 51–52.

13. M. D. Marcus, "The Regulatory Point of View: ISDN in the United States," *Telephony* 10 (March 1985): 32–34.

14. Irwin Dorros, "The New Future—Back to Technology," *IEEE Communications Magazine* 25 (January 1986): 57–61.

15. Joseph Pelton, "Joining the Global Village: Linking Low Cost Domestic Satellite Networks into the Global ISDN" (Paper presented to the Satellite VI Conference, Washington, D.C., February 1987), 11.

16. Trudy E. Bell, "Telecommunications," *IEEE Spectrum* 27 (February 1990): 31–32.

17. Miller, "Integrated Services," 33.

18. Mike Hart, "The Future of PC Communications," *Telecommunications* 24 (June 1990): 75–78.

19. Touche Ross Report, quoted in Graham Finnie, "Switching the U.S. on to ISDN," *Telecommunications* 23 (July 1989): 66–69.

20. Bill Bauer, "Private Integrated Networks: A Trigger for Public Demand," *Telecommunications* 22 (October 1988): 41.

21. Gerhard Zeidler, "ISDN: Vistas and Application" (Paper presented to Asia Telecom, Singapore, April 1989).

22. David Rogerson, "Tariff Policy and ISDN," *Telecommunications* 21 (October 1987): 87–92.

23. Anania and Solomon, "User Arbitrage."

24. Survey by ICL (International Computers Limited), "ISDN Deployment in the U.S.," *Telecommunications* 24 (June 1990): 20.

25. John McDonald, "Deregulation's Impact on Technology," *IEEE Communications Magazine* 25 (January 1987): 63–65.

26. Paul Slaa, *ISDN as a Design Problem. The Case of the Netherlands* (The Hague: Netherlands Organization for Technology Assessment, 1988), v-xiii.

27. Loretta Anania, "The Protean Complex: Are Open Networks Com-

mon Markets?" (Paper presented to the 8th Annual International Telecommunications Society, Venice, April 1990).

28. Rolf Wigand, "Integrated Services Digital Networks: Concepts, Policies and Emerging Issues," *Journal of Communication* 38 (Winter 1988): 29–47.

29. J. Dunogue, "Numeris: The French ISDN," *Electrical Communication* 64, no. 1 (1990): 15–20; Oliver Lubliner, "ISDN Development in France," *Telecommunications* 23 (July 1989): 19–24.

30. Graham Finnie, "Lighting up the Local Loop," *Telecommunications* 23 (January 1989): 31–40.

31. Thang Nguyen Tat, David Fisher, and Anders Bergland, "An Evolution Path to ATM," *Telecommunications* 24 (July 1990): 41–46.

32. William Stallings, "CCITT Standards Foreshadow Broadband ISDN," *Telecommunications* 24 (May 1990): 89–96.

33. COM (86) 205 Final.

34. Ian Mackintosh, *Sunrise Europe. The Dynamics of Information Technology* (Oxford: Basil Blackwell, 1986).

35. Heinrich Armbuster, "Worldwide Approaches to Broadband ISDN," *Telecommunications* 23 (May 1989): 49–54.

36. Slaa, *ISDN as a Design Problem*, vi.

37. Dennis Gilhooly, "The Politics of Broadband," *Telecommunications* 22 (June 1988): 58.

38. Geoffrey Mulgan, "The Myth of Cost-Based Pricing," *Intermedia* 18 (January/February 1990): 21–27.

8

The Politics of Television Standards

From the first development of radio, the history of broadcasting has been closely linked to business and politics. However, unlike radio, television broadcasting has been a nationally based technology. This national basis has resulted from the technology itself and the ability of manufacturers to achieve sufficient economies of scale in national markets. The characteristics of Very High Frequency (VHF) radio waves allow their reception in only a 50-mile radius from the transmitter. Hence, television broadcasting has needed an extensive network of relay stations to give national coverage. In turn, these technological characteristics have enabled national standards to be imposed, and have ensured that the development of television has been linked to concepts of national sovereignty and domestic industrial policy. DBS has altered this technological insularity.[1] It induces the need for standardization beyond national borders. The politics of this wider standardization, at the regional and international levels, provide the focus of this chapter.

The aim of the new generation of television technologies, of satellite broadcasting and High-Definition Television (HDTV), is to provide sharper pictures with better detail, and to provide stereo-quality sound. However, unlike their predecessors, these new technologies challenge traditional methods of transmission and production as well as determine reception equipment. In the words of Michel Carpentier:

> HDTV technology will bring immense possibilities to the audio-visual sector regarding picture quality, production costs and flexibility.

By facilitating the digital treatment of imaging it will be both an interface between TV and cinema and an advance on the current "high definition" audio-visual technology, namely 35mm film.[2]

Because of this technological potential, international standardization is desirable in studio production, in the international exchange of programs (by recording, including transfer from or to cinematographic film, and by satellite and terrestrial emissions), and in cable transmission.[3] Decisions made on technical standards in the 1990s are likely to determine the pattern of television—and film—costs of production, distribution, and reception for the next three decades. The range of impact of these standards therefore involves a number of mass-media industries, some of which are considered essential to national economies.

Moreover, because HDTV could have a wide range of applications in conjunction with digital processing and storage, the potential industrial and commercial impact of the technology is even more profound. As Martin Ernst has pointed out, the HDTV standardization debate has raised two sets of issues in the United States: one set of broadcast issues relating to home TV system standards and spectrum usage, and the other relating to trade and technology issues involving microchips.[4]

In turn, the trade and technology issues have been linked to the question of the future of the American semiconductor industry and the survival of American preeminence in computer technology. At the present time, the primary markets for semiconductors in Japan and Europe are in consumer-electronics equipment. In America they are in computers. By threatening the integration of consumer electronics with data processing, HDTV also threatens the U.S. semiconductor industry with Japanese domination. Perceived as the prime future market for integrated circuits, HDTV has strategic implications for technological leadership. The prizes being fought for are perceived as being no less than the global television, computing, and semiconductor markets. The political factors embrace no less than perceptions of domestic cultural and industrial survival.

These considerations inevitably place broadcasting standards in the geopolitical domain, impacting on international relations. On the one hand, international standardization is effective in reducing uncertainties and in allowing economies of scale to manufacturers of equipment and components. On the other hand, it seals in stone the current technological pecking order. In the case of HDTV, it would benefit the leading manufacturers and patent holders: Japanese companies.

Analyzing the politics of the adoption of the current television standards in Europe during the 1950s, Rhonda Crane noted that each nation approached the issue of compatible standards from a parochial point of view.

> The determination of whether it is necessary as well as desirable to adopt standards compatible with other nations will be based upon an evaluation of several factors involving the national interest. These include national political strategy, national technical needs, public opinion, estimates of the value of services, economic status, balance of payments, the costs of not agreeing, history and experience.[5]

As Crane suggested, "it is not a question of adopting an apolitical standard."[6] The standard adopted will always be a political artifact. It will inevitably reflect a combination of national industrial and state interests mediated through domestic and international institutions.

As in telecommunications, the numbers of stakeholders in standardization have multiplied, making international consensus more difficult. However, there has been a major difference in the standardization issues surrounding the adoption of SECAM (Sequential Color and Memory), described by Crane, and that of HDTV. In the HDTV debate, Europe has acted not as a fragmented region of various national interests, but in a coordinated fashion. The various national interests have been brought together as one European interest expressed through the European Community's commission.

In part, this new consensus reflects the European experience in the standardization of videocassette recorders (VCRs) and the dangers of leaving standards to be determined by the market. Three VCR standards competed for consumer acceptance during the early 1980s: Betamax, VHS, and V-2000. The European V-2000, marketed by Philips of Holland and Grundig of West Germany, was overwhelmed by the market penetration of Betamax and VHS from Japan, leading to the extinction of the V-2000 and the de facto industry standardization on VHS. By 1990, ten Japanese exporters had taken approximately 90 percent of the European Community's VCR market.[7] A determination not to repeat the market fragmentation of the previous television standards and not to have a de facto standard imposed on their manufacturers by market domination from overseas has motivated European actions.

TECHNICAL STANDARDS

There were approximately 12 color television standards created during the period 1928 to 1942 in the United States, the USSR, and Europe.

During the late 1950s and early 1960s, the Americans developed the National Television System Committee (NTSC) and the Europeans developed two systems, Phase Alternate Line (PAL) and SECAM. These three standards remained current in 1990. The unifying de facto standard has been that of 35 millimeter (mm) film at 24 images per second, which has been used for production and has been convertible to each television standard.

PAL, developed in West Germany, is used in Britain and most West European countries. SECAM is used in France and Greece, and NTSC is used in the United States and Japan. Whereas PAL and SECAM utilize 625 lines and a scanning frequency of 50 fields per second, NTSC uses 525 lines and a scanning frequency of 59.94 fields per second. In general, PAL and SECAM give greater picture clarity than NTSC, but the latter's 59.94 scanning frequency gives less flicker.[8] Although technology seems to have made this factor less important, the systems are related to the domestic electricity supply. The United States and half of Japan use 60Hz (the other half of Japan uses 50 Hz), and Western Europe uses 50Hz. Each system carries the disadvantage that color information (chrominance) is interleaved with brightness information (luminance), producing a shimmering of the picture when it carries a lot of detail, and "cross color" when, for instance, a performer is dressed in a striped shirt.

The MAC (Multiplexed Analogue Component) standard improves picture quality by separating chrominance and luminance. A time-compressed analog picture signal is combined with a data burst, which carries sound, data, and digital synchronization signals. MAC standards also offer the possibility of easy encryption and control of subscriber access, together with high-quality digital sound and other data services. MAC standards were developed by the Europeans exclusively for satellite television, but are also being adapted for optic fiber and cable transmission.[9]

HDTV is a standard for television production originally developed by the Japanese. Hi-Vision of the NHK offers a production standard that aims to give video pictures of similar quality to 35mm film. It comprises a 1,125-line system with 60 fields per second scanning and a 16:9 aspect ratio (the ratio of frame width to frame height). The 1,125 standard gives both an approximate doubling of vertical resolution and allows a 9/5 and 15/7 down conversion to Europe's 625-line system and the NTSC 525-line standard.[10]

Because the bandwidth needed for HDTV would be 50 MHz (compared to 6MHz for a single television channel) and is therefore very large, the Japanese have developed their own transmission system for satellite broadcasting, Multiple sub-Nyquist Sampling Encoding (MUSE). This is a compression technique that reduces the required bandwidth to 9MHz. This transmission standard (developed by NHK) allows one satellite channel to carry an HDTV signal together with more than four audio channels. However, HDTV/MUSE is not compatible with existing NTSC transmissions, nor with PAL or SECAM. It would therefore require the replacement of all television sets.

The bandwidth needed by HDTV can be handled both by high-powered DBS satellites and medium-powered fixed satellites, but where the spectrum is limited, it is also suited to fiber optic cable with its inherent wide bandwidth. As a result, the debate on HDTV standards is also a debate on whether wideband B-ISDN is the most apt method of delivery—and this debate in turn involves the competing interests of telecommunications carriers, cable TV, and broadcasters.

The Europeans have also produced their own HDTV standard. Called HD-MAC, and also known as "EU95," it is based on 1,250 lines and a scanning frequency of 50 fields per second. It is designed to be compatible with existing terrestrial television sets in Europe and the MAC transmission system.[11] The intention is to finalize EU95 by the early 1990s, ready for full-scale DBS transmission for use on the *BSB*, *TVSAT*, *TDF1*, and *Olympus* satellites (see chapter 5).

The debate between these standards officially takes place within the ITU and its subcommittee, the International Consultative Committee for Radio (CCIR). As with other ITU agencies, the CCIR is a forum where decisions are made on the basis of consensus. Therefore, for a standard to be approved, it must gain unanimous support. As in the case of ISDN, the problem with the CCIR is that the four years required for official approval of standards allows the de facto adoption of standards while de jure international standards are still being agreed. Additionally, in a fast-moving technological area, even while one set of standards are being debated, new alternatives may arise that make the previous discussions obsolete.

It is possible in such fast-moving technological areas legitimately to reject a standard as being too early in the technology's life cycle. The strategy allows those lagging behind in the technology to catch up, but risks the imposition of a de facto standard. The danger of such an imposition is, however, considerably less if the market is actually under the control of regulation by government. Because broadcasting is such a market, the Europeans risked little in delaying adoption of an international HDTV standard. Even were their standard not to be adopted internationally, the European market provides sufficient economies of scale for the transmission and equipment industries.

This chapter describes how political and economic pressures have influenced decisions over these two standards. Because DBS broadcasting has not yet become important in the United States, the MAC standard debate, while intergovernmental, is specifically an intra-European debate. In contrast, the HDTV debate originally lined Japan and the United States up against Europe. It has subsequently provoked a split between Japanese and U.S. strategy, with Europe attempting to bring the Americans into their political camp.

As was described in the previous chapter on ISDN, difficulties are apparent for any technology that has been developed separate from the market. As a result, alternative standards more attuned to the consumer market are being canvassed. In this case, it is the Japanese who are more concerned with technology push and the Europeans who are more market-led in their innovation, while domestic conflicts within the United States hamper its adoption of a new standard.

MARKETS AND INDUSTRY STRUCTURE

The debates on international standardization and the positions taken by the various government participants have to be seen in terms of the changing industry structure in the United States and Europe. Faced with the Europe-wide success of Japanese manufacturers in the late 1970s, nationally based European consumer-electronics companies merged across national borders. Thomson of France took over the television tube interests of Telefunken of West Germany, and in 1982 bid for control of Grundig of that same country. When that bid was blocked by the German cartel office, Philips of the Netherlands raised its stake in Grundig to 31.5 percent, taking management control. With the sale of Thorn-EMI's subsidiary, Ferguson, to state-owned Thomson in 1987, the European-owned consumer-electronics industry was split between two large groups—Thomson (French) and Philips (Dutch)—both with West German interests.

In 1987, Philips had a 21 percent share in the European market for color TV sets, and a further 13 percent through its control of Grundig. Thomson took 13 percent, with a further 5 percent through its takeover of Thorn-EMI. The rest of the market was shared between a number of other companies, with the Japanese taking 14 percent. However, with sales of sets only growing at 2 or 3 percent per year, and a total of 48 manufacturing plants, including 10 Japanese plants, the European market has been plagued with overcapacity.

Because of Thomson and Philips's predominance among European manufacturers, they have been important actors in the definition of European strategy. Both companies are vertically integrated and are semiconductor manufacturers. Both have argued that consumer electronics is the major user of microchips in Europe, and that if the market were lost to Japan then so would the microchip industry disappear.[12]

While Philips is the largest manufacturer of color TVs in the world, with 6.2 million units produced in 1986, in the same year the Japanese manufacturers together produced more than 18 million sets. Although imports of Japanese sets were limited by quota to 1 million out of a market of 15 million, taken together with Japanese domination of the European VCR and compact-disc market, European companies legitimately feel threatened.

However, the geographical positioning of Japanese electronics company investment within Europe has tended to reduce their importance as political actors. The largest proportion of that investment has been in Britain, where in 1990 it accounted for about $2.1 billion of investment and the employment of 20,000 people, and contributed to an export surplus of about $92.8 million in TV production.[13] Since much of this trade is intra-European, while important to Britain, the Japanese contribution is less important to Europe as a whole.

While the industrial interests involved in HDTV standards have been relatively homogeneous in Europe, those in the United States are fragmented. In manufacturing the Japanese are dominant, but subsidiaries of Thomson and Philips take about 30 percent of the American market for televisions. The only American manufacturer, Zenith, takes 13 percent of the television market and manufactures off-shore. In the late 1980s, the company was actually under considerable pressure to sell its color television business. As in Europe, the television market has matured, and annual growth has slowed to about 1 percent in a market worth about $7,600 million in 1990, or just over one-fifth of the total consumer electronics market. It is also noticeable that whereas half the sales of television sets within Europe are small portables, that market has also matured in the United States.[14]

The HDTV standardization debate has also involved the American programming industry. With exports of about $3.2 billion in 1988, of which almost half goes to the largest European countries, the motion picture and television program industry is important to the United States. Existing fragmentation of national standards has meant that films and video have all had to be converted to be compatible with national television systems—an obvious handicap to exports. Current 35mm film is said to lose definition when converted for television, and video-recordings suffer significant loss of quality in later generation copies. Therefore, if a new production standard were to replace 35mm film, either it would need to be international in its application or it would be necessary for it to be easily convertible into any television standard.

The question of HDTV standards has also been relevant to the ongoing battle between broadcasting and cable interests, in which broadcasting has been losing market share to cable. HDTV was seen at first as a means by which networks might fight back by upgrading the quality of their transmission. However, the wide bandwidth required for its use by broadcasters raised questions about the allocation of the radio spectrum and about ensuing opportunity costs for competing interests, such as cellular mobile telephony.

Finally, unlike Europe, or Japan, the major market for semiconductors in the United States is that of computer equipment. Semiconductor and computer manufacturers are predominantly American-owned. The semiconductor industry has previously been active in seeking protection from Japanese competition, while the computer industry sees itself as having been disadvantaged by that protectionism. To some extent, HDTV has unified the two. It seems that the problems of the computer-equipment industry and the fall in profits during the latter 1980s of all the major companies induced the industry to link the HDTV issue to the issue of national technological leadership. With the involvement of the U.S. Department of Defense, trade and technology issues have come to dominate the domestic debate.

THE MAC DEBATE

Standardization on the basis of national markets meant that in 1983 Philips had to supply over 100 different types of TV sets to meet differing European standards. Until 1981 it was assumed that DBS broadcasts in Europe would be based on the transmission of conventional television signals; namely, 625-line pictures using either the PAL or SECAM color system. Both systems, developed in the 1950s, are designed for terrestrial broadcasting on the basis of AM (Amplitude Modulation) rather than FM (Frequency Modulation), which is used for satellite television. Unfortunately, broadcasting on FM tends to produce much picture noise (or grain) on heavily colored parts of the image.

With a view to efficiently employing the extended bandwidth of 27 MHz available to satellite users, in Britain the BBC and Independent Broadcasting Authority (IBA) pursued separate lines of technological development. The BBC concentrated on an extension of the existing PAL system. In contrast, the IBA developed new technology, the Multiplexed Analogue Component (MAC), which would allow the emergence of

HDTV systems and would be suitable for pan-European use.[15] The MAC system, incorporating separate component signals, is suitable for large screens, high-definition displays, and high-quality signals. Because of its technological superiority over the BBC's extended PAL system, in 1982 a U.K. government committee recommended it as the technical standard.[16] Then, the IBA developed a further improvement to the MAC system, the C-MAC standard.[17]

In 1983, the European Broadcasting Union chose C-MAC as the European standard.[18] The French, however, were unhappy with C-MAC because it required too large a bandwidth for transmission to cable head-ends. France also argued the need for compatibility between the French D2-MAC and the British C-MAC.[19] By late 1984, the British and French seemed prepared to compromise on D2-MAC as the standard for the redistribution of satellite signals to cable head-ends. Then, however, at an EBU meeting in Spain in April 1985, the French threatened to walk out unless the EBU agreed to document the D2-MAC as a full broadcast standard. Hence, although the C-MAC version is technologically superior to D2-MAC, the EBU compromised, agreeing on both the D2- and C-MAC versions as EBU standards. The problem is that while MAC is designed for enhanced television, the D2-MAC can carry only half the number of data channels of C-MAC. This deficiency translates into four high-quality sound channels instead of eight, and into a greatly reduced capacity for teletext or data services.[20]

Holding out against the imposition of the D2-MAC standard, the United Kingdom at first, through the IBA, indicated that it would use C-MAC as its standard. The British government, supported to some extent by the European Commission, also backed C-MAC, and conflict between France and Britain delayed the European Commission's directive on satellite broadcasting standards. This was issued in 1986 only after it was found that C-MAC and D2-MAC were compatible (theoretically at least).[21] The commission's Directive imposed a common family of standards for satellite transmission on member states (the MAC family).[22] However, it was left to national administrations to decide among D-MAC, D2-MAC, C-MAC, or B-MAC (another variant adopted by the Nordic countries).

Generally speaking, because of its failure to launch a British DBS satellite, the U.K. government was not in a strong position to impose C-MAC on the rest of Europe. Neither has there been the market incentive of a major British manufacturer pressing it to do so. In contrast, French policy was linked to their satellite development and to domestic industrial policy.

The whole debate on MAC standards demonstrates that the superiority of a technology or standard does not necessarily lead to its immediate acceptance. Politics plays a predominant role. The debate also illustrates that while, in order to overcome its lag in terms of competition with Japanese and American firms, Europe talks of a common, less fragmented approach, in point of fact, nationalism continues to play an important role. Europe is still a group of sovereign states each pursuing its own national interest.

FRENCH INDUSTRIAL POLICY: FROM SECAM TO D2-MAC

There are parallels between French concerns and strategy surrounding SECAM in the Charles de Gaulle era of the 1960s and those in the 1980s, when a Socialist government led the fight over D2-MAC. In both cases there was international interest in adopting a single television standard for all of Western Europe. The competition was politically intense; the nation whose system was selected as the standard would gain markets, revenue, and political prestige.[23] All these factors were relevant to French strategy on both occasions.

However, in the D2-MAC debate, the French were actually in a weaker technical position than in that over SECAM. Whereas in the 1970s, the EBU had been unable to pronounce one standard better than another, in 1985 it decided that the British C-MAC was superior to the D2-MAC. The French were able to threaten to walk out of the meeting unless the EBU adopted the D2-MAC standard simply because their satellite-building alliance with the West Germans also encompassed the standards issue. In contrast, in the SECAM debate the French had competed with West Germans and allied themselves with the USSR.

On both occasions, if the French standard were not chosen as the European standard, France was still assured of a large enough market to create demand pull for the national champion company: Thomson CSF. Both in the SECAM debate, where France was allied with the USSR, and in the MAC debate, where its alliance was with West Germany, it was evident that enough economies of scale existed for a viable manufacturing industry. However, in the D2-MAC debate, reflecting both increasing European-wide cooperation at the company level and community influence against national discrimination, Thomson was allied with Philips of the Netherlands. Philips not only is the largest European consumer-electronics company, but also has large-scale interests in West Germany and France. The differences in strategy reflect the growing strength of the Franco-German alliance within the Community and the marginalization of the British.

THE MANUFACTURING PROBLEM

Reception-equipment manufacturers have a technological and industrial stake in the question of which standard within the MAC family should be used. As in many community issues where intergovernmental politics provoke economic fragmentation, the exigencies of the market have forced cooperation between companies. Philips and Thomson have formed a consortium together with Salora (Finland), Fuba (West Germany), and Logica (United Kingdom) to create one European Satellite Television Transmission and Scrambling system. Meanwhile, a rival consortium, the Anglo-Nordic Group of Philips (United Kingdom), Plessey (United Kingdom), Tandberg (Norway), and Nordic VSLI, have been working on a "multi-MAC chip" to serve the various standards.

When demanding acceptance of the D2-MAC standard from the EBU, the French argued that because of the different orbital positions of the two satellites, two dishes would in any case be required to receive both TDF1 and BSB. Clearly, however, the failure to agree on one European standard affects the viability of programmers, who are thereby limited in their market. It also affects the price of dishes, which cannot be manufactured to the same economies of scale, thereby impacting on the time needed for the build-up of subscriptions to satellite TV. Manufacturers have spoken of a modest production of 100,000 dishes in the first year, 100,000 in the second, and eventually 1 million in the third, but estimates of the potential European market put it at billions of dollars.[24] The French aim to create these economies of scale in reception equipment by public purchasing. The DGT announced in 1989 that it would buy 1 million D2-MAC dishes (over perhaps five years) in relation to the channel Canal Plus, which was planning to use D2-MAC for its encryption.[25]

Commercial considerations coupled with the delay in launching British DBS led to the eventual adoption of D-MAC standards by BSB. In 1989, the British announced that they had switched to D-MAC. The reasons given for the choice of D-MAC rather than D2-MAC primarily concerned the opportunities the standard gave for the provision of data services. (BSB had been successful in gaining a license for data transmission in 1989.)[26]

Following the launch of its service by BSB in 1990, a four-stage diffusion model was adopted, with the first stage consisting of a satellite dish plus a set-top converter box, in which customers receive no advantage from the MAC standard. The advantage is gained by the programmer, who can encrypt transmissions easily. The second phase is expected "to start very soon after the beginning of the service." In this second phase, sets will be available to encoders built in. The third will involve the production of sets with wide-screen format, and from the start of the service BSB announced it would transmit a film channel in wide-screen format. The intention was clearly to give an incentive to subscribers to purchase sets. In the fourth phase, "some productions may become available in HDTV format and . . . the full picture quality potential associated with this can be conveyed to the viewer." However, there is doubt about whether the improvement in picture quality in the first stages will mean that the progression to stage four and HD-MAC will be advantageous.[27]

By the beginning of 1990, no European manufacturer had managed to produce the D2-MAC or D-MAC packet decoders at a price and quality level sufficient to meet consumer demand. Mass production is not expected before 1992. In the meantime, both Thomson and Philips plan releases of "stage three" sets in late 1990, with wide-screen format and digital sound. However, these sets will be priced initially at around $1,700, and will arrive in a market primarily for small sets. The two companies will combine R&D on HD-MAC technologies in a program costing $6,000 million, for which they are seeking funding from the European Commission. However Philips's financial crisis, which became evident in the spring of 1990, is likely to delay this program. Moreover, Thomson is weak in several of the component technologies, such as liquid crystal displays and videorecorder technology. Neither does either company have a strong record in design. Hence, despite European adoption of MAC standards (specifically to deny the Japanese the possibility of utilizing their home market for sales), there is considerable doubt whether the two large European manufacturers are capable of meeting the challenge of the technology in the time available.[28]

Neither is a wide range of programs available. Thomson acknowledged in 1990 that if BSB were to fail, then so would MAC standards. By 1990, with the exception of BSB, the only programming in MAC format was a culture channel and a pay-TV channel provided by Canal Plus on the French satellite *TDF1*. Canal Plus, which effectively controls access to the satellite, refused to open up channel slots to West German broadcasters unless West Germany undertook to work with D2-MAC.

For the West Germans, the problem comes from the state of the economy in East Germany and the fact that PAL broadcasts would have a wider audience there. The public service broadcasters in particular have been anxious to use an upgraded form of PAL on the new West German satellite *TVSAT2*. President Mitterand of France demanded in April 1990 that the West German chancellor reaffirm his commitment to the European Commission's directive. While Chancellor Helmut Kohl made that undertaking, the West German public broadcasters have fought the decision. They threatened to move to *Astra* in order to use PAL,[29] and in May 1990 the BSAT channel became the first German public service broadcaster to move to *Astra 1A*.

In fact, *Astra* may well have made MAC standards redundant. The German private broadcasters originally lined up for *TVSAT2* have moved to *Astra*, where they can join Rupert Murdoch in broadcasting in PAL. As a satellite outside the DBS allocation, *Astra* evades the EC Directive. The primary immediate advantage of MAC was in its encryption potential, but advances in technology have now made PAL encryption secure. With a review of the EC Directive due in late 1990, a movement is in progress to abandon MAC as a compulsory feature of DBS broadcasting,[30] a movement that has gained momentum from the merger of Sky and BSB and the merged company's decision to transmit on PAL.

THE INTERNATIONAL POLITICS OF HDTV

The Japanese were the first to proceed with HDTV in the early 1970s, primarily as a replacement for their terrestrial NSTC system, whose reproduction qualities were poor. For the last two decades they have been working on HDTV. The program has been linked with their space policy and their determination to build communications satellites utilizing indigenous technology. Their first DBS satellite was launched in 1983 in order to bring television transmission to outlying areas where the reception of terrestrial signals was difficult. Japan gained a headstart on the other nations with its Hi-Vision system, which was developed by the public broadcast NHK in collaboration with Japanese industry, notably Sony. The intention is to link HDTV into other consumer-electronics products combining computers, recording equipment, and image storage. The standard is a production and studio standard, and does not cover transmission and reception by television sets in viewers' homes.

The Japanese spent $700 million in developing their 1,125-line system in the hope of it becoming the world standard. The system gained support from some American broadcasters, notably CBS. Despite the fact that the system was incompatible with NTSC, its selling point was that it would be a universal medium for the electronic interchange of programs freely around the world.[31] The CBS network claimed that despite higher equipment costs, an HDTV production system using videotape was cheaper overall than 35mm film. Suzanne Neil has suggested that the adoption by the United States of the Japanese standard was partly the result of the dominance of the views of television program producers and partly the desire of the newly created Bureau of International Communications and Information Policy within the U.S. State Department to gain political legitimacy. Together, this alliance of bureaucratic and industrial interests established American support for the Japanese standard.[32]

The CCIR Meeting of 1986

Before the CCIR's quadrennial meeting in Dubrovnik, Yugoslavia, in May 1986, the EBU's technical committee had expressed qualified support for the Japanese system, reserving the right to change its opinion once more was known about the precise means of broadcasting HDTV in Europe. Only France abstained at the meeting, while 15 members voted for the Japanese standard. This decision, taken on technical ground by public broadcasters, was in contradiction to the decision already taken by the United Kingdom, France, West Germany, and the Netherlands at the intergovernmental level, stating that they would oppose the adoption of the Japanese standard at the CCIR meeting of 1986. Opposition was led by the European Commission, but the community had no standing within the CCIR, where delegates are from CCIR member states.

In particular, the Europeans were worried that the adoption of Hi-Vision as a production standard would inevitably determine transmission standards and would demand the replacement of all European TV sets. Since Japanese companies held the patents to the new technology, they could dominate the European television reception market. The Europeans contended that the Japanese system utilized old technology, that because it was based on 60Hz it would disadvantage all those countries using 50Hz electricity supply, and that more research was needed. The British argued for an Extended C-MAC developed by the IBA, which allowed an evolutionary approach to HDTV.

The common European position came after six months of meeting and discussions, especially among the United Kingdom, West Germany, France, and the Netherlands. These countries were able to unify in response to a perceived threat to the manufacturing industry in Europe, despite the fact that they were still wrangling among themselves over D2-MAC versus C-MAC. At the CCIR meeting, the Europeans were granted a two-year breathing space to come up with an alternative to the proposed Japanese system. Immediately following that meeting, the European Commission issued its directive on MAC standards.

The European Response

The European Commission justified its involvement in the MAC and HDTV debates in terms of Article 130 of the 1985 Single European Act, which required the community "to strengthen the scientific and technological basis of European industry and to encourage it to become more competitive at the international level." The development of HDTV standards is therefore linked to the commission's industrial policy for Europe.

The commission and the manufacturers have worked together in developing a European HDTV standard. In 1986, the commission brought together manufacturers, broadcasters, the film industry, the EBU representatives, and the administrations involved into an HDTV forum. Companies are working together in a Eureka Program, a cooperative venture of companies from 19 European countries, including those in EFTA as well as the EC. Eureka 95 on HDTV was formed in June 1986. The initiative was taken by West Germany's Bosch, Philips of Holland, Thomson of France, and Thorn/EMI of the United Kingdom. These major companies were later joined by Nokia of Finland and a further 27 firms each specializing in a particular area of development. These partners have already spent $200 million on research.[33]

Other work on HDTV has taken place through the European consortium on component chips, JESSI (the Joint European Submicron Silicon project), and the RACE program, which is working toward standards for a wideband telecommunications network. The intention is to technically integrate HDTV into the future network. Hence, the HD-MAC (or EU95) HDTV standard will be suitable for both satellite and terrestrial transmission. The community plans to spend $480 million on the development of a 1,250-line, 50Hz HDTV system that would be compatible with both MAC transmission standards and existing television sets. Unlike the Japanese standard, the European standard must be compatible with current (mostly European) technologies and products.

At a CCIR meeting held in Geneva in November 1987, the European case was advanced by the decision that MAC standards should be officially recognized as standards capable of being used for HDTV in the future. Hence MAC, originally designed for satellite television, may be utilized for terrestrial broadcasting. At the same time, the EC's Commission proposed to the Japanese authorities that a mixed EC/Japanese working party should be formed in order to prepare a single world standard. This would follow the procedure that the two adopted in relation to competing standards in compact disc technology developed by Sony and Philips.

In April 1989, when it became clear that an HDTV launch strategy was needed, the Council of Ministers passed a decision on HDTV that had five objectives:

1. to ensure that European industry will develop all the necessary technology for HDTV services;
2. to promote EU95 as a global standard;
3. to promote EU95 for worldwide use;
4. to promote the introduction of HDTV services in Europe as soon as possible after 1992; and
5. to ensure that the European film and production industry will gain a competitive position in the HDTV world market.[34]

In the three years since the CCIR Dubrovnik meeting, the European countries had progressed from a defensive reaction against the Japanese proposals for a world standard to putting forward a global standard of their own.

In July 1990, 14 European electronics companies, program makers, and broadcasters set up a program termed Vision 1250. The group included Thomson and Philips, together with the BBC, Thames Television of Britain, and RAI of Italy. The intention is to make HD-MAC production facilities available to broadcasters in order to create a stock of programs. In the same month, the EBU and ETSI established a joint technical committee to define pan-European transmission standards for microwave and satellite (in effect, to bring D2-MAC and D-MAC together), and to work with Cenelec, which represents the interests of the electronics industry.[35] A further Eureka proposal has been made by France for a project to strengthen the production industry. The commission's RACE and ESPRIT programs are also likely to gain increased funding for the development of HD-MAC chips.

The U.S. Response

Following the impasse in the 1986 CCIR, although the U.S. State Department continued to support the Japanese standard, other industrial and political actors became somewhat less enthusiastic about it. The international context had altered considerably due to a burgeoning American trade deficit. The domestic debate on HDTV became linked to the issue of American technological leadership, industrial competitiveness, and exports. This cooling down on the Japanese format has mainly been caused by the awakening to the potential implications of adopting NHK/MUSE on the part of the electronics companies, terrestrial broadcasters, and Hollywood filmmakers. FCC and congressional hearings have brought the issue to the top of the policy agenda.

Following the CCIR, the FCC was petitioned early in 1987 by 58 broadcasting organizations and companies to address the implication of HDTV spectrum allocation. These terrestrial broadcasters were concerned that they would be shut out of advanced television systems unless they were allocated more spectrum space.

In its Notice of Inquiry, the FCC characterized the possible high-definition systems in three ways: those incompatible with NTSC; those compatible but demanding additional spectrum space; and those compatible but demanding no more than the current 6MHz. The commission also inclined to the view that a service that was integrated with NTSC and that eventually entirely might replace it was preferable to a completely new service. By November 1987, the National Telecommunications and Information Administration (NTIA) had also publicly announced its support for a system compatible with NTSC. In other words, only one year after the CCIR meeting in Dubrovnik, the Japanese system had ceased to have general support.[36]

In its docket of September 1988, the FCC made clear that it would not authorize systems that utilized any spectrum capacity beyond the 6 MHz already allocated to broadcast usage. Hence, the Japanese MUSE system would not be authorized.[37] Because of the realization that spectrum bandwidth of the amount required for broadcast HDTV would not be available, the broadcasters had by then also swung against the NHK/MUSE format. Already suffering from declining audiences, they were concerned that the cable operators could utilize HDTV for further market gains on the basis of picture quality. Therefore, terrestrial broadcasters and, most important, the 1,700 independent TV stations, which were concerned at the threat of losing ground in terms of both technology and audiences, lobbied for alternative systems to a fully HDTV format.

Hollywood also awoke to the costliness of a change in the production standard and the potential impact on its exports. A change from the universal standard 24 frames per second of the commercial cinema to 30 frames per second, while compatible with the 60Hz distribution standard proposed for HDTV, would mean that all exports to Europe would need conversion for transmission to PAL countries.[38] A further reason for Hollywood's change of heart was the continuing war between video and film companies. Because HDTV was incompatible with existing 35mm film, the Hollywood film companies feared that lucrative film archives would lose value.

These diverse pressures led to a search for alternative distribution standards that would provide an enhanced picture but would not require the wholesale replacement of existing reception equipment, and would also require only 6 MHz of spectrum bandwidth. In January 1988, the FCC announced that it would set up an Advisory Committee on Advanced Television, consisting of representatives from all the interested parties. This committee began in 1989 to review alternative Advanced Television Systems. The major contenders are Philips, Thomson, Zenith, and the Massachusetts Institute of Technology (MIT). Because the new standard must be compatible with NTSC, it is almost inevitable that the United States will have a different standard than Europe and Japan.

By the latter 1980s, the realization had set in that television could also be utilized in computers with compact-disc technology. Once HDTV was established, the Japanese electronics companies might use their technology to wipe out the American semiconductor and computer industries. In late 1988, the U.S. Defense Department allocated $30 million from other projects to research and development in HDTV in response to the semiconductor companies' requests, and it seemed that the George Bush presidential administration might give further financial support to HDTV development. The prospect of cuts in defense funding following Eastern European developments led the semiconductor industry to write to President Bush in November 1989 pleading their case: "HDTV has become a symbol of our national willingness to compete on the cutting edge in the strategic industries and technologies of the Nineties."[39]

As detailed in chapter 1, U.S. government funding of research and development is legitimized through the linkage between high technology and American national leadership. Outside military applications, it is difficult for a culture so heavily based on economic liberalism to legitimate direct support for industry. HDTV is no exception. The American Electronics Association (AEA), which includes in its three thousand members major companies such as AT&T, Apple Computer, IBM, and Motorola, presented a report to Congress in May 1989 claiming that if the United States sold fewer than 10 percent of the world's HDTVs, it would lose half its share of the personal computer and chip markets. Even to merely maintain its strength in these markets it needed to control over half the HDTV market. The association asked for a government-backed program of $100 million per year for five years to reclaim the consumer-electronics market for American companies.[40] However, the strategy to gain government funding backfired due to a report from the Congressional Budget

Office, which argued that funding was not needed, and counter-lobbying by Japanese and European equipment companies that had no wish to see American companies reenter the consumer electronics market. By the end of 1989 the government had reviewed its assessment of the economic impact of HDTV and had back-tracked on any financial commitment.[41]

Nevertheless, the fear of Japanese entry into the computing market via high-resolution technology remains. The argument is that there is a near-term global market in industrial electronic cinematography and scientific imaging, and that to allow the Japanese to get a foothold in this market would be to allow them into the computer work-station market. Following on from work done by William Schreiber at MIT on the possibilities of an open-architecture "smart" receiver, a new grouping of academics and industrialists has been formed from CATV, film making, computer graphics, telecommunications, and signal processing. Called the Committee on Open High-Resolution Systems, its aim is to input computing and graphics expertise into the HDTV standards debate, and to design "friendly" standards that would allow room for change as the technology changes. The argument of this group is that the Japanese and the European systems are both based on outdated technology that is not computer-compatible, and that adoption of either would once again involve the replacement of reception equipment in a few years time.[42] In effect, the committee is attempting to technologically leapfrog over the Japanese and give American industry a head start by bypassing the weak consumer electronics industry for the strong American computer industry. The most logical outcome of this group's success would be the passage of HDTV reception-equipment manufacture to computer companies.

The Japanese Response

With both the Americans and Europeans reluctant to approve the 1,125-line HDTV format as the worldwide standard, the Japanese have attempted to impose it as a de facto standard, working from the production of recording material. They argue that their system is intended primarily for production rather than transmission, thereby attempting to ease European fears that they are attempting to impose a transmission standard. The Japanese have also attempted to attract European program makers by arguing that a global standard will help the latter's trade and exports in the international marketplace. To attract European manufacturers, the Japanese suggest that transmission and production standards can be separated. They have also offered to work with non-Japanese companies to produce equipment suitable for HDTV—despite the fact that NHK holds current patents.[43] The Japanese have also demonstrated that their transmission standard is compatible with both a 50Hz and a 60Hz electricity supply.[44]

In the United States, the Japanese have responded to the cooling off on HDTV by providing equipment to film makers at ultra-low prices. One may also interpret Sony's acquisition of Columbia Pictures as part of a Japanese strategy to influence the Hollywood community's negative reactions against HDTV. In 1989, Sony set up a workshop to develop methods of mixing HDTV and film. It has also established an electronic decoder to transfer HDTV to film, and a mobile production facility to undertake selected projects with studios and postproduction companies. All these actions indicate that the Japanese are attempting to alter the film community's perception of HDTV.

In addition, in December 1989, support for the Japanese position came from several American chip makers who announced plans to develop chips for HDTV sets. In effect, the companies agreed to become subcontractors to the Japanese.[45] The Japanese seem to be winning acceptance in the United States through industrial and financial muscle and the fact that many HDTV applications are in the corporate sector in stand-alone systems. Hence, de facto standardization in this sector is possible.

However, even within Japan, where it must gain market acceptance, HDTV is having a mixed reception. Electronics companies have produced only a small number of HDTV sets, and none seems keen to be first out on the market.[46] NHK broadcasts for one hour each week in an HDTV format on the *BS2* satellite regardless of the fact that few people can receive the signal. Although these broadcasts will increase when the *BS4*, a DBS satellite, is launched in 1997, the limited range of programming delays market penetration. In addition, there is strong opposition from local commercial Japanese broadcasters, who see DBS as a major threat to their interests, and from the development by commercial broadcasters of systems compatible with NTSC. It seems unlikely, therefore, that HDTV will penetrate the Japanese market quickly.

The CCIR Meeting of 1990

At the international level, the 1986 CCIR defeat was an embarrassment to the Reagan administration, which reacted with hostility toward Europe. The Bush administration softened their line, and in 1989 the Europeans attempted to capitalize on rising U.S. anti-Japanese sentiment with a proposal for formal U.S.-European cooperation on HDTV. In 1989, increased opposition within the domestic economy, together with representatives from Congress (challenging the State Department's authority to determine a domestic television standard), computer companies, and the new academic group on high-resolution systems prevailed on the department to block any action on the HDTV standard at the CCIR 1990 meeting. The United States formally withdrew its support at the international level for the Japanese system, and the State Department announced its intention to seek a further delay in the CCIR decision on a world standard until 1994.

Within the CCIR, in Study Group 11, which was concerned with production and satellite transmission, discussions have been primarily aimed at defining the characteristics of HDTV, at depackaging the various stages of production, and working at agreement on what may enable compatibility between the competing field-rate standards. Two potential mechanisms of compatibility are being studied: a common image format, which defines an image with a standard number of lines and pixels but allows different field rates or scanning methods, and a common data format, allowing different numbers of lines and pixels and different field rates but resulting in the same data rate.[47]

In March 1990, the final meeting of the CCIR's Interim Working Party on HDTV decided not to agree on scanning standards at that time. The Europeans want their D-MAC standards accepted as the global standard; the Japanese want theirs adopted; and the United States wants neither. Unless the Japanese are able to impose a de facto standard through entry into the programming-production market, three regional market blocs are likely to develop.

CONCLUSION: THE CONSUMER INTEREST

Just as ISDN has been the product of technical personnel, so the push for HDTV has come from the technology and the trade, and increasingly from governments concerned at the implications for competitive advantage. Consumers have not been involved. However, new technologies and new standards do not make money unless they bring perceivable and understandable benefits to the consumer.

While it is true that both MAC and HDTV will bring superior picture quality to the viewer, the viewer must perceive this quality as being worth the extra expenditure on equipment. For example, a BBC survey in Britain revealed that while 19 percent of respondents would be interested in having a large-screen TV set in their homes, this proportion dropped to 5 percent if the additional cost were $480 more than existing equipment.[48] In 1990, some HDTV sets, such as the Toshiba Hi-Vision 32-inch model, were selling for an estimated ¥5 million (about $35,000). Even in Japan, where consumers value new technology, housing costs are taking increasing proportions of disposable income, and such prices are likely to limit market demand until mass production cheapens the product.

In the United Kingdom, where there is less cultural acceptance of new technology (leaving aside the question of cost), the BBC survey found that 75 percent of households were definitely not interested in a large-screen TV. Part of the problem in establishing a mass market is that the large-screen TV needs a larger viewing distance and a dimly lit room, while the audience surveys have demonstrated that viewing tends to be done in conjunction with other activities, and not in darkened rooms. In addition, many modern houses in the West as well as Japanese apartments are too small for an HDTV set.

In fact, picture quality may not be what consumers care about most. They want better programs, and programs, particularly in HDTV format, are missing. By 1990, only a few productions were being made for HDTV.

In Europe, the main focus of the HDTV program has been on broadcasting transmission, the intention being to reclaim the consumer-electronics market from the Japanese. In contrast, the concern in both the United States and Japan is for the other 70 percent of the potential market, involving HDTV applications to computing.

The future of MAC standards in Europe is tied up with the future of DBS satellites, a future that has become considerably more problematic since the demise of BSB and the transfer of five German language channels to *Astra*. One view is that DBS satellites represent the only way in which smaller European countries will be able to utilize HDTV. The other is that such high-powered satellites have no economic future, which instead rests with low- and medium-powered satellites delivering to cable head-ends. However, the European Commission's desire for a pan-European broadcasting satellite, for which it is considering asking for spectrum allocation at the ITU's WARC 91 meeting, as well as the massive investment that has already been made in MAC standards, suggests that MAC will not be allowed to die. Additionally, the commission is proposing to standardize reception equipment in the fixed service satellite band, which will bring *Astra* and Eutelsat's proposed pan-European satellite under its regulation.

At the same time, HD-MAC over optic fiber is becoming increasingly attractive. This explains the cooperation between ETSI and the EBU, transferring broadcasting technology into telecommunications. Since personal computers are expected to be the terminals for B-ISDN in Europe, a strategy of broadband HDTV via HD-MAC would link European efforts with the computer market, while European instead of national DBS satellites would enhance the EC's autonomy.

42. Richard J. Solomon, "Dissent: HDTV: Digital Technology's Moving Target," *Intermedia* 18 (March-May 1990): 58–61.

43. See "NHK Still Searching for Single Standard," HDTV Special Report, *International Broadcasting* 12 (January/February 1989): 32–33; see also Anne Eckstein, *L'Europe et l'avenir de la television* (Brussels: Club de Bruxelles, 1989).

44. Mitsutoshi Hatori and Yoshiro Nakamura, "The 1125/60 Standard: The Japanese Blueprint for Worldwide HDTV," *Telecommunications* 23 (September 1989): 31–35.

45. Jurgen, "High Definition Television," 40.

46. S. Baker, "High Noon for Hi-Vision," *Cable and Satellite Europe*, October 1989, 38–40.

47. ITU, Press Release.

48. *Television Week*, 27 July 1989, 18.

49. *Cable and Satellite Europe*, May 1990, 63–64; July 1990, 42–44.

In the United States it seemed unlikely that a new standard would be found until in June 1990 General Instruments proposed a digital compression standard with 1,050 lines fitting into 6MHz. However, Hughes, with which Murdoch, NBC, and Cablevision, is planning a DBS service, has carried out tests with the Japanese format. The Japanese standard may yet become a de facto standard.[49]

If the Japanese are correct in their view that the major market for HDTV is not in the television market itself but rather in its linkage to computers, one may see a similar de facto standardization to that of the computer industry, with the Japanese predominating. In that case, as with the computer industry, it will be only when corporate users demand communications facilities and compatibility that an international standard will ensue. In the meantime, there may well be three regional standards, each of which affects supply, not demand.

NOTES

1. Mahindra Naraine, "Direct Broadcasting Satellites: New Technologies and Traditional Concepts" (Paper presented to the British International Studies Association, Bristol, 17 December 1985).

2. Michel Carpentier, Director General of DG XIII, Telecommunications, Information Industries and Innovation, European Commission, "An Action Plan for HDTV in Europe," *Telecommunications* 23 (September 1989): 23.

3. International Telecommunications Union (ITU), Press Release, reproduced in *Transnational Data Report* 13 (February 1990): 27–29.

4. Martin L. Ernst, "HDTV Issues: Rallying Cry or Whimper?" *PIRP Perspectives*, Program on Information Resources Policy, Harvard University (Cambridge, Mass.: PIRP, 1989).

5. R. J. Crane, *The Politics of International Standards: France and the Color TV War* (Norwood, N.J.: Ablex Publishing, 1979), 8.

6. Ibid.

7. M. English, "The European Information Technology Industry," in *European Industry: Public Policy and Corporate Strategy*, edited by A. Jacquémin (Oxford: Oxford University Press, 1984), 227–73.

8. NTSC's nickname has been "Never the same color."

9. Ronald Jurgen, "High Definition Television Update," *IEEE Spectrum* 25 (April 1988): 56–62.

10. D. Fisher, "High Definition Television on the Brink," *Television Journal of the Royal Television Society* 25 (May/June 1988): 113–16.

11. Carpentier, "Action Plan," 24–25.

12. Guy de Jonquieres, "Against the Odds," *Financial Times*, 19 June 1986.

13. Kiyoshi Seki, "The Japanese Contribution to the U.K., Past, Present and Future" (Speech to the Confederation of British Industry/Electronics Industry of Japan Conference, Japanese Electronics Industry and Britain, London, 28 February 1990).

14. Ronald Jurgen, "Consumer Electronics," *IEEE Spectrum* 27 (February 1990): 39–41.

15. P. Powel, "DBS Transmission Standards for the U.K.—Proposals for the IBA and the BBC," *International Broadcasting Engineering* 13 (July 1982): 24–25; M. D. Windram, R. Marcom, and R. Hartley, "Extended-Definition MAC," *IBA Technical Review*, no. 23 (November 1983): 27–41.

16. United Kingdom, Home Office and Department of Industry, Part Report, *Broadcasting by Satellite*, Report of the Advisory Panel on Technical Transmission Standards (London: HMSO, 1982).

17. M. D. Windram, R. Marcom, and R. Hartley, "Extended-Definition MAC," *IBA Technical Review*, no. 23 (November 1983): 28.

18. EBU, *Specification of the Systems of the MAC/Packet Family*, EBU Document Tech. 3258, 1986, amended by Document SPB 438, EBU, Geneva.

19. D. T. Dosh, "D and D2-MAC/Pacquet, System-members of the MAC-TV Standard Family with Closed Base Band Representation," *Rundfunktech* 29 (September/October 1985): 229–46.

20. K. Lucas and M. Windram, "Standards for Broadcasting Satellite Services," *IBA Technical Review*, no. 18 (March 1982): 12–27; F. Torsteensen, "C-Mac puts Forward its Case," *Cable and Satellite Europe*, May 1986, 32–35.

21. *The Guardian*, 24 June 1986.

22. Commission of the European Community, *Proposal for a Council Directive on the Adoption of Common Terminal Specification of the MAC/Pacquet Family of Standards for DBS*, COM (86) Final, Brussels, 22 January 1986.

23. Crane, *International Standards*, 6–8.

24. "Battle of the Standards," *The Times*, 24 May 1989, 38; *Cable and Satellite Europe*, November 1988, 46–48.

25. *Cable and Satellite Europe*, January 1989, 34.

26. M. D. Windram and G. J. Tonge, "The D-MAC Transmission

System for Satellite Broadcasting in the U.K.," *Electronics and Communication Engineering Journal* 2, no. 1 (February 1990): 11–16.

27. Ibid., 15–16.

28. Guy de Jonquieres and William Dawkins, "Power Game with Much to Lose," *Financial Times*, 17 July 1990.

29. Michael Skapinker, "Battlelines Drawn on the Small Screen," *Financial Times*, 21 May 1990.

30. Jean Luc Renaud and Gwyn Morgan, "Nothing but MAC Trouble," *Cable and Satellite Europe*, May 1990, 58–62.

31. Raymond Snoddy, "Battle Hots Up over New TV Standard," *Financial Times*, 7 May 1986.

32. Suzanne C. Neil, "The Politics of International Standardization Revisited; The United States and High Definition" (Paper presented to the Seventh Bi-Annual Conference of the International Telecommunications Society, June 29–July 1, 1988).

33. On Eureka, see John Peterson, "Eureka and the Symbolic Politics of High Technology," *Politics* 9 (1989): 8–13.

34. Carpentier, "Action Plan," 24–25; Klaus Grewlich, "HDTV: The Struggle for Telepresence," *Transnational Data Report* 13, April 1990, 17–23.

35. A. Watson Brown, "Hype, Hope and Clarity," *Television Journal of the Royal Society* 26, no. 6 (1989): 314; *Telecommunications* 24 (July 1990): 27.

36. Jurgen, "High Definition Television," 59.

37. U.S. Federal Communications Commission, *In the Matter of Advanced Television Systems and Their Impact on the Existing Broadcast Service*, MM Docket No. 87-268, Tentative Decision and Further Notice of Enquiry, Released 1 September 1988.

38. For a comment on Hollywood's conservatism in relation to technology, see "HDTV. One Step—Two Steps," *Intermedia* 17 (October/November 1989): 6–7.

39. Loise Kehoe, "U.S. to Fight for Stake in New Generation TV Market," *Financial Times*, 13 January 1989; *Broadcast*, "U.S. Group Seeks HDTV Resolution," 3 November 1989, 10.

40. "America's Billion-Dollar Boob-Tube Battle," *The Economist* 311 (27 May 1989): 91–92; D. Cripps, "A Good Old-Fashioned Soap Opera," HDTV Special Report, *International Broadcasting* 12 (April 1989): 48–52.

41. Brown, "Hype," 312.

9

Conclusion: The Convergence of Broadcasting and Telecommunications

This book is about how technology push has impacted on the social organization of the technology of broadcasting and telecommunications. It is about the potential convergence of those two technologies into one information distribution network, bringing together HDTV and ISDN via optic fiber and satellite.

The prime questions raised by these applications of technology are related to who has access to the use of the technological hardware and the ensuing information provision, and who has control of the networks, the information, and the social organization of the technology. To whose benefit is the organization of the new technologies, and at whose cost? What interests gain power, and through what mechanisms? Is the technology elitist in the distribution of benefits that it generates? Does the technology further widen the divide between rich and poor through the economic and political interests that it generates? Does the technology widen the area of control over individuals, or does it buttress and extend the concept of democracy?

Governments intervene to push technology and innovation through massive research and development programs. They intervene because other governments do so, and because the pay-back period on any innovation has decreased and the sums of money involved are too great for any one company to risk. They intervene to promote high technology because technology is linked to competitive advantage in world markets, and hence to economic and political power. They intervene to promote and to protect their companies in a world where the industrialized countries' economies are increasingly penetrated by others. In general, intervention to create demand for innovatory products is more difficult than intervention to supply them, so the majority of funding goes to supply, and little goes to mechanisms to aid technological diffusion.

The mechanisms that activate supply include R&D expenditure, market restructuring, and standardization. These attempts to foster supply can be either national or cross-national, as in the case of the European Community. In each case, the motivation is to produce economies of scale in manufacture and operation; to utilize the world as a market, thereby reducing unit costs.

Until the mid-1980s, the politically salient sector was that of information technology, primarily relating to components and computing, and that of satellites, linked to defense. It was the component and computing industries that were financed by the U.S. Department of Defense, and it was the dominance of American and Japanese companies in these technologies that threatened the autonomy of Europe. It was these sectors that produced the perception of a technology gap to be filled by indigenous production and innovation. Moreover, it has been the technological linking of these sectors with those of telecommunications and broadcasting that has brought the latter sectors into the domain of geopolitics.

The technology itself has undermined governments. End-to-end networks delivered by satellite or cable permeate the nation-state, reducing economic control. Moreover, the technological standardization of network interfaces and regulations regarding access reduce the autonomy of each state. As actors proliferate, it becomes more difficult to gain consensus in international institutions, and the global standardization of products takes longer than the strides in the technology itself. Regional fora are faster in their work, can be used as protectionist forces, and give sufficient economies of scale. The potential movement toward cooperation between regional standards bodies is a movement of the industrialized states to reassert control over their economies, to delink them from the international.

However, this concern with competitive advantage, with regional blocs, and with the utilization of technology for techo-nationalist industrial advance focuses attention on the interests of large companies. It ignores the social organization of the technology within the nation-state. It ignores the system of rights and obligations to citizens. Divorcing the economic (markets) and the technological from the political allows technological competition, national security, and national autonomy to be used as the rationale for market restructuring. Technology subsumes politics. The distributional aspects of technological organization go undebated.

In part, this lack of debate is due to the international fora for decision making. The ITU, despite its political importance, retains its image as a technical institution. Even its plenary meetings are closed to the press. PTTs, manufacturers, and governments combine in national delegations to fight for their national interests. At the European level, technical decisions are taken within ETSI, with membership drawn from PTTs, manufacturers, and large users. Again, there is no accountability to a wider public. The EC itself is a system of trade-offs between national governments, each concerned with their industry's competitive advantage. While European-wide industrial lobbies are influential in decision making—partly because the commission itself can utilize them in alliances against the member states—consumer lobbies are weak. Neither is it possible for consumer organizations to represent the citizen's interests; rather they represent the citizen in only one role.

Nonetheless, the technical decisions taken in these fora at the international, regional, and national levels, made outside the party political process, are not simply about "techniques." They also concern how the technology will be organized in terms of access and control. They concern the distribution of costs and benefits within nations resulting from the introduction of a technology. The parameters of national political debate and decision making may be foreclosed.

Three trends predominate. First is the globalization of multimedia companies and of network operators seeking new opportunities for economies of scope and scale. Second is the desire of governments for competitive advantage in high technology. The third is political decision making within technical and regulatory fora at the international and national level. Out of this combination of alliances between large-scale capital and state bureaucracies have come the technologies of direct broadcasting, ISDN, and HDTV. Research and development funds, market restructuring, and standardization all serve the same interests, albeit in different combinations for different technologies.

Commenting on the future of communications, the U.S. Office of Technology Assessment has pointed out to Congress that there are three models it might adopt in attempting to organize the distributional aspects of communications technologies: a market model, an industrial policy model, or a social welfare model. The OTA argues that a market model in which policy-making has passed to private actors has arisen in the United States. They do not see that the form of industrial policy in the United States, of support through defense, is as much an industrial policy as that in Europe, and is linked to the market mode. Inevitably there are trade-offs between the three, simply because governments are now held responsible for both the health of the economy and the welfare of their citizens.[1] Those trade-offs are changing as the previous goals of access, accountability, and diversity of information change.[2]

To a large extent, the technologies of broadcasting and telecommunications used to be nationally autonomous, with regulation that protected them from foreign entry. Their economic potential was subjugated to organization in the larger interests of public information, access, and control. Broadcasting has been a national, cultural matter, organized since the 1930s in the United States on the basis of regulated franchises operating in the public interest and in Western Europe as national public service monopolies. In both cases, the state intervened to regulate the sector, in terms of the content of information, ensuring diversity of opinions, and in terms of market structure, ensuring access. In the United States, broadcasters were accountable to the FCC. In Europe, public ownership ensured that political accountability. Funded in the United States by advertising and in Europe by the license fee or a combination of that fee and advertising, the systems ensured the fast diffusion of television. Even the poorest groups of citizens have televisions. In the United States, a plurality of information sources was seen as the buttress of democracy, while in Europe, a plurality of opinion and "balanced" output fulfilled the same function.

Similarly, although there has been a disparity between income groups evident in telecommunications, the policy of all governments has been to increase penetration. Low access costs increased such penetration, ensuring that the network was of the greatest utility to all. Payment was made as a subscriber for connection and then for rental and call charges. Call charges were often related to the time used and the distance, and where there was pressure on equipment, they were differentially priced by time of day. Local call charges and access have been supported by transfers of revenue within PTTs between long-distance and residential services. However, as it is more expensive than television, the telephone has had a less complete penetration.

In both sectors this traditional pattern of universal access has been altered by new technology and new forms of organization and payment. The new distribution technologies have also been allowed to alter patterns of accountability and diversity.

In the United States, cable TV has encroached on network TV as the main information distributor. Relaxation of controls has reduced accountability—franchise renewals are automatic—and local citizens can no longer appeal to the FCC. The new form of organization has increased subscription prices, created a pay-per-view elite, and increased concentration between media. New DBS operators can also own cable companies, creating a private monopoly of long-distance and local broadcasting of a kind forbidden in telecommunications.

Numbers of programs have increased, but only within a narrow range of subject matter. Minorities have been excluded both from access and from representation within the media. Hence, access, diversity, and accountability have all been reduced. Neither is there any consensus that the state should regulate cable TV or cross-media ownership. In the words of Robert Britt Horowitz, "Open entry, in conjunction with the deregulation and structural rules, essentially grants complete property rights in a resource that hitherto had been considered public."[3]

In Europe as well, changes have taken place. The monopolies of public service broadcasters have been altered, and airtime given over to advertising has increased. Commercialization of the public service broadcasters has impacted on their information, education, and representational functions. Moreover, in similar fashion to the United States, new modes of distribution through cable, satellite, and video have created a second and third income-related tier of viewers. These developments have been encouraged by the European Community on the grounds of increased plurality of information. However, unlike in telecommunications, the question of limitations on access and content of a concentrated market structure have not arisen.

In the United States, in telecommunications, the previous consensus on universal access was revoked by the FCC, which moved to impose the costs of the local network on individual customers. These moves were rebutted by both Congress and state regulators. The RBOCs have been obliged to take note of their local regulators, and to participate in trade-offs allowing them to hold tariffs on residential service in return for profits on enhanced services. In general, the trade-offs within the American political system have helped to retain basic telephone service for the poor.

In Europe, the penetration of the telephone is less than that in the United States. As much as 50 percent of the population of some EC countries are without a telephone.[4] In Britain, the regulatory movement is toward imposing the costs of network modernization onto individual consumers. This movement has been put forward for European-wide implementation by the EC under the technical rubric of "cost-based" tariffs. The intention is that individuals should pay more for access to the telephone. The primary intention is for PTTs to generate revenue from those sectors of its network that are demand-inelastic—the local network.

Over the top of this basic service have been layered other services that are charged at higher prices, such as cellular mobile radio and ISDN. Given the high up-front costs and critical mass necessary to break even, it seems unlikely that cellular radio will reach beyond about 5 percent of the population. At least using current technology, cellular radio will not become the cable television of telecommunications or replace wired service, although it will compete with cable TV.

ISDN reflects the interests of PTTs in modernizing their networks in order to prevent the migration of large customers to private networks. It is possible to argue that by modernization, PTTs protect their individual customers who would otherwise pay increased charges as network traffic decreased. However, because they have developed the technology separately from the market, PTTs must price it at a cost that users will pay. That price is based on previous prices, not on the cost or architecture of the technology itself. Hence, the rest of the users of the network pay increased charges for the benefit of new customers who are offered the utilization of the technology.

To a large extent, universal service has been set in stone—relating only to voice service. Universal access to other services is seen as uneconomic for PTTs. In both the United States and Europe, the goal of universal access has extended beyond basic telephone service only in France, where a videotex service, based on Minitels (cheap terminals), has been developed. However, despite their widespread use, Minitels do not make a profit for the PTT.[5]

On the one hand, therefore, the patterns of universal access and accountability in broadcasting are being eaten away by the introduction of cable TV and DBS. On the other hand, in telecommunications, technological upgrading has bypassed the individual user. In both telecommunications and broadcasting, market restructuring favors large suppliers. Diffusion of the technology goes only as far as business users and the more wealthy individuals.

ISDN and the convergence of telecommunications distribution with that of television have the potential to give control of the technology back to the user. Broadband allows a number of services to be provided, both interactive and passive. Television can move from a stream of information over which the user has no control into an interactive mode. Increased bandwidth could increase the diversity of program content and widen access to the media.

However, on current trends the opposite is happening. Diversity is being reduced. Partly, this reduction in diversity is the result of alterations in market structure, the entry of cable and satellite programmers each competing for quick take-up and advertising revenue. It is also due to the economics of broadcasting, where economies of scope and scale are important, and where competition in adjacent markets creates homogeneity of product. Finally, in part it is due to the increasing commercialization of public service broadcasters in Europe, where the maturation of the market for reception equipment has meant that the built-in growth of the license fee no longer provides the revenue to meet inflation.

Without new regulations to control private monopolies of access to television programming, without government commitment to universal access, and without an equal commitment to maintaining a diversity of opinions, broadband presents a threat. It offers immense opportunities for control of individuals by large companies. The QUBE experiment demonstrated how broadband could be utilized to segment populations into consumer targets. Hence, broadband could be a further means for governments to deliver citizens up as consumers to advertisers. It could also be the means of transferring the control of content evident in broadcasting to the control of the content of communications between individuals. Such control is already evident in Britain, where "adult sex" telephone calls are being recorded for the regulator, Oftel, in order to establish whether they constitute obscene material.

The potential integration of broadcasting and telecommunications is related in both the United States and Western Europe to the growing demand for spectrum from mobile telephony. It is also related to the potential competitive advantage seen to arise from High-Definition Television and the market it could create for component manufacture. As currently construed, HDTV requires the large bandwidth available either via satellites or optic fiber. As they interlink with the information-technology sector, broadcasting and telecommunications gain strategic saliency in the competition between regional blocs, and their traditional linkage with defense and national autonomy become reactivated.

In the short term, broadband delivery of television is a means whereby the PTTs can modernize the local network—the most expensive part. It is also a strategic response to the potential competition for this inelastic part of their revenue from radio-based technologies and cable television. In Europe, broadband is also seen as the technological means for integration. It is part of the social reconstruction of a European versus a national identity. The interests of the EC and of PTTs coincide. However, at the European level, broadband is still seen as a means of gaining PTT revenue, as an adjunct to telephone service, and not as a replacement for both the current distribution of telecommunications and television or as the major means by which citizens will access information.

How then should broadband be regulated—as television or telecommunications? Television regulation has tended to allow spectrum use by private monopolies in geographical areas, for commercial service, coupled with national public service broadcasting. Television regulation has also encompassed content, with heavier regulation for public service broadcasters than for the new entrants of cable and satellite TV.

Telecommunications regulation, on the other hand, has concerned the protection of voice service. Divisions have been made in services between basic ("reserved," in EC terminology) and others, and between long-distance and local service. However, broadband is a digital network, not only connecting a variety of machines but also allowing the usage of varying amounts of bandwidth by the user. There is no means by which voice and data can be separated, while the concepts of local and long distance are contradicted by the very concepts of the technology. How then should broadband operators be regulated?

One answer is that they should be regulated as common carriers, with television program channels provided by third parties. However, experience in Britain suggests that the common carrier format is unrealistic. Cable TV companies rejected it out of hand when it was proposed by the government in its 1990 reorganization of broadcasting. Moreover, it is exactly this separation that has driven American telecommunications companies to exit the United States for Britain and France.[6]

No company wishes to take the financial risk of building infrastructure only to have no say in the programs that determine its return on that infrastructure. Hence, a form of regulation that allowed the provider of the infrastructure to also provide programs, on the lines of either separate subsidiaries or separate accounting would be needed. In other words, the telecommunications operator would also become a broadcast program supplier.

Second, there would be a need for open access to other program suppliers. One could argue that Open Network Provision–type arrangements could be used for this purpose, with broadcasting seen as a further value-added service—a tele-service, in the terminology of the European Commission. Additionally, access would have to be policed, access charges for programmers determined, and some form of rate of return regulation introduced.

However, what of the broadcasting regulation currently in force in every country except the United States? The implication is that, as in the United States, where most viewers receive network television via cable TV rather than off-air, distinctions between programmers would have to cease. In other words, public service television would become one or a number of channels among many. With the delivery system unified, distinctions in regulation would become less legitimate, as would separate financing, thereby increasing the commercialization of public service broadcasting.

How then would people pay? There are two possibilities. Based on telecommunications pricing, one method is for payment by use—by numbers of data bits passed, so that facsimile would be cheaper than voice, and high-definition television would be very expensive. Payment by usage would exclude the poor. Its likely impact is signaled by the current pay-per-view method for certain televised films.

The second is based on television pricing, by subscription. It is this second option that was suggested by RACE. A universal access charge four times the cost of current access charges is the PTTs' proposal. If broadband is to be universal, this charge would replace current telecommunications and television access charges, together with subscription for cable or satellite TV. At today's prices in Britain the proposed tariff is more expensive than those three charges taken together. If the television license fee were to be added to the broadband tariff, then broadband would be an expensive medium that could not be universal except with public finance. In order for the poor to be included, public investment would be needed.

How likely is the scenario of broadband replacing off-air broadcasting and cable TV? The British might have been the first to adopt the system, given the pressure from American companies to open up telecommunications to cable TV competitors. However, the government has indicated opposition to the licensing of BT to carry television to the home. BT is selling its cable TV interests. In the United States, broadband also depends on the relaxation of regulation to allow telephone companies to provide programs, or on their working together with cable companies to do so.

Nevertheless, although no one is certain when the crossover point will come, optic fiber will soon be as cheap as copper wires to put into the local network.[7] The RACE project aims to complete its work by 1995, which will give a further impetus to broadband. However, on a European-wide basis, it seems unlikely that broadband will replace public service broadcasting in the short term. Not only are PTTs in many countries far from a digital network, but the preconditions in each of the countries vary.[8] As with the liberalization of telecommunications and the introduction of ISDN, political, economic, social, and cultural factors will outweigh the technology. It will be opposed by stakeholders in the current distribution system, cable TV companies, and satellite broadcasters, as well as public service broadcasters. Ranged against them are the PTTs, the component and optic fiber manufacturers, the trade unions, and the European Community. Linked as it is to HDTV, to information technology, and to the future of European industry, broadband in Europe is a matter of competitive advantage and technology push.

The massive failure of the EC has been in its concurrence to and initiation of these trends. Despite tinkering at the edges with programs such as STAR, the European Community has failed to address the question of what rights citizenship of Europe entails. While itself extending its power and autonomy through the liberalization of private interests and the undermining of its member states, it has dramatically failed to address the question of democracy in Europe. In both broadcasting and telecommunications, its policies mimic those of the United States, but without the safeguards of competitive institutions, which produce public debate. It emphasizes economies of scale rather than diversity; large-scale technology push rather than diffusion and access. Hence, it undermines the very innovation and the very notions of European democracy it wishes to promulgate.

The political concept of the citizen with fundamental rights and obligations has been ellided into the concept of consumer, where rights are determined by payment. The legacy of the Reagan and Thatcher years is that the terms of public debate have been altered. Even in societies such as West Germany, where consensus and social welfare have predominated, unification has seen a movement away from public solutions to public problems, toward concern with strategic and industrial interests. MAC standards and the technological protectionism erected against the Japanese by the French have ranked higher than public service broadcasting to Eastern Germany.

However, while the European Community fails to address such questions of citizens' rights, its regulation has undermined the ability of national governments to organize technology according to political priorities. No member state can protect itself from broadcasts of any kind from another state. Power is passed to the private interests, who remain unregulated.

There exists, then, a movement in both the United States and Europe toward nonaccountable techno-industrial policy-making. The new technologies are imposed through the market mechanism, with choice reduced for those who cannot pay. The restructuring of markets via the mechanism of liberalization gives an impetus to growth through the injection of new private capital. However, it also extends government control while removing government responsibility. The failure of structural regulation to control the activities of business leads to discrimination in the behavioral regulation extended over companies. It leads to increased politicization of the sector as companies lobby to be allowed entry into one market segment or another. The result is a form of corporatism at the level of the company.

The success of the company and the success of that section of the state to which it is linked become synonymous.

This book began by arguing that technology is not a determinant of social organization, that each country adopts such technologies at different speeds and with different emphases on organization. However, the theme of the book points to the advantages held by large-scale international capital in the process of defining new markets. In these circumstances, no matter what the ideology of the incumbent government, it is possible to obscure the gains to particular groups through the mythology of "technological advance."

The purpose of this book has been to point out that hidden within debates on technology, whether it be the introduction into the market of new technologies or their standardization, are political issues concerning the distribution of welfare. The book has been concerned with that distribution on an international and national level within the United States and the European Community. It has argued that research and development, market restructuring, and standardization are all facets of a supply-side industrial policy on the part of governments, which is intended to place their economies ahead in the race for international competitive advantage and international power. Such initiatives ignore the complementarity between the use of advanced telecommunications and the diffusion of information technology.[9] Such initiatives carry with them the disadvantage that they do little to alter the conditions that prevent participation in those technologies by the mass of the population. They do nothing to fill the democracy gap.

NOTES

1. U.S. Congress, Office of Technology Assessment, *Critical Connections* (Washington, D.C.: Government Printing Office, 1989).

2. Philip Whitehead, "Reconstructing Broadcasting," in *Bending Reality. The State of the Media*, edited by James Curran, Jake Ecclestone, Giles Oakley, and Alan Richardson (London: Pluto, 1986), 149–56.

3. Robert Britt Horowitz, *The Irony of Regulatory Reform* (Oxford: Oxford University Press, 1989), 281.

4. Nicholas Garnham, "University Service in Telecommunications," in *European Telecommunications Policy Research*, edited by N. Garnham (Amsterdam: IOS, 1986), 26–38.

5. Diana Green, "The Political Economy of Information," in *France and Modernisation*, edited by John Gaffney (Aldershot, England: Avebury, 1988).

6. Michael Botein, "Can Fibre-Optic Broadband Networks Be Regulated?" *Intermedia* 17 (December 1989): 35–39.

7. Geoffrey Mulgan, "Monograph on the Convergence of Telecommunications and Broadcasting in the U.K." (London: Centre for Communication and Information Studies, Polytechnic of Central London, 1989); Larry Stone, *The Prospect of Broadcasting and Telecommunications Technological Convergence: A Dilemma for Coherent Industrial, Regulatory and Competition Policymaking in the U.K.* (Unpublished Master's dissertation, City University, London, 1989).

8. Alan Rudge, "The Broadband Revolution: British Telecom's Vision of the Future Broadband Network," *Information Technology and Public Policy* 8 (Winter 1989): 12.

9. C. Antonelli, "The Diffusion of Information Technology and the Demand for Telecommunications Services," *Telecommunications Policy* 13 (September 1989): 255–64.

Selected Bibliography

Anania, L. "The Protean Complex: Are Open Networks Common Markets?" Paper presented to the Eighth Annual Meeting of the International Telecommunications Society, Venice, 1990.

Anania, L., and R. Solomon. "User Arbitrage and ISDN." *Intermedia* 16 (January/February 1988): 25–31.

Armbuster, H. "Worldwide Approaches to Broadband ISDN." *Telecommunications* 23 (May 1989): 49–54.

Arnold, E., and K. Guy. *Parallel Convergence. National Strategies in Information Technology*. London: Frances Pinter, 1986.

Bagdikian, B. H. *The Media Monopoly*. Boston: Beacon Penn, 1983.

Bauer, B. "Private Integrated Networks: A Trigger for Public Demand." *Telecommunications* 22 (October 1988): 41–47.

Beesley, M. *Liberalisation of the Use of British Telecom's Network*. London: HMSO, 1981.

Beesley, M., and B. Laidlaw. *The Future of Telecommunications*. London: Institute of Economic Affairs, 1989.

Berlin, G. V., and S. Wyatt. *Multinationals and Industrial Property. The Control of the World's Technology*. Hemel Hempstead: Harvester-Wheatsheaf, 1988.

Bittner, J. R. *Broadcasting and Telecommunication. An Introduction*. Englewood Cliffs, N.J.: Prentice-Hall, 1985.

Bloch, E. "Managing for Challenging Times: A National Research Strategy." *Issues in Science and Technology* 11 (Winter 1986): 20–29.

Bogason, P. "Continuity and Change in the Role of the State in Danish Telecommunication." Paper presented to the Scandinavian Association Workshop on State and Governance in Historical Development, Uppsala, Sweden, 1990.

Booz, Allen, and Hamilton. *Strategic Partnerships as a Way Forward in European Broadcasting*. London: B. A. & H., 1989.

Botein, M. "Can Fibre-Optic Broadband Networks Be Regulated?" *Intermedia* 17 (December 1989): 35–39.

Brandt, C. "The Social Construction of Information Technology." Paper presented to the European Consortium of Political Research, Amsterdam, April 1987.

Broadcasting Research Unit. *The Public Service Idea in British Broadcasting: Main Principles*, 2d ed. London: BRU, 1988.

Bruce, R., J. Cunard, and M. D. Director. *From Telecommunications to Electronic Services*. London: Butterworths, 1986.

Bureau Européen des Unions de Consommateurs. *Comments on the EEC's Green Paper on the Development of the Common Market for Telecommunications Services and Equipment*. Brussels: BEUC, 1988.

Calhoun, G. *Digital Cellular Radio*. Artech House, 1988.

Carpentier, M. "An Action Plan for HDTV in Europe." *Telecommunications* 23 (September 1989): 23–26.

Cecchini, P. *The European Challenge. 1992. The Benefits of the Single Market*. Aldershot, England: Wildwood House, 1988.

Charles, D., P. Monk, and E. Sciberras. *Technology and Competition in the International Telecommunications Industry*. London: Pinter, 1989.

Chatham House. *Europe's Future in Space*. Royal Institute International Affairs, Chatham House Special Paper. London: Routledge and Kegan Paul and RIIA, 1988.

Commission of the European Communities. *Proposal for a Council Directive on the Adoption of Common Terminal Specification of the MAC/Pacquet Family of Standards for DBS*, COM (86) Final, Brussels, 22 January 1986.

Commission of the European Communities. *Proposal for a Council Directive on the Co-ordination of Certain Provisions Laid down by Law, Regulations of Administrative Action in Member-States Concerning the Pursuit of Broadcasting Activities*. Com (86) 146, Final, Brussels, 29 April 1986. Amended Final Version, Com (88) 154, Final. *Official Journal of the European Communities*, 24 November 1989.

Commission of the European Communities. *Television without Frontiers. Green Paper on the Establishment of a Common Market for Broadcasting, Especially by Satellite and Cable*. Communication from the Commission to the Council, COM (84) 30, Final, Brussels, 14 June 1984.

Commission of the European Communities. *Towards a Dynamic European Economy: On the Development of the Common Market for Telecommunications Services and Equipment*. Green Paper. COM (87) 290, Brussels, 10 June 1987.

Cooke, W. R. "Broadcast and Cable Deregulation in the United States." In *La déréglémentation des télécommunications et de l'audiovisuel*, CNRS, International Colloquium. Paris: CNRS, 27–28 May 1986.

Council for Science and Society. *UK Military R&D*. Oxford: Oxford University Press, 1986.

Council of Economic Priorities. *Star Wars. The Economic Fallout*. Cambridge, Mass.: Ballinger, 1988.

Council of Europe. Steering Committee on the Mass Media. *Draft European Convention on Transfrontier Television*. Strasbourg: CoE, 30 June 1988.

Crandall, R., and K. Flamm, eds. *Changing the Rules: Technological Change, International Competition and Regulation in Communications*. Washington, D.C.: The Brookings Institution, 1989.

Crane, R. J. *The Politics of International Standards: France and the Color TV War*. Norwood, N.J.: Ablex Publishing, 1979.

Cripps, D. "A Good Old Fashioned Soap Opera." HDTV Special Report. *International Broadcasting* 12 (April 1989): 48–52.

Curran, J. *Bending Reality: The State of the Media*. London: Pluto Press, 1986.

Dang Nguyen, G. "The European Telecommunications Policy or, The Awakening of a Sleeping Beauty." Paper presented to the European Consortium of Political Research, Amsterdam, April 1987.

Dang Nguyen, G. "France, Telecommunications—Intervention at the Crossroads." In *Handbook of Information Technology and Office Systems*, edited by A. E. Cawkell. Amsterdam: Elsevier, 1986, 519–38.

Dang Nguyen, G. "Industrial Adjustment and the EEC Policy for Telecommunications." In *Telecommunications: National Policies in an International Context. CPR '86*, edited by N. Garnham. London: Polytechnic of Central London, 1986, 187–220.

Dasgupta, P., and P. Stoneman. *Economic Policy and Technological Performance*. Cambridge: Cambridge University Press, 1987.

Demac, D. A. (ed). *Tracing New Orbits*. New York: Columbia University Press, 1986.

Diamenscu, D., and J. Botkin. *The New Alliance. America's R&D Consortia*. Cambridge, Mass.: Ballinger, 1986.

Dorfmann, N. *Innovation and Market Structure. Lessons from the Computer and Semi-conductor Industries*. Cambridge, Mass.: Ballinger, 1987.

Dosh, D. T. "D and D2-MAC/Pacquet, System-Members of the MAC-TV Standard Family with Closed Base Band Representation." *Rundfunktech* 29 (September/October 1985): 229–46.

Drake, W. "WATTC-88 Restructuring the International Telecommunications Regulations." *Telecommunications Policy* 12, no. 3 (1988): 217–33.

Dunogue, J. "Numeris: The French ISDN." *Electrical Communication* 64, no. 1 (1990): 15–20.

Dutton, W., J. Blumler, and K. Kraemer, eds. *Wired Cities: Shaping the Future of Communications*. London: Casel, 1987.

Dyson, K., and P. Humphreys. "The Political Implications of Broadcasting from Outer Space: The German Dimension." Paper presented to the European Consortium Planning Sessions, Barcelona, March 1985.

Dyson, K., and P. Humphreys, eds. *The Politics of the Communications Revolution in Western Europe*. London: Frank Cass, 1986.

Dyson, K., and P. Humphreys, with R. Negrine and J. P. Simon. *Broadcasting and New Media Policies in Western Europe*. London: Routledge, 1988.

English, M. "The European Information Technology Industry." In *European Industry: Public Policy and Corporate Strategy*, edited by A. Jacquemin. Oxford: Oxford University Press, 1984, 227–73.

Ernst, M. L. "HDTV Issues: Rallying Cry or Whimper?" *PIRP Perspectives*, Program on Information Resources Policy, Harvard University. Cambridge, Mass.: PIRP, 1989.

EBU (European Broadcasting Union). *Specification of the Systems of the MAC/Packet Family*. EBU Document Tech 3258, 1986, amended by Document SPB 438. Geneva: EBU, 1988.

European Parliament. *Realities and Tendencies on European Television: Perspectives and Options*. Com (83) 229 Final, 25 June 1983.

European Parliament, de Vries Report. *Report on the Economic Aspects of the Common Market for Broadcasting*. Com (84) 300 Final, Document A 2 102/85, Brussels, 30 September 1985.

Faulhaber, G. *Telecommunications in Turmoil. Technology and Public Policy.* Cambridge, Mass.: Ballinger, 1987.

Finnie, G. "Lighting up the Local Loop." *Telecommunications* 23 (January 1989): 31–40.

Finnie, G. "Switching the US on to ISDN." *Telecommunications* 23 (July 1989): 66–69.

Fisher, D. "High Definition Television on the Brink." *Television Journal of the Royal Television Society* 25 (May/June 1988): 113–16.

Foreman Peck, J., and J. Müller, eds. *European Telecommunications Organisations.* Baden Baden: Nomos Verlagsgesellschaft, 1988.

Forester, T. *High Tech Society.* Oxford: Basil Blackwell, 1987.

Friedman, D. *The Misunderstood Miracle. Industrial Development and Political Change in Japan.* Ithaca: Cornell University Press, 1988.

Garnham, N. "The Media and the Public Sphere." *Intermedia* 14 (January 1986): 26–38.

Garnham, N. "Universal Service in European Telecommunications." In *European Telecommunications Policy*, edited by N. Garnham. Amsterdam: IOS, 1986, 123–74.

Gilhooly, D. "The Politics of Broadband." *Telecommunications* 22 (June 1988): 51–96.

Golding, P., G. Murdoch, and P. Schlesinger, eds. *Communicating Politics, Mass Communications and the Political Process.* Leicester: Leicester University Press, 1985.

Grande, E. "The Influence of Party Politics and Government Strategies on Telecommunications Policy." Paper presented to the Telecommunications Policy workshop, Max-Planck Institut fur Gesellschaftsforschung, Cologne, 3–4 December 1987.

Green, D. "The Political Economy of Information in France." In *France and Modernisation*, edited by John Gaffney. Aldershot, England: Avebury, 1988, 124–37.

Guback, T. *The United States Filmed Entertainment Industry.* Report to the European Institute for the Media. Manchester:November 1986.

Haglund, D., ed. *The Defence Industrial Base and the West.* London: Routledge, 1989.

Hills, J. *Deregulating Telecoms. Competition and Control in the United States, Japan and Britain.* London: Frances Pinter, 1986.

Hills, J. "Dynamics of U.S. International Telecom Policy." *Transnational Data Report* 12 (February 1989): 14–21.

Hills, J. "Foreign Policy and Technology: The Japan-U.S., Japan-Britain and Japan-EEC Technology Agreements." *Political Studies* 31 (June 1983): 205–23.

Hills, J. *Information Technology and Industrial Policy.* London: Croom Helm, 1984.

Hills, J. "Neo-Conservative Regimes and Convergence in Telecommunications Policy." *European Journal of Political Research* 17 (January 1989): 95–113.

Hills, J. "Techno-Industrial Innovation and State Policies on Telecommunications in the United States and Japan." In *State Policies and Techno-Industrial Innovation*, edited by Ulrich Hilpert. London: Routledge, in press.

Hills, J. "Universal Service: Liberalization and Privatization of Telecommunications." *Telecommunications Policy* 13 (June 1989): 129–44.

Hollins, T. *Beyond Broadcasting: Into the Cable Age.* London: BFI, 1984.

Horowitz, R. B. *The Irony of Regulatory Reform.* New York: Oxford University Press, 1989.

Hrbek, R. "Technology Policy as an Engine of Integration in the EC." Paper presented to the 14th World Congress of International Political Science Association, Washington, D.C., September 1988.

Hsiung, J. C. "Direct Broadcasting by Satellite in the USA." *Telecommunications Policy*, 9, March 1985, 49–61.

Hudson, H. "Satellite Broadcasting in the United States." In *Satellite Broadcasting*, edited by R. Negrine. London: Routledge, 1988, 216–33.

Hughes, G. "Massed Production." *Cable and Satellite Europe*, April 1989, 48–51.

Humphreys, P. "Satellite Broadcasting Policy in West Germany—Political Conflict and Competition in a Decentralised System." In *Satellite Broadcasting*, edited by R. Negrine. London: Routledge, 1988, 107–43.

Humphreys, P. "Whither European Broadcasting?" *EBU Review* 39 (March 1988): 36–39.

International Telecommunications Union, Committee on Telegraph and Telecommunications. *CCITT Red Book*. Volume II, Fascicle II.1. *General Tariff Principles. Charging and Accounting in International Telecommunications Services.* Geneva: ITU, 1985, Recommendations D.100–D.155.

Johnson, N. "Regulating American Style." *Intermedia* 15 (July/September 1987): 31–33.

Jurgen, R. "Consumer Electronics." *IEEE Spectrum* 27 (February 1990): 39–41.

Jurgen, R. "High Definition Television Update." *IEEE Spectrum* 25 (April 1988): 56–62.

Kay, J. A. "Myths and Realities." In *1992 Myths and Realities*, edited by the Centre for Business Strategy. London: London Business School, 1989, 1–45.

Kitahara, Y. *Information Network System*. London: Heinemann Educational Books, 1983.

Kleinsteuber, H. G., D. McQuail, and K. Siune, eds. *Electronic Media and Politics in Western Europe*. Euromedia Research Group Handbook of National Systems. Frankfurt: Verlag, 1986.

Komiya, M. "Integrated Services Digital Networks in the U.S. and Japan: A Comparative Analysis of National Telecommunications Policies. *Pacific Telecommunications Council '86 Proceedings*. Honolulu: PTC, 1987.

Kuhn, R. *The Politics of Broadcasting*. London: Croom Helm, 1985.

Lucas, K., and M. Windram. "Standards for Broadcasting Satellite Services." *IBA Technical Review*, No. 18 (March 1982): 12–27.

McDonald, J. "Deregulation's Impact on Technology." *IEEE Communications Magazine* 25, January 1987, pp. 63–65.

MacDonald, S. "Stunting the Growth? Information, Technology and U.S. Export Controls." Paper presented to the Information, Technology and New Economic Growth Workshop, Tokyo, 12–13 September, 1988.

Mackintosh, I. *Sunrise Europe. The Dynamics of Information Technology*. Oxford: Basil Blackwell, 1986.

McKnight, L. "Technical Standards and International Telecommunications Regimes." Paper presented to the International Studies Association, Washington, D.C., April 1987.

McQuail, D., and K. Siune, eds., *New Media Politics*. London: Sage, 1986.

Maddock, E. *Civil Exploitation of Defence Technology*. London: HMSO, 1983.

Magnant, R. *Domestic Satellite: An FCC Giant Step toward Competitive Communications Policy*. Boulder, Colo.: Westview Press, 1977.

Martin, J. *The Wired Society*. Englewood Cliffs, N.J.: Prentice-Hall, 1978.

Miller, J. "Cable Policy in Europe: The Role of Transponder Broadcasting and its Effects on CATV." *Telecommunications Policy* 11 (September 1987): 259–68.

Miller, R. "Integrated Services Digital Network. Telecommunications in the Future." *Online* 11, March 1987, 27–38.

Molina, A. H. *The Social Basis of the Microelectronics Revolution*. Edinburgh: Edinburgh University Press, 1989.

Morgan, K., B. Habor, M. Hobday, N. von Tizelma, and W. Walker. *The GEC-Siemens bid for Plessey: The wider European issues.* Working Paper No. 2. Centre for Information and Communication Technologies, Science Policy Research Unit, University of Sussex. Brighton: University of Sussex, 1989.

Morgan, K., and D. Pitt. "Coping with Turbulence, Corporate Strategy, Regulatory Politics and Telematics in Post-Divestiture America." In *European Telecommunications Policy Research*, edited by N. Garnham. Amsterdam: IOS, 1989, 19–39.

Mosco, V., and J. Wasko, eds. *The Political Economy of Information.* Madison: University of Wisconsin Press, 1988.

Mulgan, G. "Costs and Prices in the ISDN and Broadband Networks: A Case of Whatever You Can Get away With?" In *European Telecommunications Policy Research*, edited by N. Garnham. Amsterdam: IOS, 1989, 217–42.

Mulgan, G. "Monograph on the Convergence of Telecommunications and Broadcasting in the UK." London: Polytechnic of Central London, Centre for Communication and Information Studies, 1989.

Mulgan, G. "The Myth of Cost-Based Pricing." *Intermedia* 18 (January/February 1990): 21–27.

Murakami, T. "ISDN: Advancing towards the 21st Century." Paper presented to the Asia Telecom, Singapore, April 1989.

Naraine, M. "Direct Broadcasting Satellites: New Technologies and Traditional Concepts." Paper presented to the British International Studies Association, Bristol, 17 December 1985.

National Science Board. *Science and Engineering Indicators 1987.* Washington, D.C.: Government Printing Office, 1988.

Negrine, R., and S. Papathanassopoulos. *The Internationalisation of Television.* London: Pinter, forthcoming.

Neil, S. C. "The Politics of International Standardisation Revisited; The United States and High Definition." Paper presented to the Seventh Bi-Annual Conference of the International Telecommunications Society, June 1988.

Neu, W., and T. Schnoring. "The Telecommunications Equipment Industry. Recent Changes in Its International Trade Pattern." *Telecommunications Policy* 13 (March 1989): 25–37.

Noam, E. "International Telecommunications in Transition." In *Changing the Rules: Technological Change, International Competition and Regulation in Telecommunications*, edited by Robert W. Crandall and Kenneth Flamm. Washington, D.C.: The Brookings Institution, 1989, 257–97.

Noell-Smith, G., ed. *The European Experience.* London: BFI, 1989.

Noll, M. "The Effects of Divestiture on Telecommunications Research." *Journal of Communication* 2 (Winter 1987): 73–80.

Nora, J., and A. Minc. *The Computerisation of Society.* Cambridge, Mass.: MIT Press, 1980.

Oettinger, A. "The Formula Is Everything: Costing and Pricing in the Telecommunications Industry." Cambridge, Mass.: Harvard University Program on Information Resources Policy, 1988.

Organization for Economic Cooperation and Development. *International Trade in Services. Audiovisual Works.* Paris: OECD, 1986.

P. A. Consulting Group, *Manufacturing into the Late 1990s.* London: HMSO, 1989.

Papathanassopoulos, S. "Beyond the Directive." *Cable and Satellite Europe*, April 1990, 42–46.

Papathanassopoulos, S. "Broadcasting and the European Community." In *International Political Economy of the Communications Policies*, edited by K. Dyson and P. Humphreys. London: Routledge, in press.

Patrick, H., with L. Meissner, ed. *Japanese High Technology Industries. Lessons and Limitations of Industrial Policy*. Seattle: University of Washington Press, 1986.

Pavitt, K. *Patterns of Technological Change—Evidence, Theory and Policy Implications*. Papers in Science, Technology and Public Policy, Science Policy Research Unit, University of Sussex, Brighton: University of Sussex, 1983.

Peacock Committee. *Report of the Committee on Financing the BBC*. Cmnd. 9824. London: HMSO, 1986.

Pelton, J. "Satellites and Fiber Optics in an ISDN World." *Space, Communications and Broadcasting* 6 (June 1989): 361–66.

Perez, C. "New Technologies and Development." In *Small Countries Facing the Technological Revolution*, edited by Christopher Freeman and B. A. Lindall. London: Pinter, 1988, 85–97.

Peterson, J. "Eureka and the Symbolic Politics of High Technology." *Politics* 9, no. 1 (1989): 8–13.

Pianta, M. *New Technologies across the Atlantic. U.S. Leadership or European Autonomy*. Hemel Hempstead, U.K.: Harvester Wheatsheaf, 1988.

Pipe, R. G. "WATTC Agrees on New Telecom Rules." *Telecommunications* 23 (January 1989): 19–21.

Porter, V. "The EC: Broadcasting, Competition Policies and National Sovereignty." *Intermedia* 18 (June-July 1990): 22–26.

Porter, V. "The Re-Regulation of Television: Pluralism, Constitutionality and the Free Market in the U.S.A., West Germany, France and the U.K." *Media, Culture and Society* 11 (January 1989): 5–27.

Powel, P. "DBS Transmission Standards for the U.K.—Proposals for the IBA and the BBC." *International Broadcasting Engineering* 13 (July 1982): 24–25.

Rhodes, M. "Industry and Modernisation. An Overview." In *France and Modernisation*, edited by John Gaffney. Aldershot, England: Avebury, 1989, 66–95.

Richeri, G. "Television from Service to Business: European Tendencies and the Italian Case." In *Television in Transition*, edited by P. Drummond and P. Paterson. London: BFI, 1985, 21–36.

Roessner, J. D. *Government Innovation Policy: Design, Implementation, Evaluation*. Basingstoke, U.K.: Macmillan, 1988.

Rogers, E., and J. Dearing. "The Japanese Experience: Tskuba City." Paper presented to the 40th International Communication Association Annual Conference, Dublin, June 1990.

Rogerson, D. "Tariff Policy and ISDN." *Telecommunications* 21 (October 1987): 87–92.

Roobeek, A. J. M. "The Forgotten Dimension in the Technology Race." Paper to the International Conference on the Theory of Regulation, Barcelona, June 1988.

Rothwell, R., and W. Zegveld. *Reindustrialization and Technology*. Harlow, U.K.: Longman, 1985.

Rushing, F., and C. Ganz Brown, eds. *National Policies for Developing High Technology Industries*. Boulder, Colo.: Westview Press, 1986.

Rowland, W. D. "Continuing Crisis in Public Broadcasting. A History of Disenfranchisement." *Journal of Broadcasting and Electronic Media* 30, no. 3 (Summer 1986): 251–74.

Rowland, W. D., and M. Tracey. "The Breakdown of Public Service Broadcasting." *Intermedia* 16, nos. 4 and 6 (Autumn 1986): 32–42.

Sassoon, D. "Political Market Forces in Italian Broadcasting." *West European Politics* 8 (Spring 1985): 67–83.

Scherer, J. "Historical Analysis of Deregulation: The European Case." Paper presented to "La déréglémentation des télécommunications et de l'audiovisuel," CNRS: International Colloque, Paris, 27–28 May 1986.

Schmandt, J., F. Williams, and R. H. Wilson, eds. *Telecommunications Policy and Economic Development*. New York: Praeger, 1989.

Seymour-Ure, C. "Media Policy in Britain: Now You See It, Now You Don't." *European Journal of Communication* 2 (September 1987): 269–88.

Sherman, B. L. *Telecommunications Management: The Broadcast and Cable Industries*. New York: McGraw-Hill, 1987.

Slaa, P. *ISDN as a Design Problem. The Case of the Netherlands*. The Hague, Netherlands: Organization for Technology Assessment, 1988.

Smith, R. L. "The Birth of a Wired Nation." In *Readings in Mass Communications. Concepts and Issues in the Mass Media*, edited by M. Emery and T. C. Smythe. Dubuque, Iowa: W. M. C. Brown Publishers, 1983, 247–59.

Stallings, William. "CCITT Standards Foreshadow Broadband ISDN." *Telecommunications* 24, May 1990, 89–96.

Stockholm International Peace Research Institute. *Yearbook 1984*. London: Taylor and Francis, 1984.

Stone, A. *Wrong Number. The Breakup of AT&T*. New York: Basic Books, 1989.

Streeter, T. "Policy Discourse and Broadcast Practice: The F.C.C., the U.S. Broadcast Networks and the Discourse of the Marketplace." *Media, Culture and Society* 5 (July 1983): 247–62.

Sweeney, G. "The Information Networks Designed to Support Technological Innovation in Less Favoured Regions of the Community." Paper presented to the 40th International Communications Association Annual Conference, Dublin, June 1990.

Sweeney, G., ed. *Innovation Policies. An International Perspective*. London: Frances Pinter, 1986.

Sylvesten, T. "Public Service Television in the 'Information Age': Choices, Strategies and Prospects for the Future." *Nordicom Review*, no. 2 (1988): 47–48.

Tatsuno, S. *The Technopolis Strategy. Japan, High Technology, and the Control of the Twenty First Century*. New York: Prentice-Hall, 1986.

Taylor, P. *The Limits of European Integration*. Worcester, U.K.: Croom Helm, 1983.

Torsteensen, F. "C-Mac Puts Forward Its Case." *Cable and Satellite Europe*, May 1986, 32–35.

Tunstall, J. *Communications Deregulation: The Unleashing of America's Communication Industry*. Oxford: Basil Blackwell, 1986.

Tunstall, J. *The Media in Britain*. London: Constable, 1983.

Tydeman, J., and E. Kelm. *New Media in Europe*. London: McGraw-Hill, 1986.

Ungerer, H., with N. Costello. *Telecommunications in Europe*. Luxembourg: CEC, 1988.

United Kingdom. Home Office and Department of Industry. Part Report. *Broadcasting by Satellite*. Report of the Advisory Panel on Technical Transmission Standards. London: HMSO, 1982.

U.S. Congress. House. Majority Staff of the Subcommittee on Telecommunications, Consumer Protection and Finance of the Committee on Energy and Commerce.

Telecommunications in Transition: The Status of Competition in the Telecommunications Industry. 97th Cong., 1st Sess. Washington, D.C.: U.S. Government Printing Office, 1981.

U.S. Congress. Office of Technology Assessment. *Information Technology R&D. Critical Trends and Issues.* Washington, D.C.: Government Printing Office, 1985, 4.

U.S. Congress. Office of Technology Assessment. *Technology, Innovation and Regional Economic Development.* Washington, D.C.: U.S. Government Printing Office, 1983.

U.S. Department of Commerce. NTIA; *Telecom 2000.* Washington, D.C.: Government Printing Office, 1988, 305–50.

U.S. Federal Communications Commission. *In the Matter of Advanced Television Systems and Their Impact on the Existing Broadcast Service.* MM Docket No. 87-268, Tentative Decision and Further Notice of Enquiry, Released 1 September 1988.

Vedel, T. "La 'déréglémentation' des télécommunications en France: Politique et jeu politique." In *La Déréglémentation des Télécommunications et de l'Audiovisuel,* Colloque International, Paris, May 1986.

Vernon, R. "International Investment and International Trade in the Product Cycle." *Quarterly Journal of Economics* 80 (May 1966): 190–204.

Vibert, F. *Europe's Constitutional Deficit.* London: Institute of Economic Affairs, Inquiry 27, November 1989.

Webb, C. "Theoretical Perspectives and Problems." *Policymaking in the European Community,* edited by H. Wallace, W. Wallace, and C. Webb. London: J. Wiley, 1983, 1–42.

Webber, D., J. Moon, J. Richardson, and M. Rhodes. "Information Technology and Economic Recovery in Western Europe. The Role of the British, French and West German Governments." *Policy Sciences* 19 (October 1986): 319–46.

Whitehead, P. "Reconstructing Broadcasting." In *Bending Reality. The State and the Media,* edited by James Curran, J. Eccleston, G. Oakley, and A. Richardson. London: Pluto, 1986, 149–56.

Wigand, R. "Integrated Services Digital Networks: Concepts, Policies and Emerging Issues." *Journal of Communication* 38 (Winter 1988): 29–47.

Windram, M. D., R. Marcom, and R. Hartley. "Extended-Definition MAC." *IBA Technical Review,* no. 23 (November 1983): 27–41.

Windram, M. D., and G. J. Tonge. "The D-MAC Transmission System for Satellite Broadcasting in the U.K." *Electronics and Communication Engineering Journal* 2 (February 1990): 11–16.

Zysman, J., and L. Tyson, eds. *American Industry in International Competition.* Ithaca: Cornell University Press, 1983.

Index

About the Authors

JILL HILLS is a Reader in Politics at the Social Science Department, City University, London. Her previous books include *Deregulating Telecoms: Competition and Control in the United States, Japan and Britain* (Quorum Books, 1986), and another on information technology and industrial policy.

STYLIANOS PAPATHANASSOPOULOS has been a Visiting Fellow at City University, London, and a Research Fellow at London's Broadcasting Research Unit. He has written extensively on European broadcasting with particular reference to the development and impact of the news media.